GILBERT
HIS LIFE AND STRIFE

GILBERT

HIS LIFE AND STRIFE

by

Hesketh Pearson

ILLUSTRATED

HARPER & BROTHERS   PUBLISHERS   NEW YORK

GILBERT His Life and Strife
Copyright © 1957 by Hesketh Pearson
Printed in the United States of America

Library of Congress catalog card number: 57–8176

TO
JOAN AND JAMES THORNTON

Contents

○━○━○

Illustrations

❦

Acknowledgments

❦❦❦❦

I am deeply indebted to Mr F. B. Cockburn, executor of Miss Nancy McIntosh's estate, for placing at my disposal all the private papers of Sir William Gilbert in her possession, and for giving me permission to quote whatever I thought necessary for the purpose of this book. His generous act has enabled me to tell the life-story fully and intimately.

Gilbert's hitherto unpublished correspondence, and the letters from Sir Arthur Sullivan which he kept, afford fresh aspects of the famous quarrel between the two, the bitterness of which, as now revealed, was due not to a carpet but to an affidavit. Many of Sullivan's letters make their first appearance here by kind permission of Mr Howard G. Dunkley and Mr Gerald Russell, trustees of the Will of the late H. T. Sullivan. Other letters from Sullivan were printed in his Life by Herbert Sullivan and Sir Newman Flower, and are quoted in my biography of Gilbert by the courtesy of Sir Newman Flower.

As usual, my wife's assistance in studying quantities of papers, discovering data and copying documents, has saved me months of labour.

Since this work is based on the above-mentioned private papers I have not thought it necessary to supply a list of lesser authorities, but those who are interested will find a fairly complete bibliography at the end of my *Gilbert and Sullivan*, originally published in 1935. To the list should now be added Mr Leslie Baily's *The Gilbert and Sullivan Book* (1952) which I have found helpful.

Lastly my thanks are due to Mr P. G. Wodehouse for allowing me to quote from his description of Gilbert telling a lunch-time story.

CHAPTER 1

'The Villain of the Piece'

❦❦❦❦

The man who was to give more familiar quotations to the English language than anyone since Dickens was born at a moment when the sayings in *Pickwick Papers* were beginning to gain currency throughout the English-speaking world. William Schwenck Gilbert first opened his eyes on November 18th, 1836, in the house of his grandfather at No. 17 Southampton Street, Strand, London. Seven months after his birth the throne of Great Britain was occupied by Queen Victoria, whose early reign was chiefly notable, in the realm of entertainment, for the novels of Dickens, and whose later reign was principally enlivened by the libretti of Gilbert.

In the seventeenth and eighteenth centuries the paternal ancestors of Gilbert were yeomen, living at Shipton Bellinger or nearby on the borders of Hampshire and Wiltshire. He liked to think that an eminent sixteenth-century navigator, Sir Humphrey Gilbert, who founded the first English colony in North America, was among his forebears, but no evidence of this is forthcoming, and the only recorded navigator in his family was himself, though he seldom sailed his yacht out of sight of the English coast. His great-grandfather, tired of tillage, started business as a grocer in London, on the south bank of the Thames, and his grandfather, described as a tea-merchant, made enough money to take a house in Southampton Street, Strand, to buy property in Hammersmith, to gain the acquaintance of Sir Joshua Reynolds and Dr Samuel Johnson, and to leave his children sufficient to live upon, appointing as their guardians and trustees John Samuel and Mary Schwenck, the last of whom was our William's great-aunt and godmother, bestowing upon him the name she bore.

One of the tea-merchant's sons was the father of the subject of this book. Also named William, he started life as a naval surgeon, retired soon after inheriting his patrimony, and married a Scotswoman, Anne, the daughter of Dr Thomas Morris. He was a tall, handsome, kindly but choleric person, with a strong sense of the ridiculous and a marked tendency to be so. He hated the Roman Church, intemperance, fashionable doctors, and paying rates. In fact he would not have been content without something to make his blood boil and could scarcely have existed in any system that did not call for radical reform. After his son, William Schwenck, had begun to make something of a name as a writer, he decided to do the same. He did not think much of the young man's ability: 'If he can write, anybody can!' William senior promptly commenced a literary career, and a stream of works poured from his pen. Two of them were widely-read in the eighteen-sixties: *Shirley Hall Asylum* and *Dr Austin's Guests*. The first of these and two others, *The Magic Mirror* and *King George's Middy*, were illustrated by his son. But though they have some humour and more humanity, the style in which they are written would not recommend them to a modern reader. Their author apparently thought well of them, because he lost his temper on finding that the proofs of one had been carelessly corrected by the printer, tearing up every copy of the entire edition; and when a hostile criticism of another appeared in *The Saturday Review*, he called on the editor with the purpose of chastising him. Taking advantage of his seniority, he freely criticized the literary efforts of his son, who jibbed at the parental comments, their interchanges being a source of mirth to such friends as heard them. To enquire whether this single example in history of a father following in the footsteps of his son had any connection with the topsyturvy world created by the latter, were perhaps to consider the matter too curiously.

From the letter of a relation dated December 26th, 1836, we learn that W. S. Gilbert's mother was 'not a little proud of him'. The baby was christened at St Paul's Church, Covent Garden, on January 11th, 1837, and spent most of his childhood travelling about the continent with his parents and three small sisters. Whenever in London the family lived in their own house, 4 Portland Place, Hammersmith, where the air was supposed to be good for infants. The boy was born with a remarkable memory, for late in life he could recite innumerable French songs he had heard in early childhood, and when visiting Naples at an advanced age he recognized a long, high, light-coloured wall and some of the scenery he had passed at the age of two, when a couple of charming Italians stopped his nurse, told her that they had been sent by the baby's father to fetch him, removed him to their mountain retreat, and demanded a ransom for his return. A sum of about £25 was sent at once; but the loss to the parents was a gain to the child, who in the years ahead used the episode in two of his operas. He was called 'Bab', short for baby, by his family, and this too became a lucrative source.

At the age of seven he received his first schooling at Boulogne, but by the time he was thirteen his parents had done enough travelling and he was sent to the Great Ealing School, where some notable people had learnt their lessons, including John and Henry Lawrence, Thackeray, Newman, Marryat and Huxley. As a schoolboy Gilbert was clever but lazy, good-looking but unpopular. He showed a disposition to domineer, and though he cared little for learning he cared still less for being beaten in competition, an attitude that compelled him to work hard in spurts and win prizes. He enjoyed reading and drawing and writing verses. He also contrived and stage-managed a number of plays for his schoolfellows, besides painting the scenery, and in one of them, a melodrama on Guy Fawkes, he played the leading part as well. Rehearsals were noisy, and recalcitrant members of the casts were dealt with in physical combat. The stage-manager discovered that when an actor was knocked down he usually calmed down and did as he was told.

The earliest verses by Gilbert that have survived were written after an attack of typhoid fever which necessitated the shaving of his head and a visit to France during convalescence. Standing in the street he watched Napoleon III and the Empress Eugénie pass in procession, and according to himself the sovereigns observed him with appreciation:

> To the Emperor she said:
> 'How beautiful the head
> Of that youth of gallant mien,
> Cropped so neat and close and clean –
> Though I own he's rather lean.'
> Said the Emperor: 'It is!
> And I never saw a phiz
> More wonderful than 'is.'

Feeling that his talent as an actor was being wasted among

boyish amateurs, he called at the theatre where Charles Kean was performing and asked for an interview. It was brief, because Kean soon discovered that the boy was the son of an old friend, and the lad was returned to his desk faster than he had come to the stage-door. At the age of sixteen he was at the head of the school and had won distinction as a translator of Greek and Latin verses. Oxford seemed to be the place for him now, but first of all he went to King's College, London. While there he made his presence felt by turning the Scientific Society into a Dramatic one, by writing satirical verses, and by drawing caricatures of his fellow-collegians and their professors which were only appreciated by those who were not caricatured.

At the age of nineteen he was over six feet tall and bursting with vigour. The Crimean War seemed to offer a chance for working off his superfluous energy, and after taking his B.A. degree he settled down to a course of intense study in order to pass the examination for a commission in the artillery. But without perceiving that the future of British light opera rested on their decision, the diplomats felt that the Crimean War had gone on long enough and brought it to a close while Gilbert was still wrestling with ballistics. 'I had no taste for a line regiment', he confessed, 'so I obtained by competitive examination an assistant clerkship in the Education Department of the Privy Council Office, in which ill-organized and ill-governed office I spent four uncomfortable years.' But he never lost interest in the conflict he had so nearly joined, was a keen student of Kinglake's *History of the Crimean War*, and at the end of his life wanted to write a book about it. He also became an officer in the home service, spending some twenty years, first as an ensign in the 5th West Yorkshire Militia, and then as a captain in the Royal Aberdeenshire Highlanders, ultimately resigning therefrom because the recurrent duties interfered with the job of writing plays. We shall hear more of this hereafter.

While working as a government clerk he left home and lived in a Pimlico boarding-house. Existence in his father's house was unpleasant. There were constant quarrels between his parents. The events leading to their later separation, to be duly recorded, suggest that they had never been happy together, and their constant travels in the early days of married life make it clear that a settled domestic existence did not satisfy them. Gilbert's father was irascible and arbitrary, his mother was callous and resentful; and Gilbert's sympathies were with his father, a condition of mind which, in a youngster who had a chivalrous regard for women, must have made life at home extremely trying.

With such a background of parental bickering and professional boredom he passed four unhappy years, lightened by visits to the theatre, practical jokes, writing verses, drawing cartoons, and flirting with girls who took his fancy. Convinced that some day he would be free of his present drudgery, he entered himself as a student at the Inner Temple and read for the law. A song that he had translated from *Manon Lescaut* was actually rendered by a popular singer at the Promenade Concerts and he went to hear every repetition of it, wondering what the promenaders would do if made aware that, standing in their midst, was the very man whose words were thrilling them. Later observation convinced him that they would not have leapt with ecstasy. Such triumphs could not be kept to himself and his companion-clerks were soon under the impression that he exercised control in the world of the theatre. One of them took the risk of asking him whether he could write an order for seats at a play. He said that he could and wanted to know whether he should write it for stalls or a box. The applicant preferred a box. An order was written, and the credulous fellow suffered the mortification of taking his family to the theatre and taking them home again, his presentation of the demand at the ticket-office having aroused hearty laughter. Gilbert dealt with his complaint: 'You asked me whether I could write you an order for the play. I replied that I could, and I did, but I never said that it would be of the least use to you.'

Although that was Gilbert's notion of a good joke, it reveals one of the salient features of his nature, and a good deal of the trouble awaiting him on life's path was caused by his passion for accuracy. Possibly his desire to be a barrister derived from this. By the process of examination and cross-examination, he believed that truth would come to light. But his nature was not fitted to the work, because of two other ingredients in his composition. 'When I have anything to say I talk *to* people, not *at* them', he once informed a friend. In fact he was incurably straightforward and outspoken. 'I am always in the habit of saying what I think, and when I think I have said too much, I am in the habit of saying *that*', he told someone else, adding as an apology, 'I expressed myself to you in terms which I should certainly not have used had I spoken in cold blood.' His quick judgments were not those of a born lawyer, and his language on the spur of the moment would have disqualified him as a barrister. He jumped to conclusions, took offence easily, and spoke violently and heatedly, expressing surprise when his words were repeated to him and asserting his innocence of what he was supposed to have said. His denials were made in good faith, for in losing his temper he lost touch with reality and his speech was subconscious.

At the end of his life he read in a newspaper some hurtful witticism attributed to him. 'But you *never* said such a thing!' exclaimed one who knew him intimately. 'No, of course not', he replied, 'but don't you know I am always *the villain of the piece*?'

CHAPTER 2

Bar and Bab

❦❦❦

Fortunately for him, Gilbert inherited three or four
hundred pounds from an aunt. 'I was one of the worst
bargains any Government ever made', he said, and the
death of his aunt saved the taxpayers his salary of £120 a year:
'I resolved to emancipate myself from the detestable thraldom
of this baleful office, and on the happiest day of my life I sent in
my resignation.'

He paid for his call to the bar, for his admission to a con-
veyancer's chambers, and for his own quarters in Clement's Inn.
Later he shared chambers with two other fellows in Pump
Court, Temple, and later still had rooms of his own at No. 1
Verulam Buildings, Gray's Inn. He practised as a barrister for
four years, or perhaps it would be more correct to say that he
waited as a barrister for that period. There was little demand
for his services, and when by chance a client came his way the
case presented no opening for an ambitious man to make a
reputation.

Having joined the Northern Circuit, he first appeared as
prosecuting counsel at Liverpool, but the Irish lady in the dock,
who had stolen a coat, declined to be cross-examined and he
had to appeal to the Recorder for protection against her voluble
counter-charges that he was drunk and disreputable. His first
brief was to defend a female charged with picking a pocket; but
when it transpired that she had made a hobby of pocket-picking,
his case looked shaky; and when no witness appeared to testify
to the saintliness of her character, it collapsed. Sentenced to
eighteen months hard labour, she threw a boot at his head and
continued to criticize his personal character until removed from
the court. The only person to express gratitude for his handling
of a case was a Frenchman who rushed up and kissed him on
both cheeks, but it was a form of gratitude with which he could
have dispensed. 'I was always a clumsy and inefficient speaker',

he confessed: 'Moreover, an unconquerable nervousness prevented me from doing justice to myself or my unfortunate clients.' He scarcely earned £100 as a barrister, and since his clients numbered about twenty in four years he could not regard the legal profession as a means to much money or considerable fame, both of which he determined to possess.

The time that he spent while waiting as a barrister was not wasted. He wrote plays with an energy that Balzac might have envied. Before the age of twenty-four he had written fifteen farces and burlesques, not one of which was accepted; and then he tried his hand at articles, poems, skits, parodies and drawings, but no editor seemed interested. At last his luck changed. In the year 1861 a paper called *Fun* was launched by one Maclean, who kept a looking-glass shop on Ludgate Hill, trading as The Commercial Plate-Glass Co. Maclean had a son named Roderick who, because Queen Victoria refused to read his poems, flourished a pistol at her in the region of Windsor Castle, and was sent to Broadmoor asylum. But Maclean has a better claim than that to a place in history. Weary of editors who regretted their inability to print his contributions, Gilbert laboured to make an article funny and sent it, together with a half-page drawing on wood, to Maclean, proprietor of the new paper which was to send *Punch* out of circulation. Maclean thought it so funny that he told his editor, H. J. Byron, to accept it. Byron, whose notion of fun was largely restricted to a pun, liked it so much that he sent a representative to Gilbert with the request that he should write articles and supply drawings for as long as he could hold a pen in his hand. Gilbert firmly believed that he had nothing more to say; but under pressure he tried again, and yet again, and at last found that even when he had nothing to say he could say it in a column of prose or verse. For ten years he wrote articles and poems for *Fun*, of which he was also the dramatic critic, and the last of his contributions to it was one of the best parodies in the language, *Rosencrantz and Guildenstern*, which ought to be in the permanent repertory of the British theatre.

The pay was poor: £1 a column, prose or verse, fractions in proportion. Every contribution was measured by the cashier with a piece of string, and novices received as much as the old hands. Those whose work appeared in 'the penny *Punch*', as they called it, included H. J. Byron himself (who was to write the most successful farce of his age, *Our Boys*), F. C. Burnand (later editor of *Punch*), Clement Scott (who achieved fame as dramatic critic of *The Daily Telegraph*), Tom Robertson (the production of whose plays was epoch-making in the history of English drama), George Augustus Sala (who became the best-known and most prolific journalist of his time), G. R. Sims (who founded *The Referee*), Artemus Ward (the famous American humorist) and Ambrose Bierce (the equally famous American short-story writer). *Fun* was first edited in a little room behind the looking-glass shop, but Maclean soon sold it to a man who abandoned it for dog-biscuits, and the paper was then bought by the engravers, Dalziel Brothers, who appointed Tom Hood as editor.

Gilbert could not live in comfort on what he received from *Fun*, and some of his writings appeared in *Punch*, *Cornhill* and *Temple Bar*, while an additional flow of dramatic criticisms by him were published in *The Illustrated Times*. No one ever worked harder than Gilbert to discover wherein his genius lay, and when its peculiar quality became manifest to everyone else he failed to recognize it, believing that his true inspiration lay elsewhere. The editor of *Punch*, Mark Lemon, made the serious mistake of refusing the first of Gilbert's Bab Ballads, 'The Yarn of the Nancy Bell', saying that it was 'too cannibalistic' for his readers. Later, Mark wanted Gilbert to write for *Punch* on condition that he ceased to write for *Fun*. Gilbert refused to consider this unless he were made a member of the regular *Punch* staff. Mark would not consider this under any circumstances, and the subject was then dropped. But Gilbert took his revenge on a subsequent editor, Burnand. 'Do you ever receive for *Punch* good jokes and things from outsiders?' asked a guest at a dinner-party. 'Oh, often!' said Burnand. 'They never appear', was Gilbert's dry comment from the other side of the table.

Nothing survives of all Gilbert's journalism, whether in line or rhyme, except *The Bab Ballads*, which greatly increased the popularity of *Fun* and justified its title. Their author thought nothing of them. Most of them were, he said, 'composed hastily, and under the discomforting necessity of having to turn out a quantity of lively verse on a certain day in each week'. When collected together in a book he remarked that he had 'ventured to publish the little pictures with them, because while they are certainly quite as bad as the ballads, I suppose they are not much worse.' Yet the ballads and their illustrations have been the delight of humorous versifiers and draftsmen for nearly a century. Though essentially English, nothing quite like them has been produced by any other Englishman. They contain both satire and nonsense, but these ingredients are merely incidental in their composition. They are simply jokes, and some people thought them jokes in bad taste. But the quality that makes them unique and may make them immortal is the sudden imaginative perception that human beings and the conditions of their existence on this planet are inherently ridiculous. While the imperfection of life is a source of sadness in the great poets, it is a source of silliness in 'Bab', who created an art of utter absurdity.

All sorts and conditions of men welcomed the Ballads. Even those who disliked verse enjoyed 'Bab', whose laughable jingles were recited and quoted in places where the usual pleasantries were of a ribald nature. At public banquets and private dinner-parties the latest 'Bab' was received with merriment and applause, and even the peers tittered when a verse was heard in the House of Lords. The Ballads burst on a public that revelled in humour and wallowed in horror. It was the period of *Our Mutual Friend* and *The Moonstone*, when the corpses of murdered people floating in the Thames and the presence of sinister Indians in the English countryside and battered bleeding heads and gruesome quicksands and wild shrieks at midnight and haunted faces in the gloaming were balanced by the comicalities of Silas Wegg and Drusilla Clack. In 'Bab' such components were fantasticated by imperturbable exaggeration and made ludicrous by close association. Thus the Ballads were timely. Some people thought them cruel, and they are certainly not kind; but the farcical ferocity in them merely indicated the ebullience of a man whose natural desire for martial action was restricted to the use of a pen. This mental savagery, together with many of the fancies in *The Bab Ballads*, found expression later on in the Savoy libretti, by which time the pure fun had become social satire and the cruelty had been refined.

Indeed the fascinating panorama of unadulterated imbecility which had inspired 'Bab' was soon lost to Gilbert's sight. The first collection of *The Bab Ballads* appeared in 1869 and was

succeeded by *More Bab Ballads* in 1873. In the early seventies
Gilbert was making a reputation as a serious dramatist, and
some of the ballads and nearly all of the illustrations were
beginning to jar upon him. On September 19th, 1875, we find
him writing to Messrs Tinsley of Catherine Street, Strand:

> I propose to publish a new edition of the 'Bab Ballads' – select-
> ing the most popular pieces from the First and Second Series, and
> illustrating them with new and carefully executed drawings by
> myself. It occurred to me that you might possibly feel disposed to
> undertake the work. If so, I shall be happy to attend to any
> appointment you may think proper to make.

The selection, *Fifty Bab Ballads* (1876), was published by
Routledge with the original drawings. Over twenty years later,
his fame firmly established, Gilbert made the new drawings for
another edition with textual corrections, which was issued in a
volume called *Songs of a Savoyard* and mixed up with the popular songs from the operatic libretti. In a prefatory note to this
edition he asserted that the original illustrations had erred
gravely 'in the direction of unnecessary extravagance'. So, for
that matter, had the original Ballads. But by the nineties he
was wholly emancipated from the careless rapture in which the
first verses and illustrations had been conceived. It was as if
the Shakespeare who wrote *The Tempest* had tinkered with the
work of the young man who had written *A Midsummer Night's
Dream*.

Though Gilbert set no intrinsic value on *The Bab Ballads*, he
wanted a good price for them. The publisher of the first edition
of the First Series was John Camden Hotten, who made his
reputation by bringing out Swinburne's poems when no other
publisher dared send them to the printer, and by pirating the
works of Mark Twain in England, adding several chapters of
his own. 'I feel as if I wanted to knock his brains out!' exclaimed
Mark when made aware of this outrage: 'Oh, not in anger; but
only to see, that is all.' Hotten also founded the firm of Chatto
and Windus. His transactions with Gilbert must have been
amusing. In August 1868 the author demanded £90 for an
edition of two thousand copies at 3*s*. 6*d*. apiece. Hotten offered
£50 for a first edition of fifteen hundred copies, telling an agent
that 'gentlemen always will persist in believing that publishers
make larger profits than they actually do'. At length Hotten

agreed to Gilbert's terms, and to pay £50 for each subsequent edition of one thousand copies. Immediately after the publication of the first edition Gilbert discovered that more than two thousand copies had been printed and instantly demanded payment for the second edition. Hotten, indignant, said that the extra 263 copies printed were for the press, the author, and so on. Gilbert insisted that a sum of £13 3*s.* was due to him, reckoning at the rate of £50 for a thousand copies, and he added:

> You must be aware that in consenting to this arrangement I am waiving an indisputable claim for £50. The mere fact of your having ordered the extra 263 copies to be destroyed is in itself evidence that you had no right whatever to cause them to be printed.

It seems that Hotten had been seized by panic when Gilbert advanced his claim and had jettisoned the copies which the press and the author were supposed to have had.

That Gilbert, who was entirely self-taught as a draftsman, had worked on certain of the blocks for the printer is clear from a letter J. C. Hotten wrote to him on August 5th, 1870:

> I am in receipt of your note respecting the 2 blocks which you designed at my suggestion. They can be had by your messenger – agreeably to my note of Jan. 1869 – upon payment of Dalziel's bill for engraving, £5.9.6.

Hotten enclosed a note to Messrs Judd & Glass authorizing the transference: 'Please deliver to messenger the wood blocks of frontispiece and vignette on title of "Bab Ballads" sent you by Messrs Dalziel on my account.' Having terminated his agreement with Hotten, who appeared to fulfil Lord Byron's description of a publisher, Gilbert gave *The Bab Ballads* to Routledge & Sons, and on the 18th July, 1870, he received £50 for a first edition of ten thousand copies at 1*s.* each, the firm insisting that they should be allowed to print 833 copies extra in order to give the customary thirteenth copy in every dozen sold to the retailer.

Among the Ballads are some verses addressed 'To My Bride (whoever she may be)', three of which portray Gilbert as seen by himself at this period:

> *You'll marry soon – within a year or twain –*
> *A bachelor of circa two-and-thirty,*
> *Tall, gentlemanly, but extremely plain,*

And, when you're intimate, you'll call him 'Bertie'.
Neat, dresses well; his temper has been classified
As hasty; but he's very quickly pacified.

You'll find him working mildly at the Bar,
After a touch at two or three professions,
From easy affluence extremely far,
A brief or two on Circuit – 'soup' at Sessions;
A pound or two from whist and backing horses,
And, say, three hundred from his own resources.

Quiet in harness; free from serious vice,
His faults are not particularly shady;
You'll never find him 'shy' – for once or twice
Already, he's been driven by a lady,
Who parts with him – perhaps a poor excuse for him –
Because she hasn't any further use for him.

In the early sixties, when Gilbert had become a regular contributor to *Fun*, then edited by Tom Hood, he felt the need
of mixing socially with his pen-peers and founded a small club.
The members called themselves 'The Serious Family' and they
met weekly, on Saturday nights, at his chambers in Gray's Inn.
Hood was appointed 'Head of the Family' and Gilbert was
called '*L'enfant terrible*'. The subscription was two guineas,
from the payment of which Gilbert was absolved 'in consideration of my undertaking to supply a rump-steak, cold boiled
beef, a stilton cheese, whisky and soda and bottled ale, every
Saturday night for the term of my natural life. Although,
financially speaking, this was one of the worst bargains I ever
made, I have never regretted it.' All the members were devil-
may-care bohemians, irresponsible free-lances, thoughtless of
yesterday and tomorrow, laughing easily at any joke, fond of
food, drink and puns, full of themselves and their doings, light-
hearted in success, not too downcast over failure, enjoying high
spirits when sober and boisterous spirits when drunk. They sang
and capped one another's stories and invented games and
retired to bed early on Sunday mornings with the comfortable
feeling that there was no need to get up till Monday. Gilbert
kept an 'Attendance Book', which for the sake of accuracy was
signed by each member on arrival, and the party usually consisted of six to ten members. The most regular attendants were
the editor Tom Hood, the dramatic critic Clement Scott, the

dramatist Tom Robertson, and several others whose names, known at the time as artists and journalists, are known no more: E. L. Blanchard, Arthur Cecil, Jeff Prowse, Henry Leigh and Paul Gray.

The man who meant more to Gilbert than all the rest put together was Tom Robertson, whose plays (*Society, Ours, Caste* and *School*) were put on by the Bancrofts in the sixties and revolutionized the British stage by introducing ordinary people, natural acting and realistic production. In those days the producer was called the stage-manager, and Robertson, according to Gilbert, invented stage-management. Not only did Robertson allow Gilbert to watch rehearsals of his plays, thus giving him a practical education of incalculable value, but he encouraged the younger man to write for the stage; and when the lessee of the St James's Theatre, Miss Herbert, wanted a Christmas play in a hurry, Robertson advised her to give Gilbert the job. She did; and his career as a dramatist opened with an 'Extravaganza', a punning sub-title, a text littered with puns, and a theme that would one day give acute discomfort to his famous collaborator.

CHAPTER 3
Purposeful Pot-Boiling

❀❀❀❀

W e do not know, we cannot guess, how many scenes, songs, bits of dialogue and odd ideas were presented or sold by Gilbert to other writers and passed off as their own in plays they had concocted; but he undoubtedly wrote the greater part of a pantomime called *Hush a Bye, Baby, on the Tree Top* (with sub-titles) and produced by W. H. C. Nation at Astley's Theatre on Boxing Day, 1866. The author's name was given as Charles Millward, a well-known writer of pantomimes, but Gilbert was responsible for most of the scenes and participated in the rehearsals.

The first piece to appear under his own name was a travesty of a French play. It had to be written in a week; and Robertson having said that he could do it, he did. One more week was given to rehearsals, and the first performance of *Dulcamara*, or the Little Duck and the Great Quack, took place at the St James's Theatre on December 29th, 1866, three days after the curtain had risen at Astley's. It was a period of puns and parodies, when the public delighted in those writers who could play the fool with words and ridicule the plots of popular French dramas and operas. In his salad days Gilbert enjoyed a good pun and used to quote with admiration Planché's quip: 'You're so well bred, you ought to be buttered.' He admired H. J. Byron's perpetrations in that kind and tried to out-Byron him in *Dulcamara*, which contains puns that would have shocked even Shakespeare. A leading female character is described as 'the little Duck, who, it is hoped, will nevertheless be found to be very long in the bill'. The arrival of soldiers is announced, with the appropriate emphases: 'I hear their *trumpets* sounding on my *drums*.' Nemorino, in love with Adina, says to her:

> *I envied e'en the fowls who comicahly*
> *Hopped round you like a feathery corps de barley.*
> *One of these Dorkings I would be, in one sense.*
> ADINA: *What! be a Dorking! Pooh, you're dorking nonsense!*

The plot is partly concerned with an elixir that has the power of making ugly men handsome; and this trick of transforming people into their opposites became an obsession with Gilbert, who did not abandon it when he emerged from his punning phase.

An established author is usually ashamed of his first work, and nine years after its production Gilbert discountenanced a revival of *Dulcamara*, calling it 'nonsense'. He went to see the revival and hissed it, replying to a managerial remonstrance: 'May an author not hiss his own play? I once thought it good, but now – well, I hiss.' At the time of the original production its success rejoiced him, for though he made little money out of it he made his mark as a playwright. At the age of thirty he was sufficiently optimistic to arrange a supper-party after the first night, and the play's reception justified it, but a sadder and a wiser Gilbert confessed that he 'would as soon invite friends to supper after a forthcoming amputation at the hip-joint'. In the rush of production no financial agreement had been made between author and manager, but shortly after business became brisk at the box-office he was asked how much he expected to be paid. 'Blindly ignorant of the value of such things, I modestly suggested thirty guineas. "Oh, dear, no," said Emden, "we never pay in guineas – you must make it pounds." Accordingly I made it pounds, and Emden said, as he handed me the cheque: "Now take an old stager's advice – never sell so good a piece as this for £30 again." And I never have.' A glance at the printed work suggests that he was overpaid, but as it ran for 120 nights the management did not feel aggrieved.

His reputation made, he began to turn out burlesques, farces, extravaganzas, pantomimes, comedies and musical sketches with a prodigality that has been unequalled since the time of Lope de Vega. At the end of his life he declared that he had written over ninety works for the stage. More than two-thirds of this output can be of no interest to us now, especially the early part of it, and we shall confine ourselves to such pieces as appear to reveal his character or to display his relationship with contemporaries or to have had some significance at the time. Two of his efforts to keep the pot boiling must be briefly mentioned for one or other of these reasons.

On December 21st, 1868, John Hollingshead opened the new Gaiety Theatre with Gilbert's *Robert the Devil*, or the Nun, the

Dun, and the Son of a Gun. Described as an operatic extravaganza, it was written in pantomimic verse and peppered with
puns, of which these are fair specimens:

BERTRAM: *You're in Boulogne – a place all Britons known to!*
ROBERT: *A very pretty spot I've been b'lown to!*
BERTRAM: *And here, at this well-known seaside,* cease hiding.

Of one character it is said: '*Men shun him* and do not *mention
him.*' With this queer entertainment Hollingshead started a
class of show that was known as 'Gaiety Burlesque'. Three
very clever performers, Nellie Farren, J. L. Toole and Edward
Terry, made the pieces successful and became a London insti-
tution at which people went to laugh as a matter of course,
just as they went to view the Royal Academy exhibition or to
see Henry Irving and Ellen Terry at the Lyceum Theatre.
With such performers John Hollingshead was able to vaunt
that he kept alight 'the sacred lamp of burlesque', though without them, judging by Gilbert's sample, the lamp would soon
have smoked itself out.

Seven months later Hollingshead produced Gilbert's first
comedy, *An Old Score*, at the Gaiety, and this was the cause of
the earliest of those querulous episodes which were to mark
nearly every stage of the dramatist's future career and which
were partly due to his own punctiliousness. The editor of a
paper called *The Tomahawk*, Arthur à Beckett, in the belief
that he had been attacked in the new comedy, wrote an article
censuring the author's character. Gilbert at once called on
Beckett, assured him that no such attack had been intended,
demanded a written apology, and got it. From the concluding
passage thereof we may infer that Gilbert dictated it:

I admit that it would have been better to have ascertained from
Mr W. S. Gilbert whether he intended to insult me before attacking him and am bound to declare that Mr W. S. Gilbert has treated
me with the courtesy befitting a gentleman. I gladly withdraw all
and every imputation I made against him at the time when I
imagined him guilty of an action of which I now firmly believe
him to be incapable.

That Gilbert's social behaviour was always scrupulously correct except when he was roused to wrath is exemplified by an
incident which he used to relate, prefacing it with the assurance
that it was 'literally true in every detail, even to the singular

coincidence at the end'. In the autumn of 1870, a fortnight
before the German army reached Paris, he left London for the
French capital at six hours' notice to act as war correspondent
to *The Observer*, for which he had written many dramatic
criticisms. At Dover, in a heavy gale, he overheard an altercation between an attractive young woman and one of the
steamer's officers. She had no passport, at that time a necessity,
and was told that she would not be allowed to land at Calais
without one. 'But I *must* go', she insisted: 'My husband is at
St Valérie, at the point of death, and I must go to him at any
cost.' Gilbert happened to have a passport made out for himself
and his wife, who had been unable to accompany him at such
short notice, and promptly offered to share it if the young
woman did not mind going ashore in the assumed character of
his wife. She was grateful, and though they kept apart on the
boat they landed together. At Calais he got her some supper
at the buffet and afterwards she asked if he would buy her a
ticket for St Valérie. In the train she explained that her husband was a naval captain and that having come away in a hurry
she only had a few shillings and two ten-pound notes. Gilbert,
well provided with cash, gave her twenty sovereigns in exchange
for her notes. On parting from one another at Boulogne they
swopped addresses.

After that he was very nearly arrested as a spy because of the
name 'Schwenck' on his handbag. 'Mais monsieur est Prussien?' said a fellow-traveller suspiciously pointing to his bag.
He explained that the name had been given him by his god-
parents at his baptism, and that he had not been consulted
when they took the liberty, otherwise he would have declined
to present himself at the font. The other inmates of the carriage
were not impressed by this explanation, so he produced his card
with the name of *The Observer* on it. This made matters worse.
'Mais, monsieur, "Observer" – cela veut dire espion.' He replied
that if he were really a Prussian spy he would hardly advertise
the fact on his visiting card. 'Monsieur', one of them said, 'un
Prussien est capable de tout!' However, he managed to convince
them that he was an English war correspondent, and they
became voluble on the subject of the campaign. Every Frenchman in Paris, they declared, would shed his last drop of blood
in its defence and every Frenchwoman would give her back
hair to make bowstrings. Without pausing to enquire whether

the safety of Paris would depend on bows and arrows, Gilbert asked one of his companions if he would remain in Paris to help in its protection. 'Non, monsieur, je pars ce soir pour Marseilles.'

Reaching Paris he put up at the Grand Hotel, where after a few days he decided to settle his bill with one of the ten-pound notes. The cashier examined it and decided it was a forgery. He was about to present the other note when it struck him that he would be in an awkward position if the cashier thought that, too, a forgery; so he paid in gold and departed for the ramparts. On his way he met a journalist friend who wanted money, his cheque for £20 having been refused at the bank because communication between Paris and London might at any moment be cut. Gilbert told him all about the ten-pound notes and said that if he liked to take them in exchange for his cheque he could do so on the clear understanding that they might be spurious. The friend took them and managed to obtain current coin for them.

When it seemed certain that no letters would get through after the investment of Paris, Gilbert was recalled, and he left by the last train. At Folkestone he met an old naval friend who, after hearing about the ten-pound notes, informed him that the woman and her husband were notorious swindlers and gave him many details concerning their activities. Some weeks later he received a letter from the husband, with the written heading 'Army and Navy Club', thanking him for his kindness to the wife and saying that they would call on returning to London to thank him personally. Gilbert went to see the secretary of the Army and Navy Club and showed him the letter, again hearing that his correspondent was a well-known swindler who passed himself off as a naval captain and frequently dated letters from the Club, the committee of which were most anxious to interview him.

Some months later Gilbert was in a box at the Princess's Theatre with his wife and a friend, to whom he had been telling this story and who thought that he had invented it. 'Not only is my story absolutely true in every detail', replied Gilbert, 'but there, by a most amazing coincidence, is the very lady in question', and he pointed to the opposite box. The truth became manifest when at the first interval a tall, burly-looking man with bushy ginger-coloured whiskers, asked to see Gilbert, who went into the lobby. 'I believe, sir,' began the visitor in a loud, quarter-deck voice, 'that you addressed my wife on board a Channel steamer six months ago.' Anticipating a row, several playgoers gathered round them. 'I am deeply indebted to you, sir, for your great kindness to her on that occasion', he continued, and the playgoers at once dispersed. 'I believe you were good enough to pay for her railway ticket', he went on. 'I must insist upon getting out of your debt as far as a mere money payment is concerned', and he gave Gilbert two florins. He then said that his wife would like to express her obligation in person and wondered if they might have the pleasure of calling.

'Unfortunately I have ascertained that you are a professional swindler', objected Gilbert.

'What do you mean, sir? Who has presumed to describe me in such terms?'

Gilbert supplied the desired particulars.

'I see', said the pseudo-captain thoughtfully.

'You appreciate the difficulty of my position?' said Gilbert.

'Perfectly.'

'If it had been otherwise – '

'Not another word, I beg.'

' – it would have given me the greatest pleasure – '

'You are most kind.'

'But – a swindler!'

'Out of the question', agreed the swindler.

'You acquit me of intentional discourtesy?'

'Absolutely. I quite understand. Good-evening.'

Gilbert saw and heard no more of them.

When the above incidents occurred Gilbert had been married for three years. The moment that the success of *Dulcamara* placed him firmly on the theatrical map he asked Lucy Agnes Turner, whom he had known for some time, to share his fortunes. The daughter of an Indian Army officer, she was eleven years younger than Gilbert and his counterpart in temperament. With fair hair, blue eyes, a neat figure and lively manner, she was an attractive girl, and everyone voted Gilbert a lucky man when the two were married at St Mary Abbot's church in Kensington on August 6th, 1867. They crossed to France after the ceremony, and it is typical of the bridegroom that in the train on the way to Folkestone he wrote one of his 'Bab' ballads. He had worked hard to secure a wife and he continued to work hard, not only to keep her in comfort but for the sake of cash and celebrity, the prosaic names for power and glory. All his writing was done with those ends in view; and though he was soon able to please himself by writing plays in verse, he started life with a succession of pot-boilers and never ceased to labour with the single aim of pleasing the public.

Their first home was at 28 Eldon Road, Kensington, but they soon moved to 8 Essex Villas, Kensington, where they remained for the next six or seven years. Three early letters of Gilbert's to his wife have been preserved, none dated but all written in 1872 or 1873, the first two while he was doing his annual training as a soldier in Scotland, the third during a brief visit to Paris in search of plays to adapt or burlesque:

Fort George

My darling Girl

Here you have a view of the barracks of Fort George – taken from the ramparts that surround them. It gives a very good idea of the size of the place, and also of its general appearance, and as I have marked the principal houses, you will feel quite at home with it. My house is the corner one, of the second row of buildings, on the right, and our regimental parade is between the second and third rows on the right. My quarters are on the ground floor, looking on to the parade ground. Of course, when we are inspected or when we do Battalion drill we come out into the big square that forms the foreground of the picture. The regiment arrived yesterday, in number about six hundred, and today has been spent in calling over the muster roll and in reading the articles of war. You will be pained to hear that if I strike a chaplain or betray the fort to an enemy I am liable to suffer DEATH.

(The rest of the letter has been destroyed, though from a sentence behind the last passage quoted above appears the phrase 'by the time you get this, dear old lady . . .')

Fort George

My darling Old Girl

You'll hardly believe that I'm writing this at 10.30 p.m. without a candle, but such is indeed the case – the nights are so wonderfully light here.

The Invernessshires marched out of barracks this morning and were disembodied at Inverness this afternoon. I went with them to Inverness and carried the knapsack of a man who had fallen out, fainting, on the road, and when the Inverness fellows arrived at the Station, they gave 'three cheers for t'chap who carried t'knapsack', and meaning your obedient servant. They seemed all very sorry to part with me – the officers, I mean – and I know I'm very sorry to part with them, for they were very jolly fellows and I had got to like them very much. We had a jolly dance yesterday at their . . . [the lower part of the sheet is cut away, but on the back of the above a phrase runs] . . . was present in my mind the whole time and I sincerely wished she had been there for I am sure she would have enjoyed it. You should have seen me dance a reel!

> Hotel de Lille et d'Albion
> Rue St Honoré
> Wednesday

Dearest Kits

I was very glad to get your letter as I have been thinking of you ever since I left. I am pretty comfortable here – very high up (5th floor) but a pleasant room when one gets to it. The weather is lovely. I have been writing all day in my room with the window open and without a fire. I went to the Porte St Martin on Tuesday and to the Opera Comique yesterday. Tonight I am going to the Folies Dramatiques to see L'Oeil Crèvé (of which I have bought the music) and tomorrow I shall go to the Chatelet to see Gulliver. I don't think I can be back before Saturday at 5 o'clock. I have sent P. Oliver the rest of the burlesque – I have had two hard days' work at it. I wonder the Stereoscopic people haven't written. Paris seems very full of French people, and more English are here than I expected to find. I shall look out for the late Miss Crampton, on the chance of her being here. I have not yet been to see Mde Hugue, and I don't think I shall renew that expensive lady's acquaintance. I have not been very dull up to this point as I have been working so hard.

I suppose you are at Curzon St. today – so I shall direct this accordingly. I don't much like being a bachelor – and I find a difficulty in getting up in the morning. I have, however, bought some chocolate to console myself with. I wish you were here, old girl.

Good-bye, my darling. God bless you – I think of you very often – and long to be with you again. My hand is quite cramped with writing. I have sent some copy to the I.T. about the Parisian theatres. Thank you for finding out Robertson for me.

Once more good-bye and God bless you.

> Ever your devoted
> old husband
> A Boy

Gilbert called his wife 'Kitten' and always treated her with affectionate playfulness. They remained a devoted pair, their natures being complementary. She never attempted to impose her will on his, but was clever enough to get what she wanted by making him wish it first. She quickly recognized that his habit of forming attachments to other women and his enthusiastic admiration for pretty faces sprang from some need in his nature, and she never displayed jealousy nor criticized his behaviour. It is possible that if their union had resulted in children his attractions outside the home would have been limited, but she no doubt endorsed the philosophy of Corporal Nym: 'Things must be as they may.' Someone who visited their house in Essex Villas came to the conclusion that Gilbert was the centre of interest for his wife's female friends. She was certainly docile, but she possessed humour, and as he never gave her serious cause for jealousy she was sensible enough to encourage his whims. There were times when her acquiescent and conciliatory but alert nature had the effect of calming his anger when exacerbated by the behaviour of others and of lessening the violence of his explosions when stung by ingratitude or dishonesty; though the reader of the ensuing pages may wonder what more could have happened without that gentle unobtrusive influence.

CHAPTER 4
Mainly Blank Verse

❍❑❍❑❍

In the seventies clean fun was beginning to compete with the salacious or slanderous innuendo so much enjoyed by male audiences at music halls and burlesques. The chief providers of chaste entertainment were the German Reeds, who with the help of a piano drew audiences that wished to be amused without feeling naughty. Respectable fathers and mothers from the suburbs could sit in the Gallery of Illustration, Lower Regent Street, with the comforting assurance that the performance would be approved by their clergy, and could laugh with abandon at Corney Grain, the great 'find' of the Reeds, who was as comical as he was free from dubiety of phrase. The success of the German Reeds was such that they were able to take St George's Hall and produce operettas. M. W. Balfe and Arthur Sullivan wrote the music for two pieces, while Gilbert wrote six one-act operettas and sketches for them. At a rehearsal of one of these, in the autumn of 1870, the composer Fred Clay introduced Gilbert to Sullivan.

It happened that Gilbert was in the process of becoming a poetic playwright. He had written a blank verse parody of Tennyson's *The Princess*, which had enjoyed a good run at the Olympic Theatre, and had then been commissioned by the manager of the Haymarket Theatre, J. B. Buckstone, to write a fairy comedy in blank verse, *The Palace of Truth*, founded on a French story. It was necessary that one of the characters should display a technical knowledge of music which the author did not possess; so he read the article on Harmony in the *Encyclopaedia Britannica* and converted a lengthy sentence therefrom into blank verse:

> *Believe me, the result would be the same,*
> *Whether your lordship chose to play upon*
> *The simple tetrachord of Mercury*

> *That knew no diatonic intervals,*
> *Or the elaborate dis-diapason*
> *(Four tetrachords and one redundant note)*
> *Embracing in its perfect consonance*
> *All simple, double and inverted chords!*

This seemed pure nonsense to Gilbert, but he wished to know whether it was as silly as it sounded, and on meeting Sullivan put the question in prose: 'I maintain that if a composer has a musical theme to express, he can express it as perfectly upon the simple tetrachord of Mercury, in which (as I need not tell you) there are no diatonic intervals at all, as upon the much more complicated dis-diapason (with the four tetrachords and the redundant note) which embraces in its perfect consonance all the simple, double and inverted chords.' Gilbert paused for a reply, but Sullivan wanted to hear the question again. Its repetition failed to enlighten the composer, who said that he would have to think it over, but doubtless dismissed it from his mind. The bare thought of having to supply an answer may have influenced his decision not to do the music for an operetta by Gilbert which German Reed wished to produce soon after their first meeting.

The Palace of Truth did well at the Haymarket, an old-fashioned candle-lit theatre, the manager of which received Royalty walking backwards, and once falling backwards, with a pair of candlesticks in his hands. In those days it had no stalls, the pit occupying the entire ground-floor of the auditorium. If the play were well received the manager appeared before the curtain and announced: 'With your kind permission the piece will be performed every night until further notice.' Authors were paid £50 an act for original comedies, and the highest salary of a leading actor was £20 a week. At nine o'clock play-goers were admitted at half-price. Stage superstitions were still rife, and an actor who brought a newspaper into the green-room was heavily fined, the entire company demanding rum-punch. Gilbert described another ancient custom prevailing at the Haymarket:

> A day or two before the production of the piece I was surprised to receive a packet containing 24 dress circle seats, 24 upper box seats, 24 pit seats and 24 gallery seats for the first night. On enquiry I discovered that by immemorial Haymarket custom these 96 seats were the author's nightly perquisites during the

entire run of a three-act play. I assured Mr Buckstone that I had
no desire to press my right to this privilege.

He preferred cash to free seats and after the play's success
was assured he insisted on a payment of four guineas for each
performance of *The Palace of Truth* during the first three months
of the run, after which the nightly payment dropped to two
guineas, being raised to three guineas a performance on tour.
The play, containing an amusing idea overburdened by blank
verse, enjoyed a long run. Two members of the cast were W. H.
Kendal and his wife Madge Robertson, sister of Gilbert's old
friend Tom. She was to become, technically, the most accomplished actress of her generation, and both the Kendals appeared
in four of Gilbert's blank verse plays, with seismic effects to be
related.

It would be tedious to enumerate all the comedies and
dramas for which Gilbert was responsible throughout the
seventies. There is nothing so dead as a play that was only
alive when acted. But his later claim that he 'held the foremost
position among dramatic authors' in his time is true. Without
counting the plays of Oscar Wilde, who occupies a niche of his
own like Sheridan 120 years before him, Gilbert was the leading
figure in the chronicle of the British drama between the production of Robertson's *School* in 1869 and that of Arthur
Pinero's *The Second Mrs Tanqueray* in 1893; and for sheer
versatility of production, whatever may be said of its quality,
no playwright has equalled Gilbert, who even adapted for the
stage a famous novel, *Great Expectations*, which was done at the
Court Theatre in the spring of 1871. He had a boundless admiration for Dickens and never left home for a night without one
of the great novelist's volumes. No other writer aroused his
unqualified enthusiasm, and he would perhaps have dramatized
Martin Chuzzlewit if his own plays had been less successful.
The stage censor of those days made a habit of toning down
what seemed to him irreverent phrases. In *Great Expectations*
the returned convict, Magwitch, says to Pip: 'Here you are in
chambers fit for a Lord.' The script was returned to the theatre
with 'Lord' deleted and 'Heaven' substituted.

The curious thing about Gilbert's more ambitious plays in
the seventies is that they deal with fairies or supernatural
happenings, and there is scarcely an ordinary human being

among their characters. A reason for this will be suggested in another chapter. What adds to their artificiality is the blank verse in which they are written. Finding that blank verse was much easier to write than prose, Gilbert wrote it too easily, and commonplaces embalmed in the verse of a mere craftsman appear more commonplace in print than when spouted on the stage. Here are two examples, the first from *The Palace of Truth* revealing the under-developed satirist, the second from *Pygmalion and Galatea* revealing the over-developed idealist, both passages exhibiting the reaction that followed the natural comedies of Robertson in the sixties:

> *O, honour, honour!*
> *Let no one take you at the estimate*
> *Your self-elected champions price you at!*
> *More harm is worked in that one virtue's name,*
> *Than springs from half the vices of the earth!*

> .   .   .

> GALATEA: *What is a man?*
> PYGMALION: *A being strongly framed,*
> *To wait on woman, and protect her from*
> *All ills that strength and courage can avert;*
> *To work and toil for her, that she may rest;*
> *To weep and mourn for her, that she may laugh;*
> *To fight and die for her, that she may live!*

> .   .   .

When compelled to supply padding for his plays Shakespeare wrote that kind of stuff, probably under the influence of sack; and since Gilbert had a poor opinion of Shakespeare, he only copied his faults. As we shall find, Gilbert was a true poet, but not in blank verse nor in prose.

His second play for Buckstone at the Haymarket, *Pygmalion and Galatea*, was produced in December 1871 with the Kendals in the leading parts. It was constantly revived and made more money for the author than any of his dramas, something in the region of £40,000. As he chiefly wrote for money, he had his reward. In his opinion the dramatist's profession 'does not call for the highest order of intellect – it demands shrewdness of observation, a nimble brain, a faculty for expressing oneself concisely, a sense of balance both in the construction of plots and in the construction of sentences'. These words were written but not published at the end of his life, and they were followed by his testament to the nature of the dramatist's calling:

A man who sets to work to cater for the entertainment of theatrical audiences is in the position of a refreshment contractor who has engaged to supply a meal of one dish at which all classes of the community are to sit down. What should that dish be? It must not be *suprême de caille* or it will be regarded as insipid by the butcher-boy in the gallery. It must not be baked sheep's head or it will disgust the epicure in the stalls. It must, I suppose, be some dish that will fit the gastronomic mean of the audience, and I take it that that gastronomic mean will be somewhere in the neighbourhood of rump-steak and oyster sauce. If I am right in this conjecture, it seems to follow that a dramatist who intends that his profession shall furnish him with an ample income should confine himself to writing plays of the rump-steak and oyster sauce description. Occasionally, and for the sake of justifying his claim to be regarded as a person of literary culture, he may soar into the empyrean and bring down from it, if he can, a work of the very highest literary excellence, and that work may find a moderate sale in book form – but as an acted drama it will fail to produce a profit.

Pygmalion and Galatea made trouble as well as money. At that time actors were far less subservient to authority than they have since become, and more than anyone else Gilbert was to bring discipline into the theatre; but he had to fight hard against the egotism of 'star' performers in the seventies, and a good deal of his reputation for caustic comment derived from the necessity of pricking the vanity of popular actors in order to make them recognize the author's position and the value of team-work. Mrs Kendal had her own way of playing Galatea and discarded suggestions by Gilbert that did not harmonize with it. As a result there were periods when they were not on speaking terms, except when she was on the stage and he was audibly criticizing her performance in a box. At a revival of the play an actress named Janette Steer received a letter from the author:

I must ask you to advance and kneel in front of Cynisca from her left, and not from her right – to throw yourself on your knees in front of her and (without making any exclamation) to fall at Cynisca's feet at the end of her speech, and not on any account to cross to Pygmalion, or indeed to do any business which was not arranged at rehearsal. If you do not comply with my wishes in these respects I give you notice that on Monday I shall apply for an injunction to prevent your playing the piece, or otherwise as I may be advised.

Janette complied with his wishes in these respects but managed to irritate him in others, receiving a further communication:

I understand that you interpolated several exclamations last night while Miss Repton was delivering her important speech at the end of the second act, thereby greatly impairing the effect of the speech and causing it to be indistinct and confused. I have instructed Miss Repton how to deal with the difficulty should it again arise. My instructions to her are to stop short at the first interruption, and to remain silent until that interruption has ceased – then to begin again, and should the interruption be repeated again to stop until the annoyance ceases altogether.

If Janette persisted in her tactics after that, the audience must have had their money's worth. Another revival in the eighties with Mary Anderson in the leading part led to temperamental scenes, the actress wishing to play Galatea in a classic style, the author demanding modernity. They disagreed over the dresses Alma-Tadema had designed, Gilbert complaining that she looked like a saint in a stained-glass window instead of a lively up-to-date girl. The fact that the audience liked the saint did not placate Gilbert, though the author's royalties due to her popularity lessened his vexation.

With the show at the Haymarket running to packed houses, he decided to raise his fees; and by insisting henceforth on regular payments and satisfactory rates for his work he gradually raised the status of the dramatist in the theatre, just as he improved the production of plays and the training of the players. On January 3rd, 1872, he wrote to Buckstone:

Having made two distinct and decided successes at your theatre, I consider that I am entitled to an increase of terms – the more so as I intend to devote at least six months to the next piece.

He now asked for five guineas a night and a run of one hundred nights guaranteed, the fee to be reduced to three guineas after the hundredth performance. He further demanded that the piece should not be seen by the public 'until three days after a rehearsal in which all the "cast" are letter perfect', a condition which, before his time, was not achieved until a week or so after the opening night, and frequently throughout the run the text was liable to variation due to the caprice or insobriety of the actors. He told Buckstone that he had already received offers to write plays for the Prince of Wales's and Vaudeville Theatres, which he had declined because, after two such successful productions at the Haymarket, 'it will be doubly worth my while to put my whole force, such as it is, into the piece that succeeds them'. Buckstone replied at once agreeing to his terms but hoping that in the event of further successes he would not increase them, as the expenses at the Haymarket were heavy, and also that if the next piece were a failure the guarantee of a hundred nights would not be insisted upon. Gilbert answered:

> I am afraid I must stick to the guarantee of 100 nights. If the piece does not succeed it will not be for want of hard and honest work on my part, and all I want is a certainty that my time and thought will not be wasted. At the same time, if the piece is a *dead* failure, you may be morally certain that I shall not have the face to hold you to the letter of your bargain. I think you may safely make the arrangement I propose, leaving it to my sense of fairness to modify the terms as to the length of the run if the piece fails through any fault of mine.

He undertook not to raise his terms in the event of future successes, but added:

> As an example of the kind of contingency I want to provide against – I should not have considered myself responsible if *Pygmalion* had proved a failure with such a fearful dead-weight as *Midas* to struggle with. I begin to think *Pygmalion must* be a good piece!

(*Midas* was a Christmas extravaganza which occupied the bill with *Pygmalion and Galatea*.) Buckstone said that he would rely on Gilbert's sense of fairness.

But a third success was scored with *The Wicked World* (January 1873) in which, though the fairies declaimed blank verse, the Fairy Queen's performance gave Gilbert an idea. 'My experience of Mrs Kendal suggests to me that she has considerable and unsuspected tragic capabilities', he wrote to Buckstone. 'I should like to write her a part either of the "Leah" or "Lucrezia Borgia" style – a powerful part with strong dramatic capabilities – a passionate vindictive devil

with some *one* accessible weak point – such as love for a child
or for some other *woman* – which weak point is to be the means
of reclaiming her. What do you say?' Buckstone probably said
nothing, because the Haymarket was a comedy house, Mrs
Kendal a comedy actress, and Gilbert a writer of comedy;
which he shortly proved by producing in collaboration a parody
of *The Wicked World*, calling it *The Happy Land* and getting it
done at the Court Theatre under the names of Gilbert à Beckett
and F. Latour Tomline, the latter pseudonym having been
used by him for many of his early articles. Three of the characters were made-up to resemble living statesmen, one of them
being Gladstone, and when the Lord Chamberlain's notice was
drawn to this he banned the piece. The necessary alterations
were made, the piece was again passed by the censor, and the
run was continued with the added attraction of guessing who
was what.

A parody of justice was also performed in the Court of
Common Pleas at Westminster Hall, when Gilbert brought an
action against the critic of *The Pall Mall Gazette*, one Enoch,
who had described *The Wicked World* as vulgar, coarse, offensive and indecent. Two passages were quoted by the defending
counsel to justify this condemnation. The first concludes the
Prologue, spoken by an actor who refers to the author as 'he':

> *But, let me ask you, had the world ne'er known*
> *Such love as you, and I, and he, must mean,*
> *Pray where would you, or I, or he, have been?*

The second passage, in counsel's opinion, suggested an immoral
exercise of love on the part of the Fairy Queen:

> *For six long hours has she retained the knight*
> *Within the dark recesses of her bower,*
> *Under pretence that his unhappy wound*
> *Demands her unremitting watchfulness.*

Buckstone, famous as a comedian, gave evidence, his appearance in the witness-box reducing the entire court to hysterical
laughter, even the judge being silently convulsed. Stupified by
the atmosphere of hilarity, the jury decided that both the play
and the article were innocent of offence; but they found for the
defendant and Gilbert had to pay £60 in costs. He was in
combative mood just then, for during a performance of this
same play he came to blows with an actor who was about to

appear on the stage through a trap-door, knocked him down, took his place at a moment's notice, and played his part without anyone being aware of the substitution.

Meanwhile he was writing a fourth play for the Haymarket, and it was understood that Buckstone should produce it early in the coming year. On hearing that the manager intended to put on another piece just before Christmas, Gilbert was extremely annoyed, and when Buckstone wrote to announce his intention, saying that the piece would only have a limited run, which would give Gilbert time to complete and rehearse his comedy, there was an explosion:

> 8 Essex Villas
> Kensington, W.
> 17th Nov. 1873

My dear Buckstone

I was extremely pained and surprised to receive your letter this morning. I had heard rumours during the past week that you had a three-act piece, by another author, in preparation for immediate production, but I paid no attention to the report as I should have considered it an insult to you to suppose you capable of such an act of duplicity. As it is, I have only to say that by the terms of our agreement, my piece was to be ready for rehearsal on the return of the company to town, and it was to be produced in the course of the month of December. To the terms of this agreement I propose to hold you most strictly. I have letters of yours in which you urge me to finish the piece without delay that it might be put into rehearsal immediately on your return to London. Accordingly the piece was got ready for rehearsal and I have been prepared to read it to the company any time during the past three weeks.

I will not dwell upon the deliberate character of the insult you have placed upon an author who has worked laboriously and conscientiously for you for nearly four years. I prefer to take my tone from your own, and place the matter on a strictly formal footing. Accordingly I hereby warn you that if my piece is not put into rehearsal forthwith and produced as soon as it is ready I shall place the matter at once in the hands of my solicitor.

> Yours truly
> W. S. Gilbert

Buckstone replied on the same day that Gilbert's new comedy

was to have been in my hands on my return to London. I have now been here more than a fortnight and have not yet received your book, and as you informed me you had not quite completed it I presumed I was suiting your convenience by giving you more time.

However, he refused to argue the matter and said that he would produce Gilbert's piece on the date agreed, arrange a reading of it during the current week, and start rehearsals at once. Gilbert did not consider that his convenience had been suited:

18 Nov. 1873

My dear Buckstone

If, in producing another author's 3-act play at a time when you were under contract to produce mine, you intended to do me a personal favour, you might have paid me the compliment of consulting me as to whether I considered such a proceeding a favour at all.

You have had many opportunities of letting me know your views since your return, but although your decision to produce this three-act piece was known a week ago in the theatre . . . and indeed wherever theatrical matters are mentioned, you only thought fit to let me know the boon in store for me yesterday.

With respect to your statement that I was to have been ready with the piece a fortnight ago, I wrote to you when you were in Birmingham telling you that three acts of the four would be ready by your return to town, and in reply you stated that you were glad to hear it and would put it in rehearsal immediately. You made an appointment with me for Monday the 3rd November at 3. I called at the theatre at that time with the MS in my pocket, but I found that you had forgotten the appointment. I then wrote to you and subsequently called on you and proposed reading the piece on Saturday the 8th. You postponed the reading till Saturday the 15th and on Thursday last again postponed it till Saturday the 22nd. And in the face of these facts you coolly charge me with having been unready to discharge my share of the contract. Let me assure you that I am fully posted up in all the circumstances that induced you to consent to produce this 3-act piece before my own drama. There is no need to say anything more about it, and I can only regret that the friendly relations that have hitherto existed between us should have been so severely injured by what I cannot help looking upon as "a stab in the dark".

I have an engagement which I cannot postpone for Wednesday. I am prepared to read the whole piece on Saturday at any hour you like to name. The cast includes Mr Kendal, Mrs Kendal, Mrs

Mellon, Mr Chippendale, Miss Amy Roselle, Mr Home and Mr Rodgers. There are one or two small parts of no importance.

Yours truly
W. S. Gilbert

Having clarified the situation to his own satisfaction, Gilbert read the play to the company and started rehearsing what was called a problem play, having taken immense pains in the writing of it. *Charity* was seen at the Haymarket in the first week of January 1874. There are few points in common between Lucrezia Borgia and the part played by Mrs Kendal, which is that of a woman who had 'sinned' – that is, who had once enjoyed sexual relations with a man without the consummation of a wedding-ring – and spends the rest of her life atoning for the deed by charitable actions involving self-sacrifice. Her 'sin' is discussed by herself and others in language that would be excessive if it had brought about the decimation of the world's population by the wrath of God. To exhibit the difference between the mid-Victorian and the modern mental attitudes to sex, this play should provide the historian's text-book. It was condemned as immoral at the time, a verdict with which, for different reasons, the present age will agree; and it was Gilbert's first failure at the Haymarket, though a popular actor of the time, Wilson Barrett, played it with some success in the provinces.

A sentimental comedietta in two acts called *Sweethearts* proved more acceptable at the Prince of Wales's Theatre in November 1874, with the famous actress Marie Wilton (afterwards Lady Bancroft) in the chief female part. This became one of Gilbert's most popular pieces, and the Kendals included it in their touring repertory the following autumn, paying two guineas for each performance. It is perhaps the one play of Gilbert's that might be revived as a period piece. He described it as a 'Dramatic Contrast', and the sentimentality is not too tearful.

But following these excursions in prose, he again lapsed into blank verse, and *Broken Hearts* appeared at the Court Theatre in December 1875 with the Kendals in the leading parts. When Wilson Barrett applied for the touring rights Gilbert reported that it had 'very strong sentimental interest', and late in life he confessed, 'There is more of the *real me* in *Broken Hearts* than in anything I have written.' At the end of the acting version these words are printed: 'Finished Monday, 15th November, 1875, at 12.40 a.m. THANK GOD!' He was concerned over the acting of a part and wrote with some heat to John Hare, who was casting the piece: 'I think my opinion as author of the part should go – not only for *something*, but for a *very great deal*.' He thought so much of the play that before it was produced he sent a printed copy to an editor, whose dramatic critic, Clement Scott, pronounced favourably on it. 'I am delighted to think that you like the piece so much', wrote Gilbert to Scott. 'I have been so often told that I am devoid of a mysterious quality called "sympathy" that I determined in this piece to do my best to show that I could pump it up if necessary', an odd way of speaking about a work in which he had laid his heart bare. The lessee of the Court Theatre was the great 'character' comedian John Hare, who produced the play with the author's assistance, though Hare might have called it resistance.

The action of the piece takes place on an island, where four maidens have sworn never to fall in love, three of them having already lost their lovers through death. Their hearts are broken, and their past sorrows and present affections are bewailed and celebrated in the blankest of blank verse, which must be read to be believed. A male Adonis arrives on the island; two of the maidens fall deeply in love with him; and after both have indulged in orgies of self-sacrifice, the exhibition of which would have turned a martyr into a sybarite, one of them eases the situation by dying. The play is a burlesque of itself, and the sentimentality would make a saint cynical. Acting in it must have been a gruelling experience, and apparently the Kendals made their discomfort vocal. Nothing is so disheartening as the reiteration of noble thoughts and selfless actions, and it is hardly surprising that *Broken Hearts* led to broken friendships. John Hare and the author quarrelled at the time, which later led to a broken friendship; the Kendals said or did something that Gilbert found unforgivable; and Clement Scott committed the crime of repeating in an article Burnand's joke that he was going to see *Broken Parts*, being sharply reprimanded by Gilbert:

Burnand's attempt at wit is silly and coarse, and your attempt to bring it into prominence is in the worst possible taste. I am not by any means a thin-skinned man, but in this case I feel bound to take exception to your treatment of me and of my serious work.

That closed the friendship between Scott and Gilbert, and when the former attempted a reconciliation some 26 years after he found that neither the joke nor a later criticism had been forgotten:

Dear Scott

Your ideas as to the duties and privileges of a dramatic critic are so diametrically opposed to mine that I think we had better let matters rest as they are. Nor do I think that the fact that you will have achieved sixty years on the 6th October is a reason for a general jubilation. I am sixty-five, and nobody seems to care.

I bear no ill-will towards you, but I have an excellent memory.

Yours truly

W. S. Gilbert

In the sentimentality of *Broken Hearts* Gilbert expressed the obverse of the savagery in *The Bab Ballads,* and each reveals the seeming contradiction in his own behaviour. His violence masked weakness, his tenderness melted rancour. When Clement Scott lay dying Gilbert was most solicitous; at the funeral he wept continuously; and afterwards he helped his old companion's widow in all sorts of ways.

Once more he succumbed to the lure of blank verse and wrote *Gretchen,* the leading idea having been suggested by Goethe's *Faust.* He worked on it steadily for ten months, finished it at 1.44 a.m. on Sunday morning the 15th December, 1878, and remained convinced for the rest of his life that it contained his best work. Henry Neville accepted it for the Olympic Theatre, and Gilbert was extremely anxious about its casting, its dressing and its setting. When Neville made arrangements with one firm of dress-makers, Gilbert wrote: 'I have had many dealings with May, and on the last occasion of his dressing a piece of mine I told him distinctly that he should never dress another – and with my consent he never shall.' He also objected to the scene-painter of Neville's choice and to certain actors. By this time Gilbert's reputation was considerable, and he did not mince matters:

Unless I am allowed the full privileges which are conceded to me in every theatre with which I am connected, *I will not put my*

foot within the walls of the Olympic. These privileges are an unques-
tioned right to make all engagements that have to be made and
an absolute control over the stage management of the piece from
first to last.

Faustus was played by the best obtainable actor of juvenile
parts, H. B. Conway, and Gretchen by Ellen Terry's sister,
Marion. On the first night, 24th March, 1879, Gilbert recorded
that 'at the end of the piece I received such a call as I never
had before'. But the season was Lent and the average takings
were £65 a night, which barely covered expenses. Though he
said that he had written it to please himself and not the public,
he was displeased with the public for not being better pleased.
It was withdrawn in a fortnight. 'I called it *Gretchen*, the public
called it rot', was his valedictory comment.

It is possible that playgoers would have called his other blank
verse plays 'rot' had it not been for the excellence of their
production. What Robertson had done for domestic drama Gilbert did for fanciful drama; and what Robertson invented Gilbert perfected. For the first time at a leading London theatre
audiences were treated to performances that were as faultless
as human ingenuity could make them. The inflections, gestures
and movements of the actors were rehearsed again and again
until the author could envisage on the stage what he had seen
with the mind's eye. He paid as much attention to the costumes,
scenery, properties and lighting as to the grouping and inter-
action of the characters, and so complete was the illusion
attained that his verse seemed poetic, his prose facile, his sentiments pleasing, his dramatis personae natural. The magnitude
of his achievement can perhaps only be appreciated by those
who have read his plays. But his influence on stagecraft was
so great that he may be called the father of modern play-
production.

CHAPTER 5

Uncivil and Military

०⚫०⚫०

The home life of the Gilberts was quiet and relatively free from the discord obtaining in so many households. It might be said that the master of the establishment released all his irritability in quarrels with actors, critics, managers, and so on, and was peaceful at the fireside from sheer exhaustion. But this would only be partly true. Gilbert had suffered as a youth from parental conflicts and knew how to appreciate a tranquil domestic life. His native shrewdness and knowledge of character, coupled with affection, guided his choice of a wife, from whom he received a devotion that included an understanding of his nature and a compliance with his wishes. He made a good husband to a good wife, a state of matrimony not so common as it sounds commonplace.

Excessively busy both at home and out of doors, he was also a regular clubman. He joined the Beefsteak Club in 1876 and the Junior Carlton a year or two before, using both of them continuously. Most of his writing was done between eleven at night and three in the morning. 'Then you have absolute peace', he said: 'The postman has done his worst, and no one can interrupt you unless it be a burglar.' But his mind was unremittingly busy, ideas striking him in the most unexpected places. The plot of his one-act play *Comedy and Tragedy* occurred to him in a carriage on the underground railway while travelling between Sloane Square and South Kensington stations. The story might have been improved if he had remained in the train as far as Hammersmith, but the playlet became popular with actors after its first representation at the Lyceum Theatre in January 1884 with Mary Anderson and George Alexander in the leading parts.

Since he usually worked into the small hours he rose late and the early morning sounds of fire-making in the adjoining house disturbed his slumbers, so he wrote to R. Furlonger Esq., 6 Essex Villas, Kensington, on February 7th, 1876:

Dear Sir,

I am sure you cannot be aware of the very distressing noise made by your servants, apparently, in raking out the cinders from the stove in the back room of your first floor, in the early morning – a process which usually lasts from eight to ten minutes. I am compelled by my avocation as an author to sit up very late at night, and the disturbance I refer to has the effect of seriously impairing my rest. I am quite certain that it is only necessary to direct your attention to the annoyance, to ensure your taking steps for its abatement.

With many apologies for troubling you on so purely domestic a matter,

I am,
Dear Sir,
Faithfully yours,
W. S. Gilbert

Mr Furlonger did not receive this in a neighbourly spirit, and another letter was sent him on the same day:

Sir

The tone of your letter, and your extraordinary admission that you wilfully make the noise I complain of with the express intention of annoying me, places any amicable consideration of the matter out of the question.

If you had represented to me that my servants disturb you by making an unnecessary noise in cleaning my library, it would have been my duty as a gentleman and as a neighbour to have cautioned them to conduct their duties more quietly. Notwithstanding the line of conduct you have thought proper to adopt, I shall at once enquire into the matter, and if I find that your complaint is well founded, I shall instruct them to be more careful. With respect to your remarks on the lateness of the hours I keep, I must reserve to myself the liberty of pleasing myself on that point.

I have only to add that as you have acknowledged in writing that you wilfully and maliciously interfere with my rest, I shall, on the very first repetition of the annoyance, instruct my solicitor to indict you as a nuisance at the Hammersmith Police Court.

I am, etc.

Gilbert then opened a correspondence with Furlonger's solicitors, stating that the noise had been made three times a week for at least three months and often for ten minutes at a time.

> You will scarcely pretend that this is a likely, a usual, or a convenient method of 'calling the attention of my servants to the noise created by them' or that any magistrate is likely to look upon it otherwise than as a most unwarrantable outrage.

Furlonger complained that Gilbert entertained parties every Sunday evening. Gilbert replied that three gentlemen had dined with him on February 6th, two on January 22nd, and apart from these he had dined out or alone every Sunday that year. He maintained that the charge against his servants was

> wholly frivolous. I myself sleep in the room adjoining that in which your client alleges that my servants make an undue noise, and on that very account they are particularly careful to make no more noise than is absolutely necessary.

He gave the names and addresses of his guests on the dates mentioned, Arthur Sullivan and Marcus Stone being two of them.

The tenant of No. 6 was duly advised by his solicitors to stop the noises; but the discomfort of living next door to a man who doubtless made his silence expressive of rage caused Gilbert to look for a house in a more gentlemanly quarter; and in the middle of 1876 he borrowed money from his banker in order to lease No. 24 The Boltons, South Kensington, a commodious residence with a tennis lawn.

Annoyances of a different kind awaited him here. He notified the man who should have supervised the alterations and decorations that he had failed to show 'such a personal interest in the matter as I was entitled to expect of you' and that consequently he would not be paid more than $2\frac{1}{2}$ per cent on the builder's account. A firm that had undertaken to adapt a settee to the new surroundings was told that

> a more clumsily finished piece of work I never saw. It is wholly unlike the sofa which was shown to you as the model for the alteration, and the quality of the stuffing, the careless manner in which it is finished and its general unsightliness make it impossible for me to allow it to stand in my drawing-room. You have removed a portion of the original fringe which you have replaced by fringe which matches neither in pattern nor quality – and you have placed fringe in the front only, although I explained to you that

the sofa was intended to stand in the centre of the room. As the sofa is quite useless to me in its present ridiculous form, I wish you distinctly to understand that I altogether decline to pay for the alterations you have made.

He also countermanded an order for matting because it was not delivered when it ought to have been.

Another exchange of incivilities occurred when his coachman attended an auction sale at Tattersalls and a horse was knocked down to him for sixty-two guineas. The firm afterwards discovered that the sale was an error and demanded the animal's return. 'If there has been a mistake at all, the mistake is yours, not mine', wrote Gilbert, 'and I must leave you to bear the responsibility thereof. I may add that the peremptory tone of your note is not calculated to induce me to make any unnecessary concession.' He later informed them: 'Had your first letter been characterized by proper courtesy I would willingly have consented to the horse being put up to auction again. As it is, I intend to keep the horse' – and any further correspondence must be addressed to his solicitors, Messrs Bolton & Co., 13 Gray's Inn Square.

Such letters were characteristic, but two occurrences in this decade were unlike him. He was given into custody by the station inspector for travelling without a ticket on the underground railway. Either he had left his season ticket at home or in the rush to catch a train he had failed to take a day ticket. Whatever the cause, he offered the inspector every facility for identification, but possibly his language was so intemperate that the offer was refused. The authorities were quick to apologize. Another uncharacteristic action was his claim for exemption from jury-service, which was granted.

Though he strongly objected to authoritative action where himself was the sufferer, he severely criticized the failure of authority to carry out its duties when he was inconvenienced. An example of each attitude is here given, the first letter being addressed to General Turner, the second to the Postmaster, South Kensington:

6 Jan. 1878

Dear Sir

Mrs Gilbert has handed me your letters in which you insist on seeing my marriage settlement before paying over the legacy of £150 left to her by the late Lucrezia Turner.

Without stopping to discuss the motive that prompted this demand, I will content myself with stating that I have consulted my solicitors on the subject who inform me that you have no claim whatever to examine the marriage settlements of legatees named in the will of which you are an executor. Acting upon their advice I altogether decline to comply with your request.

Yours truly

·   ·   ·

10 Nov. 1877

Sir

I have to complain of the systematic negligence of the postman who has charge of the early delivery in this district. It frequently happens that, through imperfect sorting, or some other cause, he has to return once, and sometimes twice, with letters that should have been delivered at eight o'clock. Today he delivered three letters at eight o'clock, a small book parcel at 8.45, and two more letters at 10.15. As today's experience is in no way exceptional, I think it is my duty to lay the matter before you. .

I am
Your obedient servant

Even Gilbert's generosity was tinctured by scrupulosity. When Paul Gray, the artist, suffered a breakdown in health and could no longer work, a subscription was opened for him at the club. 'What's the highest single sum subscribed?' Gilbert asked. 'A fiver', he was told. 'Then put down W.S.G. for one fiver and X.Y.Z. elsewhere on the list for another.' A more forceful instance of his precision was given in a letter he wrote to an actor who had expressed gratitude for his aid:

I am glad the money is likely to prove useful to you, but I am bound to tell you that if I had known as much about you, and your habits, as I have since learnt from several excellent authorities, I certainly should not have sent you one penny.

This aspect of his nature, a desire to be generous while being just, was clearly if comically revealed when someone applied for a testimonial to the character of James Saunders, a man-servant who had quitted his employment. In December 1875 he wrote to say that the man's general character was admirable, but 'a strict sense of justice' compelled him to add that Saunders had probably stolen his cigars, worn his linen, and attempted to remove his livery. In spite of which, 'I shall be glad to learn that you do not consider my charges against Saunders to be so grave as to render your employing him out of the question.' By the same post he advised Saunders:

I have just written to Mr Pender giving him my reasons in full for supposing that you took my cigars – wore my linen – and intended to take my livery. He can judge for himself what those reasons are worth. They probably do not amount to legal evidence to convict you, but to my mind they are sufficient to render it incumbent upon me to mention them in giving you a character. Mr Pender will no doubt allow you to see the letter I have written to him. I have no desire to stand in your way of getting another situation, and I shall be happy to give you an excellent general character. I shall feel it my duty however to mention the circumstances that gave rise to this correspondence, stating them in full, and leaving it to the employers to estimate them at their proper value.

In other respects Gilbert's punctiliousness was that of the age in which he lived, especially when women were concerned. Arriving at his house in The Boltons with a female friend, both of them going on to the theatre, he found that his wife was not at home, which meant that his friend had to remain in the carriage while he went indoors and changed his clothes.

His chief hobby, after his successes at the Haymarket and elsewhere had made it possible, was yachting. He bought a yacht in 1877, sold it and bought another in 1878 for £275. His purchases necessitated much correspondence over the costs of making the boats seaworthy, and the usual threats of legal action if his wishes were not carried out. The furniture and decorations were also the subject of controversy; and when in 1881 a yawl of 110 tons was built for him, the epistolary commands and countermands and calculations and criticisms might have convinced a land-lubber that he was designing an Atlantic liner. But his sailing was mostly confined to the ports and waters of England, though he adventured far enough into the Channel to become familiar with the lighthouse flashes from both shores, the watchful eyes of England and the winking eyes of France.

It pleased him to make the transition from sailor to soldier. As we have seen, he was in the Royal Aberdeen Militia, which he joined in 1865. Every year he went to Aberdeen when the regiment was in training. The commanding officer, Colonel

Innes, recalled at the end of his life that Gilbert had been neither eccentric nor genial but rather cynical. Asked whether the officers had found it interesting to have so distinguished a man among them, Innes replied: 'Oh, we did not think him very distinguished then!' Gilbert appears to have been a reasonably efficient officer, though he avoided what seemed to him unnecessary toil and discomfort. He lived at peace with his senior officers, but none of his avocations could be wholly unattended by friction and after he had been eleven years with the regiment he took exception to his mess bill. On July 25th, 1876, he wrote to Lord Inverurie, President of the Mess Committee:

> I must decline to pay for more messing than I actually enjoyed – if that term can be reasonably applied to the food that was placed before me by the messman. There is an item of £1.3.9. for beer. I never touch beer. Possibly this may include spirits. I certainly did not drink 50 glasses of brandy during the twelve days that I was with the regiment.

He named several officers who were not charged for messing when away from duty, and asked why an exception was made in his case. His complaint was forwarded to Colonel Innes, who replied: 'As to Major Turner's not being charged with a share of the mess contract, it has nothing at all to do with Captain Gilbert.' But he little knew his Captain if he thought that such a remark would settle the question. 'I must decline', wrote Gilbert, 'after this expression of opinion, to serve under an officer who is so little qualified to command gentlemen.' Having hinted to the Colonel that 'I could not help feeling that a charge of £21 for eleven days wine and abominable messing' would not appeal to the Commander-in-Chief, he paid the whole of his bill and despatched the following letter to the Adjutant:

Major Gordon Alexander, R.A.H.   17 Oct. 1876
Sir
    I have the honour to request that you will be so good as to inform Col. Innes that I propose to resign my commission in the Royal Aberdeenshire Highlanders, and to request him to forward my resignation to the proper quarter.
    I believe that by virtue of my service in the Royal Aberdeenshire

Highlanders and in the 5th West York Militia I am entitled to
retain my rank and wear my uniform.

> I have the honour to be,
> Sir,
> Your obedient servant
> W. S. Gilbert
> Capt. R.A.H.

Colonel Innes at once tried to soothe his touchy subordinate,
but 'when it seems to me that a principle is at stake I am rather
obstinate', said Gilbert, who on November 16th wrote to his
commanding officer:

> I am extremely sorry to take this step as some of my very
> pleasantest associations are connected with the regiment, and I
> have always taken a deep interest in it. I feel however that in this
> matter I have been so thoroughly misunderstood from first to
> last – and that there is so little chance of my ever having an oppor-
> tunity of qualifying my course of action – that in resigning my
> commission I am only taking a step that is consistent with my
> self-respect.

However, when the case came to the notice of the Commander-in-Chief, enough pressure was brought to bear on
Gilbert to stay his action and enable him to preserve his self-
respect. He remained with the regiment for another sixteen
months, and when he did resign he made no reference to the
misunderstanding over the mess bill:

> 6 Apl. 1878
>
> Dear Col. Innes
> I much regret to say that it has become necessary that I should
> resign my commission in the Royal Aberdeenshire Highlanders.
> With the prospect of a permanent embodiment of the Regiment
> before me, I have hitherto declined to accept definitely any com-
> mission to write pieces for London theatres during the past two
> months, but now the time has arrived when I am absolutely
> compelled to give a definite answer to three managers of theatres
> (Messrs Sothern, Neville and J. S. Clarke) as to whether I will or
> will not accept engagements to write for their theatres. If it were
> certain that the Regiment would be embodied, I should have no
> hesitation in deciding to relinquish my profession for the time
> being, but I do not feel justified in practically giving up the calling
> by which I earn my living for what is, after all, a prospect, more
> or less remote, of permanent service. I have temporized with
> these managers, my employers, until the latest moment, with the

expressed intention of declining their offers in the event of embodiment, but the time has come when they require a definite reply from me, and you will see that I have no alternative but to resign the commission I have the honour to hold in the Regiment under your command.

I am,

Dear Col. Innes,

Faithfully yours

He left the Militia with the honorary rank of Major, and thenceforth drilled actors instead of soldiers.

CHAPTER 6

Toil and Trouble

⊶⊷⊶

O
ne of the proofs that Gilbert was not only the foremost but the most successful English playwright in the seventies and eighties of the nineteenth century is that every front-line actor and actress, with two exceptions, appeared in one or more of his plays. It may be said that no other dramatist before or since his time has had his works illuminated by so many and such bright 'stars'. Apart from Henry Irving and Ellen Terry, who were about their own business of a kind outside his province, the rest of the leading lights shone in a drama or comedy by him, the more notable ones among the women being Marie Wilton (Mrs Bancroft), Madge Robertson (Mrs Kendal), Marion Terry and Mary Anderson; among the men, J. L. Toole, John Hare, Charles Wyndham, Wilson Barrett, Beerbohm Tree, Forbes Robertson, George Alexander, Arthur Bourchier and Lewis Waller, all of whom were actor-managers either then or later.

At one time or another Gilbert experienced difficulties with all the chief actors in his plays. His personality was too provocative and dictatorial for easy relations with a set of men whose vanity made them more than commonly vulnerable. His downright expressions were not reserved for the players who had won good positions on the London stage, though these came under his personal notice. Provincial actors who toured his plays quickly discovered that they could take no liberties with an author whose eye was upon them from a distance of two to four hundred miles. If they did not pay his royalties promptly, they were threatened with legal proceedings; if they attempted to do his plays without permission, they were injuncted; if they introduced 'gags' and vulgarities of their own, their contracts were terminated; if they did not give as many performances as they had agreed to give, they were served with a summons. Gilbert possessed not only a keen sense of business but a still keener sense of other people's eye to business, and when he felt that he was being treated dishonestly the culprit was soon made aware of his feeling.

Two examples out of many will illustrate his usual procedure. An actress, Carlotta Leclerc, did not pay the fees for the performances of *The Wicked World* which she had given in America. He instituted legal proceedings; and some five years later, when various provincial theatres in England announced that she would appear in *Pygmalion and Galatea*, he wrote to all the managers concerned warning them that if they allowed her to do so he would hold them responsible for the *gross receipts*. Then there was a manager named A. Montgomery, who, having agreed with the author to give *Sweethearts* at Edinburgh twenty times during his season there, had only performed it thrice, claiming that he was entitled to present it anywhere anywhen for the remaining seventeen times. Gilbert promptly threatened him with an appeal to the Court of Chancery and assured him that 'I will spare neither trouble nor expense in making you feel the full weight of the inconvenience you have caused me.' Montgomery climbed down.

Amateur companies sometimes performed his plays without bothering to make the usual business arrangements. When an instance came to his notice, he ordered the responsible person to send three guineas to St George's Hospital; otherwise he would 'place the matter in the hands of my solicitor'. At first he allowed amateurs to act his comedies without payment, but when other authors complained that such a course interfered with their rights he supported them by insisting on fees, which always went to the hospital. Other beneficiaries from his plays were the American managers, who performed them with so much profit to themselves and so little to him that he told his New York agent: 'The Museum is the best market obtainable for them in the States.' Occasionally however his agent there arranged a contract, charging a commission of 25 per cent, but ceased to be his agent after giving a printed copy of a forthcoming play to the critic of *The New York Times*. 'This is simply an outrageous and utterly intolerable liberty', wrote Gilbert, 'and one which you certainly shall never have it in your power to take again.' Trickery of any kind activated his bile. When Dr Wylde advertised an opera by Suppé called *Pygmalion and Galatea*, Gilbert apprised him that it was not the title of

Suppé's opera but that it was the title of his own comedy, and that if Dr Wylde did not select another title he would apply for an injunction.

It must be added that Gilbert was not solely concerned with his own gains and grievances. He helped and encouraged the younger generation of actors and actresses, took the part of girls who were being victimized, and gave his advice freely to any struggling player who asked for it. Do not 'refuse a part because it is small and unimportant', he urged one actress: 'If you show talent – and I am certain you will – your promotion will be rapid – not to the top of the tree, but to a very comfortable position on one of the boughs. The top may be attained in time.' Perhaps his essential kindliness was best expressed in championing those whom he thought unfairly treated. At that period actresses who were at all free with their favours were liable to be unpopular with those to whom their favours had not been extended; and as the profession was then struggling hard to be respectable, the movement in that direction was naturally supported by all who were never offered the chance of being anything else. Gilbert, though a Victorian in his beliefs, was a Christian in his behaviour, as shown by this letter:

22 June 1881

My dear Blunt

I've had to take your part over and over again of late in reference to this wretched Haymarket scandal. There seems to be a general impression that you and others signed a document addressed to Mrs Bancroft stating that you would decline to act with the poor girl whose name has been prominently mentioned in connection with the matter, and that in consequence she has been turned out of the theatre, and her character, professional as well as social, utterly blasted.

Presuming on a knowledge of your kindly character, I have taken upon myself to deny emphatically the possibility that such a statement could be true. I did not wait for your authority to do this, as I considered that it would be an insult to you to ask for it.

Very truly yours

He was never too busy to be kind, just as he was never too busy to have a quarrel. He gave a hand to ambitious dramatists as well as to hopeful actors. Once he asked Squire Bancroft to read a comedy 'written by a friend of mine, Mr Alfred Austin, the well-known poet and novelist', the literary quality of

which he pronounced excellent, the story both good and interesting. Yet his own work was enough to occupy a team of
authors and he was never late with his commitments. 'I am
always nervously fidgety about keeping any engagements', he
said. He took excessive pains with what he did, re-considering
and re-writing whole scenes in his plays, attacking every work
as if his reputation depended upon it, doing whatever he set
out to do with every ounce of his energy. He simplified his
labours as much as possible, buying a typewriter in the seventies, all the letters of which were capitals, and inventing a
contrivance whereby the telephone could be kept pressed to the
ear at any angle or at any required distance from the trans-
mitter without fatigue or inconvenience; which invention he
sent to the United Telephone Co. Ltd. in March 1882, demanding no payment. He tinkered constantly with a watch which
refused to go, sent it to the repairers five times, and ultimately
returned it to the makers with the comment that he had given
it every chance to redeem its character. Having threatened
proceedings, he got it back in six months, presumably in good
working order.

In the midst of all his labours he was able to write to the
editor of the *London Figaro* in November 1875: 'If my other
avocations will allow me time to do so I shall be happy to
contribute occasional articles to your paper.' But he never
allowed his work to interfere with his annual holidays. He and
his wife, often accompanied by a friend or two, usually spent
a fortnight at the sea. We hear of them in the late summer of
1875 at Trouville and Boulogne, where he bathed regularly and
vigorously, drove, walked, and even lazed. His life was full, and
he lived to the full in every hour of it. Yet he was by nature
economical. Unlike those authors who negligently leave cheques
lying about in the hope that other people will find them and
record the impression that they are indifferent to money, he
accounted for every penny he received and expected his money's
worth for every penny he paid. All his writing was done for
money, and he never pretended another reason for it. As a
consequence his plays, done with much effort and great care,
did not give him the inner joy experienced by authors who,
however much they may hope money will come of it, do their
work because they must. This explains why, though every
writer of ability produces a certain amount of trash, Gilbert

exceeded the excusable ration. 'I am the worst judge in the world of my own work', he once confessed. But if he had been able to forget the public his innate intelligence would have told him where his real genius lay.

Many of his quarrels were due to the feeling that he alone knew exactly what playgoers wanted and that the actors in his plays were more anxious to exploit their personalities than to do justice to the author. He did not think highly of two actors whose reputations have survived their day: Henry Irving and Beerbohm Tree. He had a strange prejudice against both, partly on account of their fantastic characters which were liable to transform the plays in which they appeared, and partly because neither had mastered the technique of speech and movement required by every practised playwright. There is no record of his personal meetings with Irving, but in the eighties Tree appeared in a revival of Gilbert's farcical comedy *Engaged*, originally produced at the Haymarket on October 3rd, 1877, and two remarks made to the actor by the author were not of a kind to ripen friendship. After the first performance Gilbert noticed that Tree was sweating profusely and said: 'Your skin has been acting at all events.' Dismissing the quip with a laugh, Tree suggested that he should have grown a moustache for the part. 'You will be able to grow an enormous moustache before you can play this part', returned Gilbert; and though their conversation then ceased to flow easily, Tree had enough sense of humour to repeat these jokes at his expense.

Incidentally *Engaged* was the most (we cannot escape the word) Gilbertian play ever written by Gilbert. The craftsmanship is impeccable; and though every character is a caricature, all are so well sketched that they constantly bring to mind the surface characteristics of personal acquaintances. But apart from this the farce has some significance in theatrical history. If future academic critics search for a possible source of *The Importance of Being Earnest*, they will find it in Gilbert's *Engaged*, which is written with the formal gravity, the exaggerated momentousness of Wilde's masterpiece. The love-making in both is done with the same mock sincerity, the same cynical mundanity and sudden changes of mood, and Worthing's entry in deep mourning for his brother Earnest is foreshadowed in *Engaged* by the entry of a black-garbed character in mourning for another who has just threatened to commit suicide.

Gilbert's situations are more outrageous than Wilde's, absurdity o'erleaping itself; and *Engaged* lacks the spontaneous wit, good nature and radiant enjoyment of pure fun which make *Earnest* unique. Nevertheless Wilde owed as much to Gilbert as Sheridan did to Congreve: that is, enough to make the reputation of a critic who cared to trace the influence, but not enough to make us feel that *Earnest* would have been materially different if *Engaged* had never been written. It is of some interest to observe that Marion Terry 'created' the part of Belinda Treherne in Gilbert's best comedy *Engaged* and fifteen years later the part of Mrs Erlynne in Wilde's first comedy *Lady Windermere's Fan*. And it is of considerable interest to record that when Gilbert's play was published he appended an 'Author's Note' which every actor who plays in *The Importance of Being Earnest*, and every producer thereof, ought to learn by heart:

> It is absolutely essential to the success of this piece that it should be played with the most perfect earnestness and gravity throughout. There should be no exaggeration in costume, make-up or demeanour; and the characters, one and all, should appear to believe, throughout, in the perfect sincerity of their words and actions. Directly the actors show that they are conscious of the absurdity of their utterances the piece begins to drag.

Writers with a rare comedic gift are seldom satisfied with its exercise. The First Gravedigger longs to play Hamlet, but Hamlet has no desire to play the First Gravedigger. Gilbert saw himself as a serious writer and thought little of *Engaged* in comparison with his drama *Dan'l Druce*, produced a year before at the Haymarket with Forbes Robertson and Marion Terry in the leading parts. It is a play of the 'second person singular' variety, containing much of 'thou' and 'thee' and 'art' and 'dost' and 'hast' and the style of language people were supposed to speak in the seventeenth century but never did. The sentiment in it is as thick as plums in a wedding-cake and quite as sickly, the drama is as heavy as a Calvinist conscience and just as silly. It harps so much on the longing of a father for a child that perhaps it reveals Gilbert's secret longing for one of his own and his occasional bitterness from the want. The immediate success of *Dan'l Druce*, which was partly founded on George Eliot's *Silas Marner*, elated its author but was not of long duration. 'With Compton in the comic part, it would have been tremendous', he wrote: 'Odell is simply damnable.' The last-named, known as 'Old Odell', remains a tradition at the Savage Club, where stories about him are still circulated, though many members are ready to assert that he was never seen on the stage. He lived to a great age, his last two or three decades being spent at the Charterhouse, from which he emerged every evening to visit the Savage Club in Adelphi Terrace and to sit by the bar in a chair that is still preserved.[1] Gilbert's concise opinion of his acting proves conclusively that he was on the stage, if also that his true *métier* was elsewhere.

The sudden decline in business at the Haymarket induced Buckstone to precede *Dan'l Druce* with something more exhilarating, and as he had the acting rights in Gilbert's play he was at liberty to do so, but it was a liberty the author advised him not to take:

16 Nov. 1876

My dear Buckstone

I understand, to my great surprise, that you propose to place *Dan'l Druce* at the end of the bill on Monday.

I must ask you to consider carefully before you take this step whether such a course of action is likely to facilitate our future transactions. If my piece don't draw, withdraw it by all means – but for Heaven's sake don't disgrace it by playing the people out with it.

The piece is not mine (I wish it was) – at least not yet – so I cannot legally interfere. I can only beg you to consider whether the proposed alteration is not, from every point of view, a most injudicious step.

Yours very truly

Wishing to facilitate their future transactions, Buckstone reconsidered the matter, and *Dan'l Druce* was performed at the same hour until it played itself out.

Most of Gilbert's work for the theatre in these years was of a satirical or farcical order. *Topsyturvydom* (1874) showed a country where everything appears to be the opposite of what it is in England; where people are born old with wisdom and grow young with ignorance; where men are women and women men; where beauty is horrible and ugliness admirable; where

---

[1] It is held at the Savage Club to be unlucky to sit in Old Odell's chair. Whether this is due to the fact that a head in marble of the old gentleman stands menacingly behind the chair, or for more recondite reasons, no one seems to know.

everything pleasant is detested and everything noxious adored. This theme ultimately became Gilbert's stock-in-trade, and a possible explanation of the almost complete absence of verisimilitude in his work will appear shortly. Even a farce should have some basis of actuality, but his *Tom Cobb* (1875) has none. It is too fatuous to be funny. He also knocked off several adaptations from the French, e.g. *The Wedding March* (1873) and *On Bail* (1877), which are about as good, or as bad, as most French farces, and are mentioned here solely because the first was done in just over a day, earning him £2500, while the second was done for Charles Wyndham, who was regarded by every leading dramatist of his time, Shaw, Wilde, Gilbert, Pinero and Henry Arthur Jones, as the finest actor of modern comedy; and indeed, in personal charm and faultless technique, his equal has not appeared since.

That Gilbert was working overtime to meet all the demands upon him is shown by a brisk exchange of letters with Wyndham, who asked why the play had not been finished on an agreed date. But Gilbert prided himself on keeping his promises. 'I am always punctual and I am not likely to be otherwise in this case', he told one manager, and his explanation satisfied his own conscience if not Wyndham's requirements. Some of his irritation with actors may have been due to the strain of overwork, but more was caused by their refusal to accept his advice without question. The quarrel with the Kendals, only patched up on the last day of his life, must have started in some such way; but his resentment against them was so strongly felt that it is probable they had flatly declined to take any notice of his criticisms and had themselves criticized his play *Broken Hearts*, the darling child of his fancy. At any rate, when the Kendals were visiting Glasgow in September 1877 they remonstrated in advance against a project of the manager who, having obtained the performing rights of *Sweethearts* from Gilbert, wished them to appear in it. 'For *private* reasons', wrote Kendal, both he and his wife refused to act in any of Gilbert's plays; but the manager replied that their misunderstanding with that author did not affect his business arrangements with either party, and insisted on their playing in the piece. They did so, with consequences we are about to learn. Ten years elapsed. In February 1888 W. H. Kendal wrote to inform Gilbert that he and his wife had been so frequently pressed to play in

Sweethearts that he wondered if it would be 'agreeable to you to let us do so on our forthcoming Autumn tour', and if so on what terms? Gilbert replied on February 7th:

Sir

Circumstances connected with the performance of *Broken Hearts* in 1875 caused me to write to you to say that I would never again allow Mrs Kendal or yourself to speak a line of mine upon the stage.

Two years later – in 1877 – I accidentally discovered that, notwithstanding this distinct prohibition, you were surreptitiously playing *Sweethearts* at Mr Bernard's theatre in Glasgow. I called your attention to this circumstance and again requested you to abstain from playing my pieces. In reply, your agent – one Arthur Sackville – wrote to me, at your direction, expressing your dislike to receiving communications from me, and requesting me not to address you again. In reply I wrote as follows:

'I have only to say that it rests with you to determine whether I am to be in correspondence with you or not. So long as you refrain from trespassing on my property, so long will you be spared the humiliation of being taken to task for so doing. But if you persist in playing my pieces, I shall be compelled (distasteful as it must be to me to enter into any communication with you) to take the necessary steps to protect my property from outrage.'

This letter you directed your agent – one Arthur Sackville – to return to me with the following superscript, written across its face –

'Sir

I am desired by Mr Kendal to inform you that, when returning any letters you may write to him in the future, he will not feel himself called upon to prepay the postage.

Arthur Sackville.'

I mention these circumstances because I cannot but suppose, from the fact of your considering it to be in any way possible that I should allow you to play my pieces in public, that the incident of our Glasgow correspondence must have entirely faded from your recollection.

I am, sir, etc.

Some of the most self-revealing passages in Gilbert's letters were not read by the recipients. In the draft copy of the above, kept among his papers, he cut out a sentence which followed his quotation of Arthur Sackville's rejoinder: 'You may be interested to know that I at once caused this letter, with its superscript, to be framed, and it has hung in my library ever since.'

Any frank approach towards a reconciliation completely disarmed Gilbert. In 1883 John Hare, with whom he had also quarrelled at the period of *Broken Hearts*, wrote to thank him for his kindness to 'our dear Effie' and to hope that he still thought kindly of Effie's parents. Hare confessed that though they had not been on speaking terms for so many years, he and his wife had always regarded the Gilberts as their oldest and best friends: 'May I ask you to shake hands and be friends again?' Such an appeal met with an instant response:

3rd Feb. 1883

My dear Hare

There could be no breach between us so wide but that the dear little messenger you sent us today could at any time have bridged it over – the more so as we thoroughly understood and appreciated the good feeling that prompted you to let your children look upon us as friends throughout our long estrangement. This privilege has been very precious to us, as all that was left of many happy associations.

Let our quarrel die and be buried, and let us agree that it shall never be referred to again by either of us.

Always sincerely yours

Considering his chivalrous attitude to women, it must have been an unusual assertion of independence in two of them that caused Gilbert to behave in so ungallant a fashion. Amy Roselle, an actress who had appeared in several of his pieces, decided in September 1877 that she would rather not repeat the experience. But she had already signed a contract to do so and Gilbert threatened her with a lawsuit if she failed to fulfil it. Rather than incur the trouble and annoyance of an action, she signified her intention of playing, 'but from your continued impertinent conduct towards me, and the gratuitous insults you insist upon heaping upon me . . . I can only think you wish me to cancel my engagement'. If such were the case, she would return her contract with the greatest possible pleasure; but if he kept her bound to the engagement, she wished him to remember that, business apart, she would have nothing to do with him: 'I must refuse to recognize the existence of men who have behaved in such an extremely ungentlemanly manner.'

But all this was a mere ripple in a puddle compared with the hurricane caused by his behaviour to Henrietta Hodson and hers to him.

Henrietta was married to Henry Labouchere, the editor and founder of *Truth*, the comments in which as the quarrel proceeded galled Gilbert so much that his solicitor's bill became a considerable item. It all started with the production of a play *Ought We To Visit Her?* under Henrietta Hodson's management at the Royalty Theatre in January 1874, the leading parts being taken by herself and Charles Wyndham. It was Gilbert's adaptation from a novel, a satire on snobbery naïf enough to have been written by a socialist M.P. But the adapter and the leading lady took up more of the company's attention than the piece, especially when Henrietta, thinking she was sitting on a chair, fell plump on the floor, and Gilbert remarked: 'Very good, very good. I always thought you would make an impression on the stage one day.' Henrietta had a will of her own that instantaneously clashed with Gilbert's, and neither of them spoke gently when provoked; in fact the real trouble seems to have been that both lost their tempers and afterwards forgot what they had said in that condition. At the final rehearsal a dispute arose that made Gilbert excessively angry. He left the theatre and 'under the influence of strong excitement', as he put it, described the occurrence to a friend of Henrietta's in words which, on reflection, appeared to him stronger than the occasion warranted. On February 4th he applied to the recipient of his wrathful communication:

Dear Miss Litton

I have received a letter from Miss Hodson's attorneys threatening me with an action for slander on the ground that I attributed 'obscene and disgusting language' to her in my conversation with you. As I am certain she must be acting under some misapprehension, I shall be much obliged if you will kindly let me know what you said to Miss Hodson in reference to our conversation concerning her, that could possibly bear such an interpretation.

I am prepared to admit that I said that Miss Hodson used the ridiculous expression 'floody bool' in reference to me and that she told me at the last rehearsal 'not to stand growling there, but to go home and go to bed as that was the best place for me'.

Very truly yours

On hearing what he had said, he wrote to Henrietta Hodson

withdrawing the expressions which had been made when his temper was out of control. Henrietta at once distributed copies of his letter to all the leading members of the theatrical profession in London, and it was eventually published in *The Hornet*. Her action did not help to restore amity.

Two years later *Pygmalion and Galatea* was revived at the Haymarket Theatre, where Henrietta was then employed. We are on somewhat unsteady ground here because Buckstone declared that her contract had come to an end and that he had terminated her engagement on account of her high salary. But it is fairly certain that Gilbert influenced his decision. 'It is impossible to stage-manage a piece when the stage manager (in this case myself) and a leading actress are not on speaking terms', he wrote. Henrietta accused Gilbert of persecuting her, and threatened him with an action for defamation of character; whereupon he informed Buckstone that 'if she consents to meet me on an amicable footing the only objection I have to her appearing in my pieces will be at once removed'. He repeated this in a letter to her. She then complained that she had not been offered the part of Galatea, but when told that she could have it her vanity was appeased and she agreed to play Cynisca. Before the rehearsals began Gilbert wrote to Henry Howe, the Haymarket stage manager, asking him to take notice that

> my conduct towards Miss Hodson at rehearsal will be characterized by proper courtesy and a due regard for her professional position, and I shall feel much obliged if you will at once check me if I should happen to be betrayed into any act or word which may smack of discourtesy towards that lady. But, on the other hand, I must claim to be protected from the consequences of any unwillingness on her part to meet my reasonable requests, and, in the event of any difficulty arising from such unwillingness, I propose to be guided entirely by your opinion.

The effect of his stern determination to treat Henrietta with proper courtesy was described by her as 'studied insult'.

Buckstone next revived *The Palace of Truth* and again terminated the engagement of Henrietta, who again accused Gilbert of persecuting her and doing his best to drive her out of the theatre. He provided evidence that he had done nothing to injure her by letting her see a letter from Buckstone. She replied: 'You are fully capable of either having dictated it to him or of having forged it to suit your own purposes.' Gilbert must have felt that his behaviour had not been wholly unexceptionable, or he would have put the law in motion at this point. Buckstone and Howe declared that Henrietta was quite capable of imagining conversations that never took place and letters that were never written. She certainly drew on her imagination when she published a pamphlet setting forth her grievances against Gilbert, who rejoined with another pamphlet explaining that her grievances were groundless. Meanwhile he hoped at least to proceed against *Truth*, in which Henrietta's husband had been criticizing him in a very penetrating manner. But an eminent counsel did not favour an action, writing:

> I do not advise Mr Gilbert to notice the attacks made upon him in the pages of *Truth*. The articles and notices before me show clearly enough that the writer is an adept in the art of offensive comment and criticism and that he has done his best to annoy and insult Mr Gilbert. But I am of opinion that proceedings by way of criminal information against the publisher and proprietor of the paper would not be successful.

The quarrel provided literary and theatrical circles with plenty of free entertainment for several years, and perhaps it was appropriate that the last professional meeting between Gilbert and Henrietta should have taken place in a charity pantomime at the Gaiety Theatre:

18 Jan. 1878

Dear Hollingshead

I understand that Miss Hodson is anxious to play a part in the forthcoming amateur Pantomime. To this, of course, I can have no possible objection, but if it is arranged that Miss Hodson is to appear in the harlequinade, I had better play some part, however insignificant in the opening, and *vice versa*. As I am not on speaking terms with Miss Hodson, the rehearsals will be facilitated by this arrangement.

Truly yours

But Gilbert appeared as Harlequin, and H. J. Byron described the novel event:

*There was laughing and cheering and shouts of surprise
As Gilbert in glittering garb met our eyes;*

And when the 'positions' he showed well he knew,
A thrill of astonishment ran the house through.

.   .   .

And Gilbert through all danced and postured with grace –
And a very determined expression of face!

Nearly all Gilbert's quarrels derived from the attrition of rehearsals. He could get on quite harmoniously with people in normal conditions; but when he wanted a thing said or done on the stage in a particular way, he went on repeating his commands, his tone becoming more and more peremptory; and as it was a relatively new thing for an author to produce plays, Tom Robertson being the first of the dramatist stage managers, Gilbert the second, the actors still thought they knew more about production and performance than the man who provided what they would have called their raw material, and regarded dictation from the writer as an affront. Robertson had a sort of gentleman's agreement with the Bancrofts to produce his own plays, author and actors blending so well that the little theatre in Charlotte Street seemed to house a family party. But Gilbert had to deal with all sorts of actors and managers, and he was the first author to fight for the dramatist's right to have his plays presented as closely as possible to his conception of them. Pinero succeeded him, and then Shaw, after whom the business fell into the hands of a new race of men called 'producers'. Gilbert's battles, then, seem unavoidable in retrospect, and perhaps it needed a man of his ruthlessly dominating nature to rescue the drama from the actors. Later, in comic opera, he achieved the supremacy for which he had fought all through the seventies.

That he could maintain amicable relations with a leading actor and win his admiration is proved by his association with Edward Askew Sothern, though in this case their friendship was not put to the test of rehearsals. Sothern had gone to America as a young man and had been offered a small part in a play called *Our American Cousin* by Tom Taylor (one day to be editor of *Punch* and a butt of Whistler's) who had already written two successful pieces, *Masks and Faces* with Charles Reade, and *Still Waters Run Deep*. The part offered to Sothern was called Lord Dundreary, which he undertook to perform on condition that he could re-write it and build it up. At first the show was a failure, but he made more and more of his part until it became the rage, Lord Dundreary being regarded in America as a typical English aristocratic idiot. He is still remembered for his whiskers. Following a delirious success in the States, the play was done at the Haymarket Theatre, London, on November 11th, 1861, with Sothern in what was now the leading part. As in America it failed at first, but on the advice of a famous comedian, Charles Mathews, the manager Buckstone advertised it extensively and it ran for some 400 nights, then a record in the English theatre. The play became the fashion on both sides of the Atlantic, and was being witnessed by Abraham Lincoln on the night of his assassination, but no actor played the zany peer with anything like the comic effect of Sothern.

Three years after the Dundreary furore Sothern displayed another aspect of his talent by 'creating' the leading part in Tom Robertson's *David Garrick*, which was to become Charles Wyndham's most popular rôle; and when in 1875 Gilbert wrote *Dan'l Druce* he thought Sothern the right man for the serious leading part. They drew up an agreement that Sothern should present it the following year, that a hundred performances were to be guaranteed at five guineas a night, and that Gilbert should have the entire control and stage-management of rehearsals. But when the time came Sothern was back in America and they entered into another agreement, Gilbert undertaking to write a play called *The Vagabond* with a part specially suited to Sothern's personality. As it was to be produced in the States and he could not supervise the preparations, Gilbert did not wish his name to appear as author; but Sothern wrote from New Orleans in November 1876 begging him to reconsider this:

> You have no idea how valuable your name is here amongst the *Brains*, and in Philadelphia and New York the production of a new play by you will create quite a stir . . . You must make me a legal document conveying the piece exclusively to me – as a naturalized American (I am one) . . . My return to London is doubtful. Peace and war are on the balance in the new and old worlds . . . matters look dangerous here, and we are all prepared for another civil war – God forbid it, for it would be *far* worse than the last one . . . With troops in the city and daily expectation of an outbreak I am averaging over £140 a night.

While writing the play Gilbert made all sorts of suggestions

and Sothern agreed with all of them except perhaps the introduction of a collie dog, which sticks to the Vagabond when
everyone else deserts him, becoming mangy and ill-conditioned
along with his master, just as previously he had been handsome
and well-kept when his master was in prosperous circumstances.

I know the danger of a dog on the stage [Gilbert admitted], but
some dogs are so easily trained that it occurred to me that the idea
was worth entertaining. Perhaps you possess such a dog – one who
obeys you and whom you could trust not to overact? In the first
act his double (for I suppose it must be a double – though perhaps
a dog in good condition might make-up 'mangy') need not be so
well trained as the situation is not so risky.

Sothern paid £2000 in advance for the acting rights for ten
years, and Gilbert was greatly disappointed when he returned
the play saying it did not suit him. 'I was as well satisfied with
it as a man who is not a damned conceited ass is justified in
being', wrote the author, adding, in reply to one of Sothern's
objections, 'I am afraid that in dealing with a widow one must
accept the fact that if she is still a virgin it is her husband's
fault rather than her own.'

Gilbert at once bought the play back from Sothern for £1000,
intending to return the rest of the money advanced out of the
fees he would obtain when the play was put on. It was produced
at the Olympic in February 1878, having been re-written and
re-entitled *The Ne'er-do-weel*. Rehearsals did not pass off without vexation. Forbes Robertson was stung into making a quip
at the author's expense that resulted in an estrangement of
thirty years, during which they were on scowling terms; and the
actor who played Quilt clowned his scenes, though warned by
Gilbert that he would wreck the play if at a certain point he did
not act with absolute seriousness. The audience were attentive
through the first two acts, and Charles Reade assured the author
that success was certain. 'Ah, but there's the third act to come',
said Gilbert. 'The third act is worthy of Congreve', replied
Reade, who had watched the rehearsals. But the third act was
performed in dumb show, the audience being more vocal than
the players, and comparisons with Congreve were impossible.
One scene 'was greeted with a storm of hisses such as I never
hope to hear again', reported Gilbert, who accused Quilt of
ruining the piece, though the actor concerned did not share his
opinion.

With a rectitude amounting to generosity Gilbert immediately wrote to tell Sothern of the failure, promising to refund the balance of the total amount advanced as soon as he could raise it by mortgaging his leasehold property. 'Your offer is more than fair', acknowledged Sothern. 'Damn the mortgage, I accept your word – alive or dead I wouldn't worry you . . . I cannot tell you how pleased I am with your letter.' The sum was duly repaid, but an enemy of Gilbert's must have indulged in tittle-tattle about it:

10 Feb. 1879

Dear Sothern

I have been exceedingly annoyed by a statement, publicly made by Mr W. H. Kendal in the Beefsteak Club, that I have acted most dishonourably towards you in the matter of my unhappy piece *The Vagabond*. Unless Mr Kendal at once apologizes for his slanderous statement I propose to lay the matter before the committee of the Club, and I shall be much obliged to you if you will favour me with your views as to my conduct to you in reference to the failure of that play.

At the same time Gilbert wrote to Kendal asking him to furnish the name of his informant and to send an explicit apology and retractation of the scandalous charge. Sothern's repudiation followed, on which Kendal denied that he had used the words attributed to him, Gilbert detailed the facts to the Club's committee, and a curtain descends on the episode.

After Sothern's death in January 1881 Gilbert helped the actor's sister, Mary Cowan, a passage from one of whose letters may be quoted:

Allow me to say that of all the people with whom I have had any dealings in reference to money since my brother's death, you have treated me with the greatest kindness and fairness, and I feel grateful to you for sparing me any trouble or anxiety.

Gilbert's experiences in the theatre caused him to take a jaundiced view of both players and playgoers, and he wrote a sketch, *Actors, Authors, and Audiences*, in which an author is tried for the offence of writing an unpopular piece. Witnesses are called for the prosecution and cross-examined by the delinquent. The manager states:

I did not read your play before accepting it, because I do not profess to be a judge of a play in manuscript. I accepted it because

a French play on which I had counted proved a failure. I had
nothing ready to put in its place. I was at my wits' end. I have
been there before. I soon get there. I have had no special training
for the position of manager. I am not aware that any special training is requisite. It is a very easy profession to master. If you make
a success, you pocket the profits; if you fail, you close your theatre
abruptly, and a benefit performance is organized on your behalf.
Then you begin again.

The leading actress says:

It is true that two minor parts were fused with mine to make
it worthy of my reputation. I did not charge for rolling the three
parts into one. I did it entirely in the author's interest. I do not
remember your objection to the mutilation of your play. It is not
a circumstance that would be likely to dwell in my mind. I have
never been hissed in my life. The parts I have played have
frequently been hissed. No one has ever hissed me.

The low comedian's evidence is punctuated with roars of
laughter:

I did my best with the part. I bought a remarkably clever
mechanical wig for it, but it was useless. In my zeal in behalf of
the prisoner I introduced much practical business; I introduced
it solely in the prisoner's interest. No doubt the prisoner remonstrated, but I knew what an audience likes much better than he
does. The part was soundly hissed – even the introduced scene
with the guinea-pig and the hair-oil . . . I consider that authors
should feel much indebted to me for the valuable interpolations
suggested by my humour, experience and good taste. Most certainly I have never been hissed in my life. The parts I have played
have frequently been hissed. No one has ever hissed me.

The actress who played the sorrowful governess explains
why that character indulged in a song and dance between her
pathetic scenes:

She might be supposed to do so in order to cheer her spirits.
I do not consider 'Father's pants will soon fit brother' an inappro-
priate song for such a character . . . I would not dance in every
scene, because that would not be true to nature. I see no objection
to her dancing now and then . . . I wore short petticoats because
the audience expected it of me. I see no reason why a governess in
a country vicarage should not wear short petticoats if she has
good legs . . . I have never been hissed. My parts have often been
hissed, but no one has ever hissed me.

Picked members of the audience are called on for their opinions:

One claims: 'I consider myself a judge of a play. I have written a play myself. It has not been acted – not yet.'

Another, a plumber, objects to a scene between the Duke and Duchess: 'I consider myself a judge of what Dukes and Duchesses would be likely to say . . . I have plumbed in the very best families. I have supplied a ball-cock to a Royal cistern.'

An officer in the Grenadier Guards declares: 'Nothing is easier than to write a good stage-play. I have written one myself. I found it extremely easy . . . My play has not been produced – not yet.'

A medical student agrees: 'I have written several plays; they have not been produced – not yet.'

A clerk in the Home Office tells the same story: 'I have written many plays – everybody has. They have not been acted – not yet.'

The prisoner's defence, given in the third person, contains a hit at what was then considered the advanced French drama: 'As a clean-minded gentleman he would no more think of drawing inspiration from M. Zola or M. Alexandre Dumas than he would think of drawing drinking-water from a grave-yard.'

This was Gilbert's serious opinion. He never liked the advanced drama, whether French, German, Norwegian or British. It made him feel uncomfortable and increased that sense of instability which resulted from the unhappy relationship of his parents about to be divulged, and which may have been partly responsible for his awkward contacts with the outside world as well as the unreality of his stage creations.

CHAPTER 7

Partly Explanatory

❦❦❦

The phrase 'incompatibility of temperament' covers a multitude of things, from nasty habits to silly behaviour, from an idiosyncratic sense of humour to habitual melancholia; but in effect it usually means that two people cannot live together because they do not like one another. Gilbert's mother and father had been getting steadily on each other's nerves for a long time, and at last they separated. There does not seem to have been any sympathy between them from the early days of marriage, because affection once given can never be wholly obliterated, though it may be so much overlaid with later emotions as to be invisible. But a sudden crisis will momentarily revive it; so we may infer from Anne Gilbert's later attitude to her husband that in her case it had not existed. His dictatorial and irascible personality must always have grated on her cold reserved nature and ultimately bred a settled resentment that no crisis could change to a warmth of feeling she had never felt. Allowing for her peculiarly repressed disposition, it is fairly certain that her indifference to him was shown in a lesser degree to their children; and when she saw her husband's domineering and quick-tempered characteristics reappearing in her son, her vexation probably made her a hostile, or at least an apathetic, mother.

In the spring of 1876 a correspondence took place between father, mother and son. Gilbert kept copies of all his letters which he thought necessary for future reference, mostly with the aid of a copying-press, though sometimes in the original corrected drafts. In a slender book, unlike the fat volumes wherein most of his letters were copied, appear his strange communications with his parents, from which it is clear that, however much their somewhat similar natures clashed, he liked his father a good deal more than his mother. His first letter explains the position.

8 Essex Villas
29 May 1876

Dear Mama,

Undeterred by your cold and formal reception of the appeals made to you by my Aunt, by Jane and Alfred, and by myself on behalf of my father when we and both his medical attendants believed him to be dying, I write to you once more to direct your attention to the lamentable circumstances in which he is placed.

It seems that he has assigned the house in Pembridge Gardens (worth £180 p.a. unfurnished, and at the very least £300 p.a. furnished) to you absolutely, and that, beyond this, he allows you £400 p.a. for your household expenses; my sisters having about £400 p.a. between them. His own net income is, he assures me, about £150 or £160 p.a.

When he made this arrangement it was when he was in a position to earn a considerable income by his pen. It now turns out that by direction of Dr Coates and Dr Didfield, who attended him in his illness, this source of profit is entirely cut off – they both say that he must absolutely resign all hopes of ever writing for profit again. Under these circumstances it becomes absolutely necessary that some new arrangement shall be arrived at, by which he will be placed in a position to live on his income modestly but like a gentleman.

To effect this I desire most seriously to submit two courses to your consideration:

1. To allow him to live in your house, assigning a sitting room and bedroom to him for his separate use, and keeping your domestic arrangements entirely distinct, or

2. To forego so much of the allowance he makes you as will raise his own net income (whatever that may be) to £400 p.a.

I will not insult you by supposing for one moment that when you have realized the position in which he is placed you will raise any objection to one or other of these courses – to either of which he is quite prepared to agree. As to the original cause or causes of your quarrel, I express no opinion one way or another. I steadily kept aloof from any discussion of that matter after I found that my proffered interposition was rejected by both sides – I contented myself you will remember by offering you my assistance either in arranging affairs with your solicitor or in effecting a reconciliation at a future time. To that line of conduct I have resolutely adhered. Whenever he has attempted to broach the question, I have invariably declined to enter into it, and if you had referred to the matter in my presence I should have done the same. But it is impossible to disregard the fact that he has been

most dangerously ill – that he is still in a very delicate state of health – that he is in his 73rd year – that he has no settled home – that his net income is about £150 a year, and that he has now no means whatever of increasing it; whereas your income and that of my sisters may be estimated, at *the most moderate calculation*, at £1000 a year. Without going further into particulars which I have perhaps no right to refer to, I may say that he has within the last fortnight given a practical proof of his great interest in your future welfare and that of his daughters. I mention this to show you that he, at all events, is not entirely lost to those feelings of regard which forty years of intimate association must have aroused in the mind of any person not absolutely lost to all feeling of humanity.

I hope you will not reply to this letter without giving it *your very gravest consideration*. If I have unintentionally misstated any of the facts of the case, I shall be glad to be put right, and in proportion to such miscalculation the proposed allowance might be reduced. But I have quite made up my mind that the last years of his life shall not be made miserable by a poverty which it is wholly unnecessary he should suffer. And I am certain that when you have fully realized the gravity of his position, you will make up your mind to the same effect. This is my reason for urging you to think the matter over, before you send a reply that subsequent events may give you reason to deplore.

Yours affectionately
W. S. Gilbert

P.S. I may add that I desire to take upon myself the entire responsibility of these suggestions.

His mother's reply might have been written by a distant and uncongenial cousin:

14 Pembridge Gardens
1st June

Dear Schwenck

You seem from your letter to infer that a quarrel was the cause of your father's leaving his home. So far from this being the case, it was the result of weeks of calm deliberation and entirely against the wishes, as he and you well knew, of your sisters and myself. He left his home of his own accord and without the slightest reason, and is of course at liberty to return if he chooses.

Yours affectionately
Anne Gilbert

Gilbert made the best of the situation and wrote to both his parents:

4th June 1876

Dear Mama,

I am very glad to hear that you do not intend to offer any opposition to my father's return home, but at the same time I cannot reconcile your statement that he left in opposition to your wishes and to those of his family with the fact that when I urged a reconciliation and offered to do anything in my power to bring it about, before the separation had actually taken place, you replied that, 'while thanking me for my proffered interposition, you would not avail yourself of it, as you had both determined never to live together again'. I am quite content, however, to read your last letter without reference to those that preceded it, and I feel quite certain, from my father's altered manner, that you will have no cause to regret your expression of willingness that he should return, though I will not disguise from you my regret that, considering all the circumstances of the case, that willingness was not expressed in more cordial language.

I may add for your satisfaction that I have spoken seriously to him on the error he committed in endeavouring to impose unnecessary restrictions on your proceedings and on those of my sisters, and I am convinced that my remarks have had a salutary effect. I have only to urge on you and on them the policy of meeting him half way.

I have written to him by this post informing him that you are quite willing that he should return. You do not particularly refer to my suggestion that two rooms of the house should be reserved for his exclusive use and that your domestic arrangements should be kept entirely distinct, but in my letter to him I have taken the liberty of assuming that you have no objection to this proposal.

I have much pleasure in expecting that if this arrangement is carried into effect I shall be relieved from the necessity – a very painful one – of urging him to reserve for his own use such an income as will enable him to live independently.

Yours affectionately

4th June 1876

Dear Papa,

I have written to Mama urging upon her the absolute necessity either of reserving two rooms of the house for your exclusive use, and keeping your domestic arrangements entirely distinct, or of foregoing so much of her allowances as will bring your income up to £400 p.a.

She replies that she is quite ready and willing to agree to the suggestion that you should return to Pembridge Gardens, in accordance with the terms of my proposal.

Under these circumstances I suppose it is only necessary to name a date for your return, that the requisite arrangements should be made. It is quite certain that this is the *very best* course you can take – indeed I believe it to be the only one that is consistent with the circumstances of the case. Your arrangements will be entirely distinct (if you choose that they should be so) and you will have no more to do with each other than two families that occupy separate flats in Victoria Street. As you agreed to my making this proposal – 'breaking ground' as you termed it – and as the proposal has been accepted unreservedly, I think you are bound by it. I shall be glad to hear from you that you are prepared to assert your position once more.

As I have opened the proceedings I would suggest that for the present any necessary correspondence may be made through me.

Lucy sends her love. We are both very glad to have such good accounts of your health.

Yours affectionately

W. S. Gilbert

His mother's next letter, which produced this extraordinary rejoinder, must have been lost or destroyed:

6th June 1876

Madam,

I am in receipt of an unsigned letter from you, dated the 5th June, in which you expressly withdraw the consent implied by your letter of the 1st June to my proposal that my father should have two rooms in his daughter's house assigned to him for his separate use. It therefore becomes necessary that I should use my best endeavours to put into effect the other alternative to which I referred in my letter of the 29th ult.

I shall proceed to Salisbury on Wednesday, and lay the whole correspondence before him. I may add that I have hitherto, in your interests, induced him to believe that when he was in danger of his life you hurried home from Paris and were unremitting in your personal enquiries after him, until he was pronounced out of danger. It will now be my duty to tell him the bare facts of the case – that you delayed two days in Paris after receiving a copy of Dr Coates' letter describing the perilous state of his health, and that on your return you exhibited no interest whatever in his then critical condition.

I have nothing more to add, except that your statement that you appealed to me to prevent the impending separation is, as you are well aware, absolutely untrue.

I am, etc

W. S. Gilbert

After that a happy or unhappy reunion was out of the question, and Gilbert's father spent the rest of his life at Salisbury, residing with a married daughter in the Cathedral Close. Before his illness he must have been a difficult man to deal with, because if he got an idea into his head nothing could get it out again. On Sundays he often called at his son's residence in Essex Villas, but as the servants were absent that day he was always told to ring the bell since the door-knocker could not be heard in certain parts of the house. But he persistently ignored the bell and went on hammering at the door, cursing when there was no reply, stamping off in a rage, and refusing to call again for several weeks. This displays his character. He expected everything to happen exactly as he wished and behaved like a spoilt child when people or circumstances did not conform to his requirements. His son, though far more adaptable, had a similar temperament and a corresponding temper, and so we can guess that his quarrelsomeness was inherited. But his touchiness, his susceptibility to unintended insult and to a hostility that did not exist, were in some sense due to a feeling of personal insecurity bred by the restless, acrimonious, unhappy and unstable conditions of a loveless home.

Life is a mystery; and however deeply we may probe into the conduct of human beings and satisfy ourselves that we have found a reason for this or that, the preponderant residue of personality remains inexplicable. Some of a man's behaviour may be tenuously traced to heredity, some to upbringing and environment; but it is safer for a biographer to exhibit his subject than attempt to explain him. Nevertheless there are two aspects of Gilbert's work that seem to derive from the unsatisfactory domestic conditions of his early life. The absence of human feeling in most of his plays, the false exaggeration of the sentiment wherever it occurs, his inability to portray real people, his constant resort to the fancies of fairyland, his frequent pictures of a topsyturvy universe; all these, taken together, suggest an internal discomfort, a desire to see things as they are not, born of his early contact with an unpleasant actuality. The other aspect of his work that appears to be related to the impressionable period of his youth is the mockery he makes in his operas of ageing females. Though this has some connection with his strong attraction for pretty women, held in check by an equally strong moral sense, the origin is possibly to be found in his total lack of sympathy with his mother, amounting in time to active dislike, his feeling revenging itself on all women whose age and insensitiveness called her to mind. In this way his mother may have been responsible for the sole appearance of realism in his operas, a disquieting feature which was to cause a rift between himself and his illustrious collaborator.

CHAPTER 8

Tentatives

❦❦❦

lthough, as we have seen, Sullivan refused to do the
music for a one-act entertainment by Gilbert which
German Reed wished to put on, he accepted a commission by John Hollingshead to provide the setting for a two-
act 'grotesque opera' called *Thespis* by Gilbert which appeared
at the Gaiety Theatre on December 26th, 1871. This was the
first piece they did together, and it failed. Neither company
nor audience were prepared for work of such quality. Though
Gilbert's method of production won Sullivan's admiration,
especially the way in which he made the chorus play a part
in the piece instead of appearing as a vocal background, it
was impossible to convert a troupe of burlesque mimes into a
caste of comic opera artists. 'Really, Mr Gilbert, why should I
stand here? I am not a chorus girl!' complained one of the
Gaiety favourites. 'No, madam, your voice isn't strong enough
or you would be.'

The collaborators agreed that no money was to be made out
of grotesque opera and went their separate ways, Gilbert to
write blank verse dramas and farces, Sullivan to compose
hymns, songs, incidental music, cantatas, and an oratorio that
gained the approbation of Gounod and Queen Victoria. Their
paths in life seemed as different as their personalities. Sullivan
had been reared in poverty. His father was the bandmaster at
the Royal Military College, and the boy had music in his
blood, producing his first anthem at the age of eight. He joined
the choir of the Chapel Royal and charmed elderly ladies and
gentlemen with his singing and his humility. Winning the
Mendelssohn Scholarship when only fourteen, he studied for
two years at the Royal Academy of Music, earning golden
opinions from the professors, and when he again won the
Scholarship he went to the Leipzig Conservatoire, remaining
there for another two years and composing his first considerable

piece of music, for Shakespeare's *The Tempest*, which was performed with applause at the Grand Public Examination. Returning to England, he made the acquaintance of George Grove, Secretary of the Crystal Palace, who appointed him Professor of Pianoforte and Ballad Singing at the School of Art there. Though at that time the work of unknown composers was never heard at the Crystal Palace concerts, Sullivan's personal popularity and professional competence broke down the convention and his music for *The Tempest* was given in April 1862, receiving the unstinted praise of Charles Dickens, who confessed he knew nothing about music, and of leading critics, who claimed to know everything. Sullivan became organist of St Michael's, Chester Square, then of St Peter's, Cranley Gardens, continuing all the while to write songs and serious music, including *In Memoriam* on the death of his father, and the most popular of English hymn tunes for *Onward Christian Soldiers*.

His rise to fame was materially assisted by his charm as an individual. In every single respect he was the opposite of Gilbert. His speech was soft; his words were gentle, his manners ingratiating, his presence soothing. He was complimentary, caressing, conciliatory. He loved company and enjoyed doing what other people liked. He was as fond of the aristocracy as they were of him. Monarchs and princes patronized him with pleasure because of the pleasure it gave him to be patronized. It was such a relief to find a serious musician who was fond of gambling and horse-racing that sporting peers began to feel there must be something in serious music, and cultured peeresses for whom Mendelssohn was the last word in composition were persuaded to change their opinion by the singular fascination of Sullivan's personality. Tall people liked him because he was short and short people liked him because he was not tall. Men found him as sympathetic and amiable as women thought him sensitive and lovable. There was no discordant note in the man or his music. The one was voted delightful, the other delicious.

His lyrical genius as a composer was again to be harnessed with the more vigorous genius of Gilbert as a librettist, and this time they remained in harness until their radically dissimilar temperaments broke the partnership. Their coming together once more was due to the intelligence and initiative of Richard

D'Oyly Carte, who was eight years Gilbert's junior, two years Sullivan's. After beginning as a musical instrument-maker in his father's business, Carte became keen on the theatre, wrote music for operettas, and in time started an agency which quickly thrived. His acute business sense was aided by a frank and agreeable manner: he could not only see where money was to be made but how to make it. He took what other people thought were risks, but he felt were certainties, his apparent hazards being backed with much cunning. His easy, companionable and humorous air concealed an eye to the main chance, for which reason he was known in the theatrical profession as 'Oily Carte'. He knew everyone worth knowing from his point of view, assessing their value to himself with precision; and his practical judgment was as sure as his sense of artistry. On seeing *Thespis* he perceived at once that the music of Sullivan was perfectly suited to the words of Gilbert, and that the latter had no rival as a producer. Given the means, the end was assured.

Early in 1875 he asked Gilbert to provide a one-act cantata, with music by Sullivan, to be played as an after-piece to Offenbach's *La Périchole* at the Royalty Theatre, which he was then managing for an actress named Selina Dolaro. It happened that Gilbert had done a stage-version of one of his stories, the music for which would have been written by Carl Rosa but for the death of his wife which caused him to return the piece. Gilbert sent the script to Carte, who liked it and asked the author to let Sullivan hear it read aloud. It was a raw morning at the beginning of March when Gilbert, his coat covered with snow, called on Sullivan and read *Trial by Jury*, becoming more and more wrathful the further he went as if he despised what he had written. But it captured Sullivan, who laughed all through it and agreed on the spot to do the music. Within three weeks it was ready for production, and was seen on the evening of March 25th, 1875. Sullivan's brother Frederic played the Judge, and W. S. Penley, later to achieve fame as the original Charley's Aunt, had his first part on the professional stage as the Foreman of the Jury. Carte's belief that Sullivan was the money-making partner, an attitude that would one day contribute to the break-up of the partnership, was shown at the outset, Sullivan's name appearing alone in the preliminary announcement and above Gilbert's in the programme.

A London management then had the curious experience of seeing a listless audience for the main item in the programme, a packed and excited house for the after-piece. Offenbach, whose music had been so popular for so many years, disappeared from the British stage at the advent of Sullivan almost as quickly as his opera disappeared from the Royalty Theatre. But another piece was substituted and *Trial by Jury* went on for some time, being withdrawn when Frederic Sullivan fell ill. He died in January 1877, his passing having inspired his brother to compose 'The Lost Chord'.

It is generally assumed that after the success of *Trial by Jury* D'Oyly Carte took the librettist and composer under his wing and that neither of them attempted to collaborate with anyone else before their regular partnership was formed. Gilbert's letters contradict this. If any manager had commissioned him to write the words for an opera, he would have written them for any competent composer. First of all Carl Rosa, who ran an operatic company, approached him once more for a libretto, this time with music by Sullivan. Gilbert answered, on October 4th, 1875, that the play he was then writing for John Hare would occupy his 'unremitting attention' till December 1st, after which a piece he had promised Sothern would keep him busy till January 1st, but

> After that date I shall be quite ready to undertake a two-act comic libretto for you, and I will undertake to get it practically finished – that is to say, I will have supplied Sullivan with the principal numbers by the 1st February. I hope this will meet your views – as I should be very sorry not to be associated with the new work. If you say 'yes' I will arrange to undertake no other work until March.

But Carl decided that popular foreign operas were more likely to be lucrative than untried British works and missed the chance of his life. Next came a famous conductor, German by origin but naturalized in England, whose opera *The Lily of Killarney* had done well:

21 Dec. 1875

To Sir Julius Benedict.

Dear Sir Julius,

I am very sorry indeed to hear that Mr Enoch's negotiations have not been attended with the success we anticipated. I have looked forward for some years to the honour of being associated with you in an operatic work – even though in the very subordinate capacity of a librettist – and I do not yet despair of seeing my hopes realized. I am afraid however that the rush of work that ensued upon the success, such as it is, of *Broken Hearts* will fill my hands and head with work to be paid for in advance, and which, on that account alone, I cannot reconcile myself to refusing. I am sure you will sympathize with my feeling on this point – if it is inartistic, it is at all events *human*. I sincerely hope that before long some impresario will entrust us with a distinct commission. With kind regards from my wife

I am,

Very truly yours

W. S. Gilbert

The chief thing for Gilbert at that time was ready money, and as Carte wanted to revive *Thespis* he agreed in October 1875 that it should be done at the Criterion Theatre before Christmas, stipulating for a fee of two guineas a night for the librettist, the same for the composer, and a guaranteed run of a hundred performances, much of the dialogue to be re-written and some of the music re-scored. Sullivan consented but added that their total fees for fifty nights must be paid down on completion of the script and score and that the guaranteed run should apply only to London and be continuous. A month after this agreement had been made Gilbert wrote to Sullivan: 'I have heard no more about *Thespis*. It's astonishing how quickly these capitalists dry up under the magic influence of the words "cash down".' But he remained on friendly terms with Carte, obtaining from him the promise of a job at the Criterion for an actress who requested that she might be released if she got a better offer elsewhere: 'I told her that I thought, in such a contingency, you would be able to reconcile yourself to the sacrifice. I hope I did not over-estimate your powers of self-denial.' He also yielded to Carte's desire that Selina Dolaro should be permitted to give a minimum of fifty performances of *Trial by Jury* at another London theatre, though he drew the line at making himself responsible for the representation, writing to her: 'It's a pity, but the piece has been so be-devilled that I have lost all interest in it.'

Nothing came of the *Thespis* revival because Carte was unable to raise the money, and early in 1876 the manager of the

Opera Comique, C. Morton, asked for an opera. Gilbert and Sullivan sent a joint reply:

Dear Mr Morton

We have considered your proposal, and we are prepared to write an opera for your theatre on the following terms:

£4.4. each per night, guaranteeing a minimum of 120 performances in town and country, within eight months of first production.

Of this, £105 to be paid to each of us in advance.

We are to select our own company.

The piece is to be in two or three acts, as we may deem to be most suitable.

The entire control of rehearsals to be in our hands.

The selection of the subject to rest with us.

Yours very truly

Gilbert was not the man to make a secret of such matters, and Carte was quick to remind him of a previous understanding between them. The first typewritten letter in Gilbert's correspondence (all in capitals) was addressed to Carte:

11 March, 1876

Dear Mr Carte

I certainly considered myself under an agreement to write a libretto for you on certain conditions. But those conditions have not been fulfilled.

Imprimis, both Sullivan and myself were to receive a sum down, before putting pen to paper. Then we were to begin on the 1st March. I wrote to you on that day to say that I was ready to begin. But you left my note unanswered for a week, and then wrote to say that there was a hitch somewhere. And then it turned out that you were going to close the theatre for a few weeks and reopen perhaps with a revived comedy, perhaps with a revived opera; but in any case our little one-act 'Bouffe' was to constitute the whole substantial attraction.

Now this won't do for either Sullivan or myself. If we're to be businesslike, you must be businesslike too. Give us a fair chance at a good theatre, and comply with our conditions precedent, and we'll work like Trojans. But we can't hold ourselves at your disposal whenever you want us.

Sullivan is in Paris and I don't know when he is expected home.

Yours faithfully

Carte was not yet in a position to pay 'a sum down' and he realized that he would have to form and manage a company of his own before he could establish the desired Gilbert and

Sullivan combination; so towards the end of that year he made a bid for the necessary capital by issuing a prospectus. Unfortunately he got the capitalists along with the capital and they were to cause him a great deal of trouble at the commencement of his career as a company director.

Meanwhile Gilbert and Sullivan were involved in another business transaction. What became known as the Westminster Aquarium was opened in 1875 on a site facing the Abbey. To help its finances many eminent people had been asked to give their names to the undertaking and to become Fellows of the Royal Aquarium and Summer and Winter Garden Society. Among others Gilbert and John Hare were approached by the manager, Wybrow Robertson, and told that for the sum of five guineas they could be enrolled as Fellows. On the understanding that this entitled them to life membership, they agreed to make the 'donation'. At a later date Gilbert received a demand for seven guineas, being the entrance fee and annual subscription of a member, as well as two guineas for his subscription as a Fellow. He replied with a threat: 'As you decline to recognize my right to a Life Membership on payment of five guineas, I shall place the matter in the hands of my solicitor forthwith.' Robertson regretted the tone of this letter, offered to pay the insignificant sum of two guineas for the Fellowship himself, and in a further note informed Gilbert that the executive committee had decided that the Council of Fellows would in future be exempted from the payment of the 'donation' but would still have to send the annual subscription as members. Gilbert declined to do so, and at last heard from the chairman of the committee, Henry Labouchere, one of whose co-directors was Sullivan, to whom Gilbert wrote in January 1876:

I have received a disgraceful letter from Labouchere, disclaiming any contract between Robertson and myself on the ground that the Company was not in existence at the time. Now as the contract between Robertson and the Council of Fellows was made with the view of bringing the Company into existence, it is rather like sharp practice to ignore it on the ground that the Company did not at that time exist. It is a disgraceful quibble, worthy of a police-court attorney.

The finances and management of the Aquarium proved to be unsatisfactory, and not only did Gilbert stick to his point, refusing to make any payment, but Sullivan soon resigned his directorship. In 1877 Labouchere washed his hands of the Company and accused Robertson in *Truth* of dishonesty. That summer the two men happened to run across one another at the annual fair in Boulogne. Robertson struck Labby on the face, Labby hurled a large glass butter dish at Robertson, the French onlookers wondered whether these droll Englishmen were playing their national game of cricket, and a legal case ended with a victory for the editor of *Truth*. Nevertheless Robertson continued to manage or mismanage the Company, for at the close of 1877 Gilbert wrote to say that, as his solicitors had been compelled to dun Robertson for the sums due on performances of *Trial by Jury* at the Aquarium, all fees must henceforth be paid in advance.

CHAPTER 9

Annus Mirabilis

◦━◦━◦

Carte's object in forming a company was to produce native light opera, and he hoped to get the support of leading British composers and librettists. The capital was subscribed by three men interested in the trade of music and one other who owned the water-carts that laid the dust of the London highways. These four, with Carte, were constituted directors of the Comedy Opera Company. They leased the Opera Comique, then situated in a maze of streets where Kingsway and Aldwych have since been built, and paid an advance of a hundred guineas each to Gilbert and Sullivan for a two-act opera, the advance money to be deducted from their fees of three guineas each a performance. Gilbert finished his part of the work in April 1877 and sent it to Sullivan. Much delay was caused by casting. Both of them had decided that the popular burlesque actors and operatic singers were unsuitable for their class of work and caused more trouble than they were worth. The average tenor was especially objectionable, being subject to exhibitions of temperament. It was their intention to train the artists they wanted for the sort of parts they wrote; and they began by picking one named George Grossmith, who had been entertaining provincial audiences of working men with songs and recitations, and another named Rutland Barrington, who had been acting in second-rate melodramas. 'I should have thought you required a fine man with a fine voice', said Grossmith after reading his part. 'No, that is just what we don't want', said Gilbert. As for Barrington, whose sense of music was far from acute, Gilbert told someone: 'He's a staid, stolid swine, and that's what I want.' Carte had the job of arranging their terms. He had no difficulty with Barrington: in those days £6 a week in a London theatre was attractive bait, and the actor was easily hooked. But Grossmith had doubts. If he appeared on the professional stage he would never again be

· 93 ·

asked to entertain the various Christian institutes that had previously engaged him, so he asked for more than he was offered. Carte suggested that they should discuss the matter over lunch. Oysters and champagne had a mellowing effect; Grossmith lessened his demand by three guineas a week; and eleven years later discovered that, apart from the annual interest on the money, his lunch with Carte had cost him some eighteen hundred pounds.

For a man of his prodigality of output Gilbert was curiously economical in the use of his ideas. Nearly all his plays and operas were either founded on *The Bab Ballads* and the stories he wrote for journals or contained notions therefrom. *The Sorcerer*, taken from one of his short stories, 'An Elixir of Love', was produced at the Opera Comique on November 17th, 1877. The cast had been carefully drilled by Gilbert, and for the first time an opera by him and Sullivan was given exactly as he saw it in the mind's eye, or as near as human fallibility permitted such a consummation. The other directors of the Company had strongly advised Carte not to engage Grossmith, who made the chief hit of the piece, while Barrington's comic clergyman settled his future career in light opera, though he had been rather alarmed over the part and hinted to Gilbert at a rehearsal that the audience would either take very kindly to an operatic cleric or hoot him from the stage. 'I quite agree with you', said Gilbert, a remark that did not remove Barrington's apprehensions.

From the first week of the six-months run Carte had trouble with his co-directors. When the takings dropped, they wanted to put up a fortnight's notice and cut their losses. When the bookings increased, they wanted to commission another opera. The sight of empty seats drove them to despair; a full house made them jubilant. Carte was continually harassed by their changes of mood, their abrogations and sanctions; and when at one moment they wished to lower the advance for the new opera to be written by Gilbert and Sullivan, he passed the information on to Gilbert, who noted in his diary for January 2nd, 1878: 'Met Carte in Strand. Directors of Opera Coy want to reduce guarantee on new piece. Absolutely declined, as not having heard from them for four weeks, concluded proposition accepted.' A fortnight later Gilbert read the plot of the new opera, *H.M.S. Pinafore*, to Carte, who was much pleased with it. Already the outline had been despatched to Sullivan in Paris.

> I have very little doubt whatever but that you will be pleased with it [wrote Gilbert]. I should have liked to have talked it over with you, as there is a good deal of fun in it which I haven't set down on paper. Among other things a song . . . for the First Lord – tracing his career as office-boy in cotton-broker's office, clerk, traveller, junior partner, and First Lord of Britain's Navy. I think a splendid song can be made of this. Of course there will be no *personality* in this – the fact that the First Lord in the opera is a *Radical* of the most pronounced type will do away with any suspicion that W. H. Smith is intended.

Gilbert did not mean to be funny, but if he had seriously thought that the First Lord's radicalism would prevent identification with W. H. Smith he would not have been capable of writing the song. But he was anxious to allay any possible suspicion on the part of Sullivan, whose friendships in high quarters might have made him nervous of satire at the expense of a cabinet minister. W. H. Smith, the well-known bookseller, was First Lord of the Admiralty in Disraeli's government; and as no one (except of course Gilbert) had any doubts about the model for the Right Hon. Sir Joseph Porter, the Prime Minister himself was soon speaking of '*Pinafore Smith*'.

Gilbert's diary, mentioned above, covers the year 1878 and includes a few entries for the early part of 1879. It is not known whether he kept a diary for any other year of his life until 1905, when he began to do so, continuing it until his death. Fortunately the one early diary deals with the most important year of his life as a librettist, the year of *Pinafore*. Some of his jottings are illuminating, but he was not the kind of man to produce a readable journal. The good diarist is interested either in himself or in other people; the great diarist is interested in both; Gilbert was interested in neither. He did not closely observe the reactions of others or his own. He was the creature of impulse, acting and speaking as he felt without the least curiosity as to the cause or consequence of his behaviour. We may therefore turn the pages of his diaries with the conviction that there will not be a trace of self-consciousness, which implies an awareness of the outside world, and that the revelations will be incidental and accidental. Such of his memoranda as contain some interest will here be quoted, with explanatory additions. The first entry concerns his play *The Ne'er-do-weel*, which he was revising. The 'M.T.' so often referred to is Marion Terry, in whose career Gilbert was then taking a keen interest. She often stayed with the Gilberts and had appeared in several of his plays at the Haymarket, where her salary was £10 a week in 1877. He rehearsed her privately in every part she played for him. The 'Mrs' throughout the diary is Gilbert's wife. They were then at 24 The Boltons. In the early part of the year he was writing songs and dialogue for *Pinafore*.

1878

Jan. 1. Lunched Neville and Lord Londesborough. *The Ne'er-do-weel* to be put in rehearsal at once. M.T. to be offered engagement. Suggested Faust and Marguerite subject.

Jan. 21. Wrote Captain's song 'I am the Captain' &c.

Jan. 25. Wrote part of song for 1st Lord.

Jan. 26. Wrote song for 1st Lord.

Jan. 27. (Sunday) Bad headache. Walked out during church time – saw man trying to steal dogs – ordered him off. Short man, reddish whiskers. Met Mrs coming out of church. Walked with her round by Alexander Sq and home to lunch . . . Headache lifted about 4. Wrote letter to *Observer* but did not send it. Stage-managed 1st act of *Ne'er-do-weel* for tomorrow. Dined (Marcus) Stone's. Good dinner. Rainy night. Row with cabman – refused to take us – made him – paid him bare fare – abusive – gave him card – number 8630 . . . Played penny bank – lost £2. Left at 12.30.

Feb. 15. Rehearsed 2 and 3 acts *Ne'er-do-weel*. Then with M.T. to lunch at Victoria station where Mrs met us. Then by 4.30 train to Brighton – arrived at ¼ to 6. Went to lodgings, 29 Bedford Square – small but clean and comfortable – dined there – Sat up writing *Ne'er-do-weel*.

Feb. 16. At Brighton. Walked out in morning to Aquarium – then to Mutton's to lunch – filthy meal – then took carriage and drove along parade. Home to meat tea – then to theatre – pantomime very well done. Then drove to lodgings – oysters.

Feb. 17. At Brighton. After breakfast walked out – sat on beach. M.T. went to call on friends in Goldsmid St – in a bath chair – we accompanied her but did not go in – return home to lunch. Then walked out – went to Aquarium –

then on pier – met Herman Merivale – went home . . .
read out loud in evening.

Feb. 18. At Brighton. Walked out in morning on beach – bought
newspaper – home to lunch – then drove out through
Hove and Shoreham – beastly drive. Home to meat tea.
H. Merivale called – he was going to dine at Mowatt's.
Went to Frikell (conjurer) in evening – atrocious entertainment – left when half over – atmosphere putrid –
saw '*the* Galatea'. Evening very warm so we sat on seat
on Esplanade. M.T. in high spirits about nothing – home
– oysters – rehearsed part with M.T.

Feb. 19. Left Brighton by 9.45 – arrived Victoria 10.15 (*sic*) –
with M.T. to Olympic. Rehearsed 1 and 2 acts *Ne'er-do-
weel*. All smooth enough. After rehearsal drove home,
leaving M.T. at Conduit St – brought her trunk with me –
she is to dine and sleep here . . . at home all evening.

The diarist wrote that the weather had been very fine every
day they were at Brighton. *The Ne'er-do-weel* was seen at the
Olympic on February 25th. He described the verdict of the
audience as 'divided'. The play was taken off, the third act
re-written, and under its original title of *The Vagabond* tried
again on March 25th, when it went 'magnificently'. But it soon
ceased to go at all.

March 6. Woke with slight gout . . . went to bed at 3 a.m. –
Gout much worse – couldn't sleep – got up at 4.30 –
lighted fire in study – read until 6.45. Then went to
bed and slept till 9.30.

March 11. Stopped ten minutes (at shop to buy a cigar case).
Then home. Row with cabman – took 6d away from
him. He is going to summon me.

March 19. Dressed for Queen's Levee . . . I went to levee – turned
back at Buckingham Palace, because no crape on arm
– went to Gorringe's to repair this omission – crape
sewn on in shop – then admitted.

April 13. Went to Portsmouth with Sullivan – on board *Thun-
derer* – Lord C. Beresford. Left by 10.30 train from
Victoria – arrived at one. Lunched on board – went
round ship – then Lord C. Beresford told off boatman
and four men to take us on board various ships – went
to *Invincible, Victory* and *St. Vincent,* making sketches
on last two – then pulled ashore to station – home by
4.40 train, arriving 7.34 – went to Beefsteak Club –
dined – afterwards to Olympic – home.

Gilbert was constantly at the Beefsteak Club and frequently had supper there after the theatre, arriving home between 3 and 4 in the morning. He did a certain amount of gambling, and the names of a few members crop up at intervals, including Labouchere and Kendal, with both of whom he seems to have been on talking terms at the Club, whatever his feelings beyond the precincts. The next entry in his diary refers to the second Afghan War:

> April 19. (Good Friday) Proposed I should go as *Times* correspondent – to war.

But Gilbert never penetrated the Khyber Pass. Instead he went with his wife and Marion Terry to Paris, seeing Versailles and St Germains, then to Antwerp and Brussels, visiting the field of Waterloo, which gave him a headache. At the beginning of May he erected a tent in his garden, where he began to play tennis most afternoons. On May 3rd he wrote out the dialogue of *Pinafore* and sent the alterations he had made in the lyrics to Sullivan. Thereafter he was rehearsing and rewriting the opera at the same time, occasionally suffering from bad headaches.

> May 24. Rehearsal in morning – to which Mrs and B went. I remained at theatre till 5.30. Then home ... Night rehearsal – everything smooth – dresses all right – remained there till 3.35 a.m. – then to Beefsteak for supper – then home at 4.30.
>
> May 25. (Saturday) Went to Opera Comique to superintend scene – remained there till 6.30 working at it – Wiseman helping. Then went to Beefsteak to dine and dress. To theatre at 8 – put finishing touches &c. Rowdy gallery, singing songs &c. Piece went extremely well. I went in and out three or four times during evening. Enthusiastic call for self and Sullivan. Then to Beefsteak. Great meeting – Beaufort, Yardley, Lyttleton, F. Locker, Labouchere, Kendal, Marshall &c. Arranged to dine with Locker on Monday.

All the notices of *Pinafore* were good, he noted, but he and Sullivan decided to cut several things and add several others. The excitement made him feel out of sorts.

> May 27. Dressed and dined with F. Locker, 25 Chesham St. Dull dinner. Home by 12. Slept on sofa. Bed 2.

This was the well-known parodist and writer of light verse, Frederick Locker-Lampson.

> June 2. (Sunday) M.T. here. Drove with Mrs and M.T. to Richmond Park – took luncheon with us – lunched in park – found thrush – found carriage which had put up at Star and Garter at gate at 6 and drove home. Dined. Read *David Copperfield* out loud – bed.

The thrush must have been hurt because they took it home, but it died next day. In June the Gilberts were looking for a country-house and tried the Henley and Haslemere districts. At the end of the month he felt ill and suggested to his wife that they should make a tour round the world. He even called at Cook's office to enquire about it and arranged with *The Graphic* to send a weekly illustrated article while away. But a holiday at Margate restored him to health and in the middle of July they went to France, bathing a lot at Havre and Trouville. At the Hotel d'Angleterre, Rouen, the supper was 'beastly', the wine 'atrocious', the terms 'extortionate', the hall porter churlish: 'Offered him 3/- – he asked 5/- – refused to give it him – he made me a present of it.' They went on to Dieppe and stayed at the Hôtel de la Plage at Tréport, where everything was good. At Boulogne 'Parson and wife from St Philips Kensington came up and claimed acquaintance – said they wanted to know me – woman especially offensive – gave them cold shoulder.' He ate a large number of cakes and bathed regularly, Victorianism having apparently crossed the Channel: 'After breakfast Mrs and B bathed together – I apart.' They returned via Folkestone on Bank Holiday, August 5th.

> Aug. 9. Went to picnic at Windsor with Opera Comique Company. Met at Paddington at 9.30 – arrived at Windsor – waited there ¾ of an hour for steam launches which had not arrived from Kingston. Then got on board and steamed to Cliefden (Cliveden) – Landed there, lunched at cottage – re-embarked – returned to Windsor and left by 5.30 train for London. Arrived there, one of chorus sick – looked after her and put her in cab – then home by 7.20.

He spent much time in his garden during August, either playing tennis or reading in the tent. In September he visited

Ramsgate to see a yacht, but was driven therefrom by tooth-ache. Soon after that he bought a yacht, *The Druidess*, in the Isle of Wight, and started in her to Ramsgate; but the weather was so rough that they had to leave her at Dover, returning to Ramsgate by train and making arrangements for someone to sail her there and for future anchorage.

On September 20th he saw Sullivan at Covent Garden and urged him to do another piece for the Opera Comique. Sullivan half-consented. On the 23rd he called for Carte and Sullivan at Covent Garden and accompanied them to view the 'site of proposed theatre in Beaufort buildings', so even then Carte was thinking of erecting a theatre for operas. That autumn Gilbert took lessons in navigation and studied text-books thereon. The entry for October 6th, a dull day spent at home in seedy melancholy, ends with the word 'Row'. By the end of that month Sullivan was as keen as he to write another opera and called for a talk on November 4th. Gilbert took advantage of the occasion to read as much of *Gretchen* as he had finished, which must have tested Sullivan's powers of endurance. A characteristic passage in the diary, which a man who cared for anything more than the passing moment would have expanded, runs: 'Sunday, 24 Nov. Breakfast with Whistler.' Nothing else except that his own wife and Albert Moore were present. At the end of that month he attended the hearings of two legal cases at Westminster Hall: Whistler *v.* Ruskin, and Robertson *v.* Labouchere.

In December he worked at the new opera, *The Pirates of Penzance*, and also at *Gretchen*. On Sunday December 8th the collaborators talked over the new piece at Sullivan's flat until 3 a.m. On the 11th: 'Worked at Faust – also at plot of operetta. In evening Sullivan dined here – went home early' – possibly to escape more of *Gretchen*. On the 30th Marion and Florence Terry lunched at 24 The Boltons:

> They left at 5, having to go home before going to theatre – went with them in Hansom to Notting Hill – left umbrella in Hansom – overtook it – went in it to Beefsteak – left umbrella again in same Hansom. Dined with A. Sullivan at Garrick – afterwards cards in his room. Present: Prinsep, Marquis of Anglesea, Fairs, Merryweather, Crabb, etc. Won £17 – home by 3.30.

The Gilberts saw the old year out with their friends John Fairs and his wife, the process being assisted by punch.

The New Year however saw their friendship out. Fairs,[1] who ran the Court Theatre, had been a close friend of Gilbert's for some years. They saw much of one another throughout 1878, though when Gilbert dined at Marcus Stone's on January 27th he put in his diary 'J. F. sulky' and on reaching home 'wrote letter to J. F. as to cause of sulkiness'. Presumably Fairs was able to give a conciliatory reason, for thereafter they met almost daily at the Club and together with their wives spent holidays, played tennis, saw plays and dined with one another. Then, quite suddenly, something occurred to ruffle Fairs. We cannot conjecture the cause, though Gilbert's letter, which is a perfect example of his instantaneous reaction to a sign of unfriendliness, suggests that 'our declared enemies', the Kendals, were the source of the mischief. Enough to say that six weeks after they had seen the New Year in, with all the embracing and hand-grasping and good fellowship it implied, John Fairs received this letter from Gilbert:

18 Feb. 1879

Sir

Your letter of this morning puts an end, as a matter of course, to all relations between us. I have no hesitation in telling you that I altogether decline to accept your explanation of the cause of your insolent letter.

When your wife called upon us, on the first of the two occasions to which you refer, I was, as she very well knows, extremely unwell – in point of fact, I was confined to the house for the greater part of the four ensuing days. Nevertheless, on that occasion, I pressed her to fix a day upon which you would be able to dine with us, and she replied 'that she would see my wife on Monday and arrange a day then'. On the second occasion (yesterday) *there were no fewer than thirteen persons in the room during nearly the whole of her visit*, and feeling sure that Mrs Fairs would remain, as she usually has done, for at least an hour, I had no hesitation in devoting my attention, for some time, to other visitors – the less, because I had proposed to myself to walk to Kensington Gore with Mrs Fairs – which, however, I subsequently found I could not do, as Mrs Fairs had ordered her carriage to wait for her. Eventually I saw Mrs Fairs into her carriage, and our parting was perfectly friendly in tone. As a minor but significant circumstance,

[1] Whose stage-name was John Hare. He had just formed a partnership with the Kendals, and their management of St James's Theatre for the next nine years became famous.

I may mention that when Mrs Fairs called on the very same day on which I am said to have exhibited a marked coolness, she examined a gold thimble belonging to my sister-in-law, and expressed a wish to have one like it. I made a mental note of the fact (being anxious to place on record my appreciation of your wife's extreme kindness to mine during her illness) and I called at your house on the ensuing Monday to obtain, if possible, the size of Mrs Fairs' thimble. Both Mrs Fairs and yourself were from home, so my intention was frustrated. I mention these matters to you that you may distinctly understand that when I express my disbelief in your excuse for quarrelling with me, I speak in perfect good faith.

I have little difficulty in assigning your course of action to one of two causes – either your mind has been prejudiced against me by the malicious utterances of persons who are interested in dividing us, or you feel that it is difficult to remain on intimate terms with us and our declared enemies – whom you have recently admitted to an exceptional degree of friendship, and to whom you have so frequently referred in terms of the utmost disparagement and contempt. You accuse me of want of generosity. Allow me to point out to you that such a charge comes with a bad grace from one who is *so* lacking in manly feeling as to lay upon his wife's shoulders the burden of an action which is the outcome of his own inability to appreciate the value of an old and often-tested friendship.

> I am,
> Your obedient servant
> W. S. Gilbert

At the same time that he was losing a friend, Gilbert was making much money. Nothing like the frenzied popularity of *H.M.S. Pinafore* had been known in the history of comic opera. It started badly because the directors of the Company again suffered from nerves. During the first eight weeks of the run notices to end it were posted and withdrawn six times. A heat-wave reduced the takings and everyone was in a panic. Carte was beside himself with anxiety. The situation was saved by Sullivan's inclusion of a selection from the *Pinafore* music in the Promenade Concerts he was conducting at Covent Garden. It was received with tumultuous applause and he repeated it frequently. Everyone now wanted to see the opera which contained such joyous music, and by the late summer of 1878 the theatre was crammed to capacity. No one could have guessed that these gay and happy tunes had been composed by a man writhing in pain. Sullivan suffered from stone in the kidney, and sometimes the agony was so great that he was almost insensible. The notes were written between paroxysms. An operation in July 1879 temporarily relieved him. While recovering from this he received strange news from Gilbert.

There had been countless disagreements between Carte and his fellow-directors, and as their lease of the Opera Comique lapsed at the end of July 1879 Carte had determined to finish with the Company and run the show alone. A year before the other directors might have agreed, but their investment was now showing a handsome profit, so taking advantage of Carte's absence in America they hired a gang of roughs to remove the scenery and properties, which they considered their own, with the intention of staging the piece elsewhere. A mob of fifty hirelings burst into the theatre on the evening of July 31st towards the end of the performance. There was a fierce fight betwixt the roughs and the stage-hands, during which George Grossmith explained the cause of the rumpus to a startled audience, and after an hour's combat the invasion was repulsed. Gilbert's account of the affair was sent to Sullivan on August 6th, by which time the peccant directors had reproduced *Pinafore* at the Westminster Aquarium. A little later they brought it to the Olympic, close to the Opera Comique, and people witnessed both versions in order to make comparisons. But two simultaneous representations of the same opera could not last for ever, and when the original production of *Pinafore* came off after seven hundred performances a partnership was formed between Carte, Gilbert and Sullivan, each of them putting up £1000 as capital. By their agreement, which was to remain in force as long as Carte retained a lease of the Opera Comique, he would receive £15 a week as business manager, Gilbert and Sullivan were to get four guineas each for every performance of their operas, and when all fees, salaries and other expenses were paid, the profits were to be equally divided between the trio.

CHAPTER 10

Pirates and Poets

❦❦❦

The *Pinafore* craze had crossed the Atlantic and dozens of companies were performing the opera all over the United States. At that time there was no law of copyright between England and America, and the moment a song or a bit of dialogue was publicly heard in one country it became the public property of another. In New York, Philadelphia, Boston and elsewhere the tunes of *Pinafore* were played by every band and barrel-organ, the jokes quoted by every newspaper and orator, until the average person was hypnotized into humming, strumming, whistling and talking Gilbert and Sullivan. In New York eight companies were performing the piece, in Philadelphia six, and in other leading cities a proportionate number, some forty being on the road. The delirium surpassed anything that had previously been known in American stage history. Liberties were taken with text and music to suit the fads of the hour, the representations being of a kind to make Sullivan weep and give Gilbert apoplexy.

Carte visited America to survey the situation and came to the conclusion that if the collaborators were to produce the piece in New York exactly as it was done in London, with some English actors in the chief parts, the original orchestration and the identical stage business, the sensation would be immense and the receipts gratifying. They agreed, and further determined to produce their new piece in New York, reaping the profits before the pirates got to work by rehearsing touring companies at the same time. 'I will not have another libretto of mine produced if the Americans are going to steal it', said Gilbert; 'not that I need the money so much, but it upsets my digestion.' Another cause of digestive trouble was his dispute with the postal authorities. He opined that New York should be charged as one word in a cable, but the Postmaster General pronounced in favour of two. On April 24th he 'called on

Sullivan to meet Carte and arrange about America. We are to start on 7th October. Shares one-third each of profits – all travelling and hotel expenses paid.' The partners now set to work on *The Pirates of Penzance*, with which they hoped to defeat the pirates of New York, and sometimes met for pleasure as well. On May 13th Gilbert dined at the Garrick Club with Sullivan, whose party included the Duke of Edinburgh, a keen musician who was the second son of Queen Victoria. Afterwards they went to Sullivan's rooms, where Mrs Ronalds sang. An American by birth, Mrs Ronalds was in every sense Sullivan's most intimate friend, whose singing of 'The Lost Chord' brought tears to his eyes. On this occasion there was piano-playing as well; and when the other guests had departed, Gilbert, Sullivan and Lord Someone (whose name is indecipherable in the former's diary) played cribbage. Gilbert lost £3 and reached home at 3 o'clock.

Taking with them Frank Cellier, conductor of the Opera Comique, Gilbert and Sullivan left England at the end of October and had such a rough crossing that Gilbert's belief in Britannia's rule over the waves began to fluctuate. Their arrival off Sandy Hook was inspiriting. A large number of steamers, decorated with stars and stripes and union jacks, with bands on board playing the *Pinafore* airs, came out to greet them; though a rival show of Nigger Minstrels sent forth a tug placarded with the words *No Pinafore!* which did its best to make the music inaudible by means of a powerful whistle. The press reporters were not far behind. They were charmed by the famous pair, describing them as simple, amiable, modest, good-natured and lively. The contrast between them was noticed: the hearty laugh and quick utterance of the tall, fair-haired, blue-eyed, rosy-cheeked, mutton-chop-whiskered Gilbert; the soulful eyes, mobile face and sensitive expression of the short, dark-haired, gentle-mannered Sullivan. The collaborators were alike in one respect only: each of them was disappointed that his serious work had not achieved the popularity of a 'frothy trifle' like *Pinafore*.

Putting up at 27 Waverley Place, New York, they were immediately subjected to the interviews, receptions, handshakings, questionings, speechifyings and invitations that are a feature of American life, while trying to prepare *Pinafore*, with a new chorus and principals, for production on December 1st.

Gilbert was told by an American impresario that he would make a fortune if he were to re-write the piece, changing H.M.S. to U.S.S., substituting the stars and stripes for the British ensign, anchoring the ship off Jersey Beach, and turning the First Lord of the Admiralty into the U.S. navy boss. Gilbert listened courteously, wondered how he could adapt the Boatswain's famous song to the new situation, and asked how this would meet the case:

> He is Ameri-can!
> > Though he himself has said it,
> > 'Tis not much to his credit,
> That he is Ameri-can!

> For he might have been a Dutchman,
> An Irish, Scotch, or such man,
> Or perhaps an Englishman!
> > But in spite of hanky-panky,
> > He remains a true-born Yankee,
> A cute Ameri-can!

The impresario joyfully proclaimed that New York would go mad over it. But Gilbert felt that the city's insanity might take unwelcome forms and dismissed the project.

When the audience at the Fifth Avenue Theatre saw the English production, they realized that they had not seen the piece before, though all of them were familiar with the tunes and most of them had witnessed several of the New York representations. The orchestration, the stage-management, the acting, everything was a revelation; and the reception by an enraptured house seemed to presage a prosperous run. But the piratical versions had made stale the public appetite, and after a week's excitement business declined. The partners started to reduce their expenses. 'We shall begin by not paying the postage of our letters home', wrote Sullivan to his mother. An early production of *The Pirates of Penzance* became necessary. Sullivan discovered that he had left all the sketches for the first act at home, so he had to re-write the lot while rehearsals started with the second act. There followed a frenzied period of composing, scoring, rehearsing and re-arranging. To add to his troubles the band went on strike a few days before the opening night, their reason being that *The Pirates* was grand opera, for playing which they were entitled to higher salaries. Sullivan bluffed them by saying that he would import the Covent Garden orchestra and in the meantime run the show with himself at the piano and Cellier at the harmonium. Both these alternatives were, he knew, ridiculous, but the mere threat persuaded the band that the piece came under the heading of light opera. The overture was not ready for the dress rehearsal, which finished at one in the morning, when Sullivan, with Fred Clay and Gilbert as copyists, set to work on it. He went to bed at 5 and got up at 9 for a band rehearsal. The strain of over-work, which lasted continuously from December 10th to the 31st, made him ill. Before the first performance, on the last day of 1879, he tried to eat but could not, tried to rest but could not sleep. His head ached and burned, and he felt half-dead. Twelve oysters and a glass of champagne failed to revive him, and with difficulty he struggled to the conductor's seat. He felt better as he lifted the baton, and when the curtain went up he forgot himself, becoming absorbed in the piece.

The Pirates had a riotous reception and at last the partners felt that they would make more money out of their work than the unauthorized investors. But they had to keep a watchful eye on their property, and after every performance the music was deposited in a safe till the next night. Members of the orchestra were offered bribes to lend their scores; experts in the audience made notes of the themes; but the authors had a good start of the pirates and maintained it by sending out three touring companies. This meant a great deal of work for them, but as it also meant a good deal of money they slaved away at their respective tasks. Having attended the opening night of their last company at Buffalo, they went with D'Oyly Carte to see Niagara Falls. 'I suppose I must find time to leave a card on Niagara', Gilbert had said. He was not one of those people who go everywhere and see nothing. He went to a place because he wanted to look at it. Having stared steadily at the frozen Falls, and knowing that some comment was expected, he said nothing. Sullivan left the other two and spent a few days at Ottawa with the governor-general of Canada, the Marquess of Lorne, who was married to one of Queen Victoria's daughters, rejoining them at the beginning of March, when they sailed for England. A month later, on April 3rd, 1880, they produced *The Pirates of Penzance* at the Opera Comique. As there were pirates in England too, a copyright performance of the piece had been given at the Royal Bijou Theatre, Paignton, by the *Pinafore* touring company on December 30th, 1879. It ran for a year in London.

Their association while in America had been highly successful but not always harmonious. Gilbert, more than a little nettled by the immense popularity of the *Pinafore* music, which he heard praised wherever he went while only the silliest of his own words were quoted, could not help displaying the superiority of wit to tunes in public; and when the partners were being entertained he was inclined to make a butt of Sullivan. No doubt he believed that his fun was good-natured, but the pointed way in which he expressed it pained the more sensitive nature of the composer, who confided in Fred Clay that Gilbert's jokes never failed to get a laugh at his expense. Their relationship was a little like that between Samuel Johnson and Oliver Goldsmith. The elder man allowed himself to hurt the younger, but would not have permitted anyone else to do so. That Gilbert was steadfastly loyal to those friends who were loyal to him is proved by a letter to his American agent shortly after *The Pirates* appeared in London:

28 April, 1880

To Horace Wall Esq.
14 Union Square, New York.

Dear Sir

I am in receipt of your cheque for £82 for fees on *Engaged*.

With respect to your remarks upon Mr R. D'Oyly Carte's character, I have thought it my duty to hand your letter to him, that he may take whatever steps he thinks proper to set himself right in the eyes of American managers.

I have only to add that all business arrangements between us are henceforth at an end. Mr French will take charge of *Engaged* and is authorized by me to advertise to that effect.

Yours truly

On the same day he advised E. A. Sothern:

I have just received a letter from Mr Wall (who was extremely anxious to have the agency of *The Pirates* in America) attacking Carte in what I conceive to be a most disgraceful manner. I have in consequence written to Mr Wall declining all further dealings with him.

No doubt Sothern had introduced Wall to Gilbert as a satisfactory agent.

The success of *The Pirates* proved conclusively that *Pinafore* had not been, as many people thought it was, a flash in the pan. The continued shouts of 'Encore' by an audience that could not have enough of the song about the Enterprising Burglar made Rutland Barrington propose that the author should provide an encore verse. ' "Encore" means "Sing it again" ', said Gilbert. While the piece was in full career a different class of work by the same authors was heard at the Leeds Festival in the autumn of 1880. Sullivan had asked Gilbert to provide a poetic version of *The Martyr of Antioch*, and for once the pair produced a solemn composition. It was an occasion when Gilbert, to quote himself, justified 'his claim to be regarded as a person of literary culture', but he preferred cash to culture, and in his next work displayed his preference.

He had been toying with a libretto founded on one of the 'Bab' ballads, 'The Rival Curates', but the thought that he might be accused of irreverence if he ridiculed clergymen on the stage prevented him from sleeping at night. Suddenly, in a wakeful hour, he thought of the aesthetes who had been pilloried in *Punch*, jumped out of bed, ran down to his library, and in an hour 'rearranged the piece upon a secure and satisfactory basis.' What used to be known as 'the Aesthetic Movement' was no movement at all but a reaction against the stereotyped art and craft of the Victorian Age. The chief rebels were following a general tendency to revolt, but there was no cohesion among them, such men as Morris, Ruskin, Swinburne, Pater, Rossetti and Whistler expressing their own individualities in totally different ways. The operas by Gilbert and Sullivan were quite as much a part of the reaction as the poems of Morris and Swinburne, the prose of Ruskin and Pater, or the paintings of Rossetti and Whistler. But what made the tendency notorious was the arrival of Oscar Wilde in London, his peculiar contribution to the art reformation being a new style of clothing. A group of disciples soon outdid the fashions he set, and the original aesthetes were made to look ridiculous by the posings and affectations of these neophytes. The so-called movement was satirized in journals and parodied in musichalls, the emphasis always being on the curious clothes and artificial utterances of a small band of exhibitionists. Although Bunthorne, the chief character in Gilbert's opera *Patience*, was at once identified with Wilde or Whistler, the satire was directed at the cult-followers of aestheticism, not at any particular aesthete. Gilbert knew that Wilde, like Bunthorne, had more innocent fun in him than a casual spectator would imagine and was enjoying his own performance while laughing at those who took it seriously. That Gilbert's instinct was right became clear in *The Importance of Being Earnest*, where the innocent fun of Bunthorne had flowered into the exquisite nonsense of Bunbury. The two men must have run across one another occasionally, since both were regular playgoers; but no account of their meetings has been preserved except that given to the present writer by Beerbohm Tree. At a supper-party in the Haymarket Theatre Wilde held the table with his conversation for about half an hour. Gilbert seized the first opportunity to pay a handsome compliment: 'I wish I could talk like you', which he followed with an acid comment: 'I'd keep my mouth shut and claim it as a virtue.' Wilde flashed back: 'Ah, that would be selfish! I could deny myself the pleasure of talking, but not to others the pleasure of listening.'

Gilbert's decision to satirize aesthetes instead of clerics was due to another cause of which he may have been unconscious. He had ceased to be wholeheartedly amused by the fundamental folly of mankind and now concentrated on the antics of particular people. This mental transition almost invariably takes place when an ambitious humorist becomes successful. A settled situation and a regular revenue are liable to check the witty man's inclination to laugh at every form of stupidity. Perhaps the only person on record who, having achieved a secure social position and an assured income, maintained his view of human beings and their systems as incorrigibly idiotic, was a clergyman, Sydney Smith, though the Scottish translator of Rabelais, Thomas Urquhart, may have been another, for he had lived through the Commonwealth and on hearing of the rapturous welcome given to Charles II at the Restoration he actually died of laughter. But these are rare exceptions, and most men of outstanding intelligence are willing to suppress their sense of the ridiculous in favour of a balance in the bank or an established place in society. The Gilbert of 'Bab' who laughed at everything was killed by the success of his plays and operas, and the Gilbert of *Patience* had become a man who would safely satirize follies that most people regarded as absurd. But that he still halted for a while between the two viewpoints is shown in his letter to Sullivan announcing his change of theme. The opening paragraph refers to the bill of their solicitors in the action they brought and won against the Comedy Opera Company, which thereafter expired:

> 24 The Boltons
> 1st Nov. 1880

Dear Sullivan

I have just received the enclosed from Lewis & Lewis and I have sent a cheque for £500 accordingly. You can let me have your half of this at your convenience.

I want to see you particularly about the new piece. Although it is about two-thirds finished, I don't feel comfortable about it. I mistrust the clerical element. I feel hampered by the restrictions which the nature of the subject places upon my freedom of action, and I want to revert to my old idea of rivalry between two Aesthetic fanatics, worshipped by a chorus of female aesthetics, instead of a couple of clergymen worshipped by a chorus of female devotees. I can get much more fun out of the subject as I propose to alter it, and the general scheme of the piece will remain as at present. The Hussars will become aesthetic young men (abandoning their profession for the purpose) – in this latter capacity they will all carry lilies in their hands, wear long hair, and stand in stained glass attitudes. I entertained this idea at first, as you may remember, but abandoned it because I foresaw great difficulty in getting the chorus to dress and make up aesthetically – but if we can get Du Maurier to design the costumes, I don't know that the difficulty will be insuperable.

> Very truly yours
> W. S. Gilbert

P.S. Let us meet to talk over the proposed change.

The theme of aestheticism was in the air, and to his consternation Gilbert read an account of a play which dealt with the same subject as his opera:

> 21 Nov. 1880

To James Albery Esq.
Criterion Theatre.

Dear Albery

I gather from the notices of your new piece, produced at the Criterion last night, and called 'Where's the Cat?', that you have made good capital out of the affectations and eccentricities of the modern school of lily-bearing poets. By an odd coincidence, I have completed the greater part of the libretto of a two-act opera (designed six months ago) in which this preposterous school plays a very prominent part. I mention this as, otherwise, you might reasonably suppose, when the piece comes to be played, that it was in some way suggested by a successful character in your comedy.

Yours very truly

P.S. I am sure you will see that it is important to me that the contents of this letter should not be made public, unless occasion should arise.

But he need not have worried. *Patience* eclipsed all the pictures and parodies inspired by the aesthetes. Produced at the Opera Comique on the evening of St George's Day, April 23rd, 1881, it ran for a year and a half, and gave aestheticism a much longer life than any other transient art tendency in history. Also it was the first of the operas to be done at the Savoy Theatre, to which it was transferred on October 10th, 1881, when Sullivan conducted and the Prince of Wales occupied a box. Carte had bought the freehold of the land and built his new theatre to provide accommodation for the larger public that now rushed to see the operas and could not obtain seats at the smaller place. The Savoy was the first London playhouse in which electric light was used for both stage and auditorium, gas being held in reserve in case the electricity failed, and at which the playgoers lined up in orderly queues at the pit and gallery entrances instead of fighting to get in. A new profit-sharing arrangement was made between the three partners, based on the previous one, and Carte estimated the rent of the theatre at £4000 a year, this being the chief expense in their agreement. Gilbert hinted that as Carte the partner was paying one-third of the rent to Carte the proprietor, it was a sound investment for Carte the capitalist. The tone of this remark hurt Carte the man.

The success of *Patience* enabled Sullivan to enjoy several holidays in 1881, one of them being a trip in a warship with the Duke of Edinburgh. They were entertained by the King of Denmark at Copenhagen, the Tsar of Russia at St Petersburg, and the future Kaiser of Germany at Kiel. The latter sang a song from *Pinafore* that was naturally popular in the German navy, 'He polished up the handle of the big front door', a performance that Sullivan thought 'too funny'. At the end of the year he visited Egypt, where he was feasted by the Khedive and other notables, and where he played 'riotous games' with the future George V and his brother the Duke of Clarence.

Meanwhile Gilbert had been working. He started on his next libretto, and in December 1881 attended to the production of his new farce *Foggerty's Fairy* at the Criterion Theatre. Taken from one of his own short stories, it is a clever bit of work that would be brilliant if it had the least connection with probability. Absurdity itself ceases to be funny when there is nothing real to be absurd about. A single sentence written in Gilbert's stilted style is amusing, e.g. 'I'm at a loss for words in which to express definitely my sense of your infamous conduct, because I am not at present acquainted with the nature of your offence.' But a whole scene in that style is wearisome. Gilbert's sense of reality, usually operative in his life, seldom functioned in his writings, though it appears now and then in a short passage, such as this from the Fairy whose advice makes Foggerty eat an ornament off a cake and change himself into someone else: 'Every age is matter-of-fact to those who live in it. Romance died the day before yesterday. Today will be romantic the day after tomorrow.'

CHAPTER 11

Great Nights

❍━❍━❍

Perhaps no works were ever produced at the cost of so much mental travail and in the course of so much physical pain as those of Gilbert and Sullivan. The libretti were written out as stories, revised, re-written, reconsidered, re-drafted, a score of times; and the dialogue and lyrics were subjected to an equally laborious process, from conception to completion, over a prolonged period. The music was often composed with astonishing swiftness, welling out as spontaneously as the words had been churned out arduously, though not seldom accompanied by bodily torments. The composer however took longer than usual over his contribution to the next Savoy opera.

The financial rewards of *Patience* were so considerable that Sullivan moved into an expensive flat in Queen's Mansions, Victoria Street, and Gilbert started to build a house in Harrington Gardens, South Kensington. Naturally the opera had been pirated in the United States, and the partners made up their minds to have their next produced simultaneously in both countries. The first act did not please Sullivan and he wanted to discuss it with Gilbert, who at the time was yachting off the south coast. They spent an afternoon together in the coffee-room of the Half Moon Hotel, Exeter, and revised the act to their mutual satisfaction. To prevent piracy and newspaper gossip, the music was locked up between rehearsals and the opera misnamed. Even the cast were kept in the dark about the title until the final dress rehearsal, when they were told that the word they had been speaking, *Periola*, must be changed to *Iolanthe* the following evening. Those concerned protested that they would almost certainly confuse the names on the first night. 'Never mind, so long as you sing the music', said Sullivan. 'Use any name that happens to come first to you. Nobody in the audience will be any the wiser except Mr Gilbert, and he won't be there.' Gilbert cannot have been there when Sullivan delivered this advice.

The really popular writer drifts with the trend of public feeling, giving the impression that he is leading it by making articulate the sentiment of the majority. In *Patience* Gilbert had shown the public exactly what they wished to ridicule in poetry. In *Iolanthe* he showed them precisely what they wished to deride in politics. The Liberal Party under Gladstone had come to power and the idea was gaining ground that the House of Lords obstructed progress. Gilbert wittily expressed the popular view in *Iolanthe*, while providing some fun at the expense of the House of Commons to placate those rich or titled playgoers who might have complained of a class distinction in grey matter. Everybody was pleased, and the opera, first seen on November 25th, 1882, was repeated for more than a year. Gilbert very sensibly refused to regard his satire as an index to his opinions. Twenty-seven years after he had written *Iolanthe* the Liberal Party were campaigning against the House of Lords and a section of it wished to use his verses as propaganda. He wrote sharply: 'I cannot permit the verses from *Iolanthe* to be used for electioneering purposes. They do not at all express my own views. They are supposed to be the views of the wrong-headed donkey who sings them.'

The collaborators had now performed a feat unparalleled in the annals of the theatre: they had produced four extremely remunerative comic operas in succession. It seemed that whatever they did together would fill a theatre for at least a year; and in those days very few plays, let alone operas, ran for half that time, one hundred performances constituting a success. They felt in 1883 that they could aestivate at ease, careless of the future. Gilbert lazily adapted his play *The Princess* to the needs of the Savoy and produced an opera in blank verse. Sullivan jibbed at first but assented at last. In May 1883, at the age of 41, he was knighted, and his birthday-party on Whit-Sunday included the Prince of Wales, the Duke of Edinburgh, a brace of peers, Ferdinand Rothschild, J. C. Millais, F. C. Burnand (editor of *Punch*) and Gilbert. Having concluded a musical entertainment, to which Madame Albani and Paolo Tosti contributed, Sullivan treated his guests to a selection of songs from *Iolanthe*. The company had gone to the theatre for the purpose, and the guests in Victoria Street listened-in with the aid of an electrophone.

That year Gilbert moved into his new house, which had been fitted up luxuriously with panelled walls, thickly moulded ceilings, richly embellished wallpapers, ornate tapestries, and some windows of stained glass. More useful additions were electric light, central heating, a telephone, and a bathroom on each floor. Delays and disappointments in connection with such an elaborate establishment were inevitable. Several tart letters were addressed to one company that supplied a dado and a chimney-piece, and on July 2nd 1883 Gilbert wrote to the firm chiefly responsible for the interior arrangements:

Gentlemen

I write to inform you that I intend to move into my house in Harrington Gardens on 1st October next, as I am selling this house from that date. To enable me to make this move it is necessary that the hall, dining-room, morning-room on half landing, library, our bedroom and dressing-rooms, 3 servants' bedrooms, and the basement should be completed. I would suggest that you put all your strength to the completion of this work, as I shall commence occupation on the 1st October, in whatever condition the premises may be. I shall also reckon demurrage as from that date, as regards the rooms I have specified, and such other rooms as may be essential to my comfort.

Yours truly
W. S. Gilbert

In the same year he took a furnished country-house called Breakspears, at Harefield near Uxbridge, for which he paid £800 per annum. Here he spent many summer weeks and spring week-ends for the next seven years, playing tennis on an outsize court and entertaining those friends who did not provoke friction, of which there was always sufficient in the theatre and the world of business.

The preparation of the next opera, *Princess Ida*, provided more friction than usual, possibly because the blank verse irritated the actors. 'Look here, sir, I will *not* be bullied! I know my lines', rasped one of them. 'That may be, but you don't know mine', Gilbert snapped back. George Grossmith was roused to exclaim indignantly 'I beg your pardon!' after one of the author's acid remarks. 'I accept the apology', Gilbert blandly replied; 'let's get on with the rehearsal.' Having repeated one scene almost twenty times, Grossmith struck: 'I've rehearsed this confounded business until I feel a perfect fool!' Gilbert soothed him: 'Ah, now we can talk on equal terms.' As usual, Sullivan was late with the music and made himself ill with overwork when time pressed. On the date of production, January 5th, 1884, he was clearly unfit to conduct. After two injections of morphia he struggled to the theatre in a semi-conscious condition. Braced by his reception he managed to get through the evening, but collapsed after the curtain-call. The opera only lasted nine months, which the authors considered a failure. The theme was not acceptable, being a variation on that of *Love's Labour's Lost*. Shakespeare's male characters and Gilbert's female characters seclude themselves from the other sex to study philosophy; but playgoers had not yet been sufficiently indoctrinated by Ibsen to regard the independent woman as pleasant or natural. Gilbert's satire was blunted by verse, though it happened that his lyrical gift was displayed at its finest in *Princess Ida*, wherein one song is as charming as anything by Robert Herrick, as perfect as anything by John Suckling, its absence from anthologies being due to editorial ignorance:

> *Whom thou hast chained must wear his chain,*
>   *Thou canst not set him free,*
> *He wrestles with his bonds in vain*
>   *Who lives by loving thee!*
> *If heart of stone for heart of fire,*
>   *Be all thou hast to give,*
> *If dead to me my heart's desire,*
>   *Why should I wish to live?*
>
> *No word of thine—no stern command*
>   *Can teach my heart to rove,*
> *Then rather perish by thy hand,*
>   *Than live without thy love!*
> *A loveless life apart from thee*
>   *Were hopeless slavery,*
> *If kindly death will set me free,*
>   *Why should I fear to die?*

The relative failure of this opera caused disruption in the partnership, though the ostensible reasons were of another kind. The one thing that bound the pair together was their dual success. Without that Sullivan would much rather write what was known as 'serious music'; namely, oratorios, grand operas, symphonies, and so on. From the throne to the professors of music, from friends to critics, he was incited to solemnity; and now that he had been knighted he felt that he must do better than set comic words to music, that he should justify his sovereign's confidence in him as another Mendelssohn. Yet his nature craved for all the things that money brought him,.and it was impossible to grow rich on oratorios. The ambition to write music that would be approved by those who believed that music should be improving, and the desire to earn enough money for the life of gambling and hospitality enjoyed by his aristocratic friends: these were the two main strands in his nature, and they were irreconcilable. Sometimes one was the stronger, sometimes the other, but the struggle between the two was never resolved. Gilbert's situation was different. Though he too felt convinced that he was made for better things than the writing of humorous libretti, he was an older man who believed that he had put his best work into his plays and was now solely concerned with comfort and financial security. Their different aims, coupled with Sullivan's sense of frustration and Gilbert's natural irritation, explains the first rift in their association.

Shortly after the appearance of *Princess Ida* Sullivan informed D'Oyly Carte that he had written his last work for the Savoy Theatre. Carte was upset but felt that Sullivan, temporarily under the weather, would reconsider his decision after a holiday; and when in March the opera showed signs of failure, he wrote to remind the composer of their contract whereby he had to give the collaborators six months' notice when a new opera would be required. He now gave this notice to both of them. Sullivan answered from Brussels that he could not undertake another piece 'of the character of those already written by Gilbert and myself'. Carte wondered what Gilbert would have to say. Gilbert said it to Sullivan: 'I learnt from Carte yesterday, to my unbounded surprise, that you do not intend to write any more operas of the class with which you and I have been so long identified.' He warned Sullivan that if they failed in their agreement with Carte they would be responsible for any losses resulting from their default, and he declared that he had already started work on a new libretto:

In all the pieces we have written together I have invariably subordinated my views to your own; you have often expatiated to me, and to others, on the thorough good feeling with which we have worked together for so many years. Nothing, as far as I am aware, has occurred to induce you to change your views on this point, and I am therefore absolutely at a loss to account for the decision.

Sullivan replied from Paris that his music was becoming repetitive, that his share of the work dissatisfied him, and that what he now wanted was a story of human interest and probability, where the comedy, drama and sentiment would be separated each from the other. 'Your reflections on the character of the libretti with which I have supplied you have caused me considerable pain', returned Gilbert:

However, I cannot suppose that you have intended to gall and wound me, when you wrote as you did. I must assume that your letter was written hurriedly. When you tell me that your desire is that I shall write a libretto in which the humorous words will come in a humorous situation, and in which a tender or dramatic situation will be treated tenderly and dramatically, you teach me the ABC of my profession. It is inconceivable that any sane author should ever write otherwise than as you propose I should write in future.

They met in April at Sullivan's flat and had a long talk. The theme of Gilbert's new libretto was not new: one variation of it had appeared in his first play *Dulcamara*, another in *The Sorcerer*, and it would continue to haunt his fancy during the remainder of his life, for it was based on a feeling, engrafted in childhood, that the world would be a better place if its inhabitants could change their natures. The version he now proposed to Sullivan was that every character in the new piece would become what he or she pretended to be by the simple process of absorbing a lozenge. Two years before Sullivan had rejected the same idea, though on that occasion the means of metamorphosis had been a coin. The substitution of a lozenge for a medal did not make the circumstance any more lifelike, and Sullivan again rejected it. A day or two later Gilbert proposed that Sullivan should write his next opera to someone else's words, since 'your objections to my libretto really seem arbitrary and capricious'. Sullivan declined to consider such a proposal. Again they met but Gilbert remained faithful to his lozenge, and though Sullivan did his utmost to swallow it he found that it would not go down. He reported as much to Gilbert, who replied:

> Anxious as I am, and have always been, to give due weight to your suggestions, the time has arrived when I must state – and I do so with great reluctance – that I cannot consent to construct another plot for the next Opera.

Sullivan regretted this decision and a frantic Carte went from one to the other for several days in an agitated attempt to reach a compromise.

With their weekly returns from the Savoy steadily diminishing, each would have seized any excuse to do another work together; and a Japanese Exhibition in Knightsbridge turned Gilbert's thoughts from his lozenge libretto. Japanese prints, designs, and what-not, were rapidly becoming the fashion, and the public would surely jump at a Japanese opera. He wrote the good news to his partner, who was inexpressibly relieved, replying that if the plot were to be devoid of super natural and improbable elements he would 'gladly undertake to set it without further discussing the matter, or asking what the subject is to be'. It cannot be said that the plot and people of *The Mikado*, which Gilbert at once started to write, are noticeably natural or probable, but at least they are not made less so by a lozenge.

Though Gilbert declared that the idea for this opera entered his head when a Japanese sword fell from the wall of his study, it seems more likely that the idea was germinating within him before that accident, the crash of the falling weapon merely fixing it in his mind. Extremely susceptible to the atmosphere of his age, he must often have envisaged a Japanese setting, because the taste for oriental prints and pots, started in England by Whistler in the sixties and advertised by himself and Rossetti in the seventies, had become fairly general by the eighties, and Gilbert knew to a fad how the popular taste could be exploited. The sureness of his instinct, coupled with the creative harmony between librettist and composer, was again demonstrated when the country went Mikado-mad.

Like all the operas, it was produced by Gilbert with the utmost care, if possible with greater care than usual because of the necessity to recover the ground lost by *Princess Ida*. Weedon Grossmith, brother of George, once remarked that the difference between the methods of production at the Lyceum and those at the Savoy was that at every rehearsal Henry Irving groped for perfection, while Gilbert arrived at each rehearsal with perfection in his pocket: the first saw what he wanted in fitful gleams, the second in a hard steady light. In other words Gilbert knew exactly what he wanted before he started to produce. He worked it all out on a model stage with wooden blocks for the actors; and though he occasionally improvised during rehearsals, all the positions, stage business, exits, entrances, even the word-inflections, were clear in his mind's eye before the practical work began.

He was an exacting but patient producer. Knowing what he wanted, he took endless pains to get it, occasionally repeating a word twenty or thirty times before the actor could speak it rightly, often doing a scene over and over again until the performers were breaking under the strain. His energy never flagged. He could show the chorus how to dance with the efficiency of a ballet-master and instruct them how to pronounce the words and maintain the rhythm with the skill of a music-master, though he always asserted that he knew nothing about music and could scarcely distinguish between one tune and another. Whenever he thought that a performer was not trying to obtain the effect he desired, his patience gave way to temper and his sarcasms were relentless; but knowing that most people can only do their best under persuasion, he seldom attempted to bully them into subjection. Nevertheless the drilling to which they were exposed was of a military kind. Nothing was left to chance, and the company had to go through its evolutions at the word of command, repeating them, as on a parade-ground, until the process became automatic. Once, at any rate, his method nearly caused disaster. George Grossmith had a highly sensitive nature, and the rehearsals of *The Mikado* shattered his nerves. To such a condition had he been reduced that, according to Sullivan, he 'nearly upset the piece' on the first night. He forestalled the repetition of such an alarming event by deadening his nerves with drugs.

Though no one would have guessed it, another martyr to first-night agitation was Gilbert, whose forebodings took the form of going the round of the dressing-rooms and imparting his last words of advice to the players, thus adding to their own misgivings. A score of things he had told and repeated to the stage-manager were recapitulated, and even the property man came in for a series of warnings. He heard the roar of applause that greeted Sullivan's appearance in the orchestra, made a final survey of the scenery and chorus, and on the rise of the curtain quitted the theatre. 'What I suffered during those hours, no man can tell', he said. 'I have spent them at the club; I once went to a theatre alone to see a play; I have walked up and down the street; but no matter where I was, agony and apprehension possessed me.'

The yells for librettist and composer when the final curtain descended on *The Mikado* were louder than usual. They entered from different sides, Gilbert with reluctance, Sullivan with readiness. The first frowned at the audience and nodded his head curtly; the second smiled with pleasure and bowed with grace. This time their success was unquestionable. *The Mikado*, produced on March 14th, 1885, ran for nearly two years and made more money for the partners than any other of their operas. Oddly enough one of its most popular songs –

> *My object all sublime*
> *I shall achieve in time –*
> *To let the punishment fit the crime –*
> *The punishment fit the crime –*

was nearly omitted. Gilbert did not like it at the final dress rehearsal and said that it must be cut out. But Richard Temple, who sang it as the Mikado, backed by the members of the chorus, begged for its retention, and the author gave way.

After the production of all his operas the relief and reaction were so considerable that, with one exception, Gilbert never again witnessed a performance from the front. Having devoted months to the writing and weeks to the rehearsals, he felt sick of a work by the time it was ready for the public. But the public, unconscious of his birth-pangs, have never shared his feeling.

CHAPTER 12

Gravity and Charm

❦❧❦❧

The Savoy triumvirate had their duties clearly assigned. The casting, dressing and staging of the operas were entirely in the hands of Gilbert and Sullivan. Carte had nothing whatever to do with all that. Although he engaged the cast, arranged for the dresses and scenery, and paid the stage-staff, he carefully followed the pair's instructions in all such matters. The scenery was modelled, the dresses were designed, the cast was chosen, entirely under the direction of the librettist and composer, their will being law. Carte did not even know the subject of a single opera until he heard it at the reading, and he never interfered, even with a suggestion, in the staging of the pieces. His job was confined to the front of the house, and he was a first-rate business-manager.

Discipline was rigidly enforced at the back of the stage, and for this Gilbert was chiefly responsible. In most of the London theatres he had been accustomed to much laxity, which resulted in scandals, jealousy and bad feeling. He determined to put an end to this by arranging the dressing-rooms of the women at one side of the stage, those of the men on the other, and by forbidding the intermingling of the sexes in one another's dressing-rooms during the intervals. They could meet and talk in the green-room but nowhere else. This did not of course protect the women from solicitations addressed to them by male members of the audience, and on one occasion Gilbert informed the youthful occupants of a box that the letter they had sent to a lady in his company was inexcusable and that they could take the choice of leaving the theatre quietly or of being thrown out. They chose the first and revenged themselves by relating the incident, after which several papers referred to 'the Savoy Boarding School' and the lady concerned received ironic messages of condolence. It was also decreed that no strangers should be allowed at the back of the stage during a performance, and the players were not permitted to receive anyone in their dressing-rooms. But as, from the early days at the Opera Comique, George Grossmith and Rutland Barrington had been in the habit of inviting their friends for a drink in their dressing-rooms after the show, they continued to do so at the Savoy as a prescriptive right, and several other leading members of the company asked if they might follow suit. After some discussion between Gilbert and the stage-manager the privilege was extended to them on condition that it was exercised reasonably; but the company as a whole were not allowed to receive friends in the theatre.

Though Gilbert could silence scandal inside the Savoy Theatre, he could not suppress rumours outside, and it came to his ears that a young officer of Hussars had bragged of his intimacy with a member of the company then playing *Patience*. At great pains and some cost he obtained the necessary evidence and tracked down the malefactor, from whom he extracted with the usual legal threats a written confession and recantation in the presence of a solicitor. This document, obviously dictated by Gilbert, expressed the offender's

unfeigned regret that on the 24th and 25th October, 1882, at the Raleigh Club, I intentionally allowed a member of that Club to infer that I had passed the night with Miss Fortescue, a lady connected with the Savoy Theatre. I desire most unreservedly to withdraw this imputation against Miss Fortescue's character, to admit that I have not, nor have I ever had, any personal knowledge of that lady, and that except in her public capacity she is a total stranger to me. I desire further to acknowledge Miss Fortescue's forbearance in consenting to stay the action she has commenced against me on my signing this unqualified apology and retraction and agreeing to pay all her costs of and relating to the said action as between solicitor and client. I hereby authorize Miss Fortescue to make such use of this apology as she may be advised. Dated this 7th day of March, 1883.

It should be said that Gilbert's own moral rectitude was in accordance with his moral attitude to others. Though bursting with vigour and unusually susceptible to female attractions, it is as certain as anything can be that he never lapsed from his conception of virtue. In these days it may be asked if it were possible that a normal and lusty man who adored the society of pretty women, spent much time with them, helped to advance their careers, and petted them, should demand no more of them than their company. The answer is that it was possible in the case of Gilbert. Most people are pagan in their desires and christian in their sentiments. Gilbert was neither one nor the other but a sort of pagan-christian in every respect. We cannot therefore say whether he shared the experience of those whose resistance to temptation in early manhood is the cause of more remorse in old age than anything else.

On one point he was never in doubt: his belief in the lozenge was almost religious, and while *The Mikado* was still packing the Savoy he again brought it up. Sullivan very courteously begged him to forget it. In January 1886 Gilbert arrived at Sullivan's flat in a snow blizzard with a non-lozenge plot. Sullivan was delighted and agreed to co-operate, but first he had to produce an oratorio for the Leeds Festival. He did so, and *The Golden Legend* created a sensation, Sullivan undergoing the unique experience of a conductor being pelted with flowers by his orchestra. This time he was called the Mozart of England and mildly reprimanded for wasting his genius on Savoy opera. Gilbert wrote: 'I congratulate you heartily on the success of the Cantata which appears from all accounts to be the biggest thing you've done.' But Gilbert was solely concerned with the little thing that he himself had done, and sent the libretto of *Ruddigore* to his partner. At rehearsals each of them thought that the other had too large a share of the work, Sullivan describing it as a play with a few songs, Gilbert convinced that the words were overshadowed by the music. At the fall of the curtain on the first performance, January 22nd, 1887, several occupants of the gallery expressed disapprobation; and the critics said it was not half so good as *The Mikado*; whereupon Gilbert suggested that they should re-entitle it *Kensington Gore*: or *Not Half So Good as The Mikado*. Though a number of alterations were made to please the public, the opera only ran for ten months. Ancestral ghosts were in the air just then, possibly because the daughters of certain impoverished peers had recently been married to wealthy Americans, and less than a month after the appearance of *Ruddigore* a magazine published *The Canterville Ghost* by Oscar Wilde; but somehow the theme failed to catch the popular fancy, and Gilbert's share of the profits on the original run was a measly £7000, which any other author would have thought a windfall.

The relative misfire touched his pride and made him feel that he had put some of his best work into the opera. So he criticized Sullivan's music in the ghost scene: 'I fancy he thought his professional position demanded something grander and more impressive than the words suggested', and further declared that it was like introducing fifty lines from *Paradise Lost* into a farcical comedy. He even resented jokes about the title. 'How's *Bloodygore* going?' asked a friend. 'You mean *Ruddigore*', said Gilbert severely. 'Same thing', was the airy response. 'Indeed? Then if I say I admire your ruddy counte- nance (which I do), it means that I like your bloody cheek (which I don't).' D'Oyly Carte's deputy business-manager at the Savoy Theatre was George Edwardes, whose productions of musical comedies were destined to supersede the Gilbert and Sullivan operas as the most popular form of entertainment, and when Edwardes had left the Savoy he told a newspaper reporter that Gilbert's refusal to alter his libretti and to make experiments had harmed a fine work like *Ruddigore*. Gilbert still felt sore over the reception of the piece and wrote to the newspaper:

> Mr Edwardes is quite right in supposing that (after polishing up my work to the minutest degree) I have not been in the habit of handing it over to a stage-manager to embellish it with altera- tions and additions at his good pleasure. If I had done so the Savoy pieces would no doubt have borne a stronger resemblance to the productions with which Mr Edwardes' name is associated, but that was not the object I had in view.

A successor to *Ruddigore* was soon needed, and once more Gilbert proffered his lozenge. Sullivan at first temporized, say- ing that he would consider the plot carefully if the other would complete a scenario. But when he read it he decided that he could not work on such an inhuman theme, and for a time it looked as if the collaboration were at an end. Then, one day, a poster of a number of beefeaters, advertising a furnishing com- pany, caught Gilbert's eye while he was waiting for a train at Uxbridge station. It gave him an idea for a human story about the Tower of London. Sullivan was greatly relieved when he heard the plot, which struck him as human, amusing and natural. Gilbert's instinct again proved sound. It was the year of Queen Victoria's Golden Jubilee, when the British Empire had reached its apogee, and the Tower of London was a symbol of England's history. In order to get into the atmosphere of the place he visited the Tower regularly, read books about it, and, since the period of his piece was to be the sixteenth century, he even went so far as to re-read Shakespeare, whose work made little appeal to him. 'If you promise me faithfully not to mention this to a single person, not even to your dearest friend, I don't think Shakespeare rollicking', he told George Grossmith. His skit on *Hamlet*, which he called *Rosencrantz and Guildenstern*, is, with the possible exception of Max Beerbohm's ' "Savonarola" Brown', the best parody of the poet ever written. It tells how Claudius as a young man had written a five-act tragedy which was laughed off the stage, all reference to it thereafter being forbidden by him on pain of death. 'Was it, my lord, so very, very bad?' asks Gertrude. 'Not to deceive my trusting Queen, it was', he replies. Unconscious that it is by his uncle, Hamlet has it performed at court and is banished to England for the crime, leaving Ophelia in the arms of Rosencrantz. It is the funniest thing Gilbert ever wrote and was originally performed for a charity matinée at the Vaudeville Theatre on June 3rd, 1891, its first professional production being seen at the Court Theatre on April 27th, 1892, with Brandon Thomas (author of *Charley's Aunt*) as Claudius, Weedon Grossmith as Hamlet, and Gertrude Kingston as the Queen.

In Gilbert's opinion Shakespeare's jesters were somewhat dismal folk whose conversation was largely enigmatical. 'Shakespeare is a very obscure writer', he informed a friend. 'What do you think of this passage? – "I would as lief be thrust through a quicket hedge as cry Pooh to a callow throstle".' The friend thought it perfectly clear: 'A great lover of feathered songsters, rather than disturb the little warbler, would prefer to go through a thorny hedge. But I can't for the moment recall the passage. Where does it occur?' Gilbert enlightened him: 'I have just invented it – and jolly good Shakespeare too!' So he determined to improve on Shakespeare and draw a jester who was unaffected in his motley and comprehensible in his speech. The result appeared in his new work, and whether Jack Point is more amusing than Touchstone, or Touchstone is more natural than Jack Point, is a moot question.

While Gilbert was writing *The Tower of London*, as he called it at first, he had one of his periodic rows with Carte, to which later reference will be made, and another disagreement with Sullivan. A comic opera called *Dorothy*, music by Alfred Cellier, had been an enormous success in the West End, and Sullivan felt that as any composer could now make a fortune out of similar products, the time had come to devote himself to serious work. He wrote from Monte Carlo to tell Gilbert so. 'I can't, for the life of me, understand the reasons that urge you to abandon a theatre and a company that have worked so well for us, and for whom we have worked so well', Gilbert replied:

> Why in the world are we to throw up the sponge and begin all over again because *Dorothy* has run 500 nights, beats my comprehension. The piece that we are engaged upon has been constructed by me with direct reference to the Savoy Company. Every member of it has been fitted to the ground, and now that the piece is half finished you propose to scatter the Company, abandon the theatre, and start anew with a new company in (I suppose) a new theatre ... We have the best theatre, the best company, the best composer, and (though I say it) the best librettist in England working together – we are world-known, and as much an institution as Westminster Abbey – and to scatter this splendid organization because *Dorothy* has run 500 nights is, to my way of thinking, to give up a gold mine. What is *Dorothy's* success to us? It is not even the same class of piece as ours. Is no piece but ours to run 500 or 600 nights? Did other companies dissolve because *The Mikado* ran 650 nights?

He closed the letter with a friendly tip:

> I hope you've been lucky at the tables. Try my system; it's very simple. Back red until it turns up twice in succession, then back black till it turns up twice – then back red and so on. I tried it a dozen different times, with Napoleons, and always won.

This letter brought Sullivan to his senses, though there was discord between the pair both before and after it was written. In the spring of 1887 Gilbert wanted a favourite singer in the operas, Jessie Bond, to appear in his play *Broken Hearts* for several afternoon performances at the Savoy Theatre. Sullivan would not consent, saying that if the theatre were lent to one of their company all the other principals might ask for the same thing and complain if refused. Jessie reported this to Gilbert, who wrote to her:

Sir William Gilbert, 1907

The Three Sleepers, 1887. (W.S.G., Maud Tree, the Playwright, Beerbohm Tree)

Captain Gilbert, R.A.H., 1874

Lucy Agnes Gilbert

The Library at Grim's Dyke. (W.S.G. taken by himself)

The Horseman. (In the Eighties)

The Motorists. (W.S.G. in right car; Lucy Gilbert in back, Nancy

The Deputy-Lieutenant

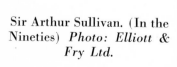

Sir Arthur Sullivan. (In the Nineties) *Photo: Elliott & Fry Ltd.*

Breakspears
Uxbridge
17 June, 1887

My dear Jessie,

I am very sorry that any difficulty has arisen with Sullivan.
In point of fact he ought to have been consulted at first – but he
was abroad at the time, and I left it to Carte to settle with him.
I suppose Carte thought it unnecessary to consult Sullivan about
a matter which concerned him in no way – nevertheless, as the
theatre can't be lent without the consent of all three, his consent
ought to have been obtained. I think he is taking a very unwarrantable and ill-advised course in interfering – but he is quite
within his rights. I wrote to him admitting this, in the hope that
my doing so might induce him to withdraw his opposition – but
I am afraid, from your letter, that he has not done so. I am very
sorry for all the trouble this has caused you. I proposed the performance entirely in your interests and I am greatly disappointed
that this hitch has occurred. I told him that I thought it unreasonable that we should lend the theatre right and left to outsiders,
as we do, and refuse it to a member of our own company who has
been with us for many years.

Yours affectionately
W. S. Gilbert

P.S. Sullivan did not consult me about lending the theatre to
the College of Music – he assumed that, as a matter of courtesy,
I should agree. Next year, however, it may be otherwise. W. S. G.[1]

The theatre was kept open with revivals during the preparation of what Gilbert now called *The Beefeaters*, the second act of
which he altered considerably at the prompting of Sullivan.
Whenever the composer found difficulty in setting the words of
any of their operas, he would say so and the necessary revision
would take place. But though he could not satisfy himself with
his attempts at Jack Point's 'I have a song to sing, O!' he liked
the words so much that he refused Gilbert's offer to re-cast the
song. At last he said, 'You often have some old air in your mind
which prompts the metre of your songs. If anything prompted
you in this one, hum it to me – it may help me.' It had been
suggested by a chanty which the sailors on Gilbert's yacht used
to sing in the dog-watch on Saturday evenings, and at the risk
of destroying the musician's peace of mind he hummed it.

[1] Copied by the author on September 22nd, 1934, from the original letter
then in possession of Jessie Bond.

'That will do – I've got it!' exclaimed Sullivan so suddenly that Gilbert wondered whether it had hurt him. The opera, finally entitled *The Yeomen of the Guard*, was staged on October 3rd, 1888, and surprised the audience because of a seriousness to which they were unaccustomed at the Savoy. It contains some of Gilbert's best verses, including Phoebe's song 'Were I thy bride' and a ballad that is worthier of a place in the Golden Treasury of songs and lyrics than many that are included:

> *Is life a boon?*
> *If so, it must befall*
> *That Death, whene'er he call,*
> *Must call too soon.*
> *Though fourscore years he give,*
> *Yet one would pray to live*
> *Another moon!*
> *What kind of plaint have I,*
> *Who perish in July?*
> *I might have had to die,*
> *Perchance, in June!*
>
> *Is life a thorn?*
> *Then count it not a whit!*
> *Man is well done with it;*
> *Soon as he's born*
> *He should all means essay*
> *To put the plague away;*
> *And I, war-worn,*
> *Poor captured fugitive,*
> *My life most gladly give –*
> *I might have had to live*
> *Another morn!*

Although the opera ran for more than a year, and both collaborators regarded it as their best work, the general feeling was that gravity did not become them so well as frivolity. On this point they were out of sympathy with the general feeling. They wanted to concentrate on serious work, not only because each believed he was capable of dealing with weighty matters but because their different temperaments were beginning to clash. At a rehearsal of their latest opera Gilbert's fussiness got on Sullivan's nerves and their tempers exploded. 'I can't stand it any longer', wrote Sullivan in his diary, though the row closed with a reconciliation. At any rate Sullivan reached a disquieting decision of which we shall hear shortly, and Gilbert had already written a modern drama with a part for Rutland Barrington, for whom there was nothing suitable in *The Yeomen of the Guard*. During the previous year the guests at Break-spears had included the actor Beerbohm Tree and his wife Maud, with whom Gilbert formed a close friendship. In the course of conversation, after saying 'I have been writing down to the public all these years', Gilbert added, 'I will show them what I can do! I am writing a comedy.' This turned out to be an attempt to dramatize real people in realistic situations, and the result is more fantastic than his own fantasies. In comparison with his realism Oscar Wilde's drawing-room comedies seem like direct transcripts from life; and in reading Gilbert's *Brantinghame Hall*, produced at the St James's Theatre on the 27th November 1888, we are made to appreciate fully the debt we owe to Bernard Shaw for lifting the English stage on to the plane of naturalism. Though the cast included Rutland Barrington, Lewis Waller, and a beautiful newcomer named Julia Neilson, the author's endeavour to show the public what he could do was not good enough for the public, whom, in his own words, it 'failed to attract'. Freed from the necessity of having to consider Sullivan, he was in a relaxed mood at rehearsals and made some of his neatest quips. One morning he asked Barrington where the leading lady was. 'She's round behind', replied Barrington, pointing to the door leading to the stage. 'I know', said Gilbert, 'but where is she?' His mood changed to one of wrath when he read what the critics had to say about his drama: 'I am determined not to expose myself again to your insolent jibes; I have written my last play', he informed one of them. It is a pity he did not stick to this resolution, for his next play caused an outburst that ended in a court of law.

While he was busy producing his play, Sullivan was meditating on his future, and Carte was building a new theatre. The collaborators had disagreed over certain things in *The Yeomen of the Guard*, Gilbert wanting more comedy, Sullivan more music, and both a freer hand in direction. The composer, whose word was law throughout his sphere except at the Savoy, at last made up his mind to abandon the sort of thing they had been doing together and to write grand opera. Early in 1889 he informed Gilbert that he wanted to do something on a larger musical scale than hitherto and to have some influence in the preparation of the libretto. He returned to the subject shortly afterwards and asked if Gilbert would prepare a libretto for a serious and dramatic work. He must have been partly prepared for the answer:

20 Feb. '89

Dear S

I have thought carefully over your letter, and while I quite understand and sympathize with your desire to write what, for want of a better term, I suppose we must call 'Grand Opera', I cannot believe that it would succeed either at the Savoy or at Carte's new theatre unless a much more powerful singing and acting company were got together than the Company we now control. Moreover, to speak from my own selfish point of view, such an opera would afford me no chance of doing what I best do – the librettist of a grand opera is always swamped in the composer . . . Again, the success of *The Yeomen* – which is a step in the direction of serious opera – has not been so convincing as to warrant us in assuming that the public want something more earnest still. There is no doubt about it, the more reckless and irresponsible the libretto has been, the better the piece has succeeded – the pieces that have succeeded the least have been those in which a consistent story has been more or less consistently followed out. Personally, I prefer a consistent subject – such a subject as *The Yeomen* is far more congenial to my taste than the burlesque of *Iolanthe* or *The Mikado* – but I think we should be risking everything in writing more seriously still. We have a name, jointly, for humorous work, tempered with occasional glimpses of earnest drama. I think we should do unwisely if we left, altogether, the path which we have trodden together so long and so successfully. I can quite understand your desire to write a big work. Well, why not write one? But why abandon the Savoy business? Cannot the two things be done concurrently? . . .

Yours truly

Sullivan did not think so. He replied that he could not write any more comic operas: the absurd plots, the preposterous parts, had become obnoxious to him. In answer to Gilbert's statement that the librettist would be swamped in serious opera, he said that the composer had been sacrificed in all the operas they had written together. This brought a trenchant response:

19th March, '89

Dear Sullivan,

Your letter has filled me with amazement and regret.

If you are really under the astounding impression that you

have been effacing yourself during the last twelve years – and if you are in earnest when you say that you wish to write an opera with me in which 'the music shall be the first consideration' (by which I understand an opera in which the libretto, and consequently the librettist, must occupy a subordinate place) there is most certainly no *modus vivendi* to be found that shall be satisfactory to both of us.

You are an adept in your profession, and I am an adept in mine. If we meet, it must be as master and master – not as master and servant.

Yours faithfully

The sense of having played second fiddle to Gilbert for so long, of having depended on the genius of the librettist for the commercial exploitation of his own, made this letter peculiarly exasperating, and Sullivan yielded to a mood of self-pity. Magnifying the differences and disagreements that had occurred between himself and Gilbert at rehearsals, he set them forth in a letter to Carte, wherein he complained that his wishes had been disregarded, his music spoilt and his time wasted by his partner's egotistical and tyrannical methods as a producer. But with the morning cool repentance came, and the next day he wrote a series of reasonable suggestions to Gilbert: that the composer's opinion should have some weight 'in the laying out of the musical situation', that he should have 'a more important share in arranging the attitudes and business in all the musical portions', and that the voices of the singers should not be wearied at rehearsals. Injudiciously, and perhaps maliciously, Carte showed the letter he had received from Sullivan to Gilbert, who had not the temperament to indulge a temporary weakness in his collaborator for seeing himself as a victim or a martyr:

31st March, '89

Dear Sullivan,

The requirements contained in your letter of the 27th are just and reasonable in every way. They are requirements with which I have always unhesitatingly complied, and indeed I have always felt, and fully appreciated, the value of your suggestions whenever you have thought it advisable to make any . . .

If that letter stood alone there would be nothing to prevent me embarking at once, in a cheerful and friendly spirit, upon the work which (subject to your approval) I have been constructing during the last 10 days. But unhappily the letter does not stand alone. It was preceded by a letter to Carte (avowedly written that its contents might be communicated to me) which teems with unreasonable demands and utterly groundless accusations – the very least of which, if it had the smallest basis of truth, would suffice to disqualify me absolutely from collaboration with you. In that most cruelly unjust and ungenerous letter you say 'except during the vocal rehearsals and the two orchestral rehearsals, I am a cipher in the theatre'. Have you no recollection of 'business' arranged and re-arranged to meet your reasonable objectives? Have you no recollection of any expressed wish of yours that was not acted upon, without expostulation, argument or demur, upon the spot?

You say that our operas are Gilbert's pieces with music added by you, and that Carte can hardly wonder that 12 years of this has a little tired you. I say that when you deliberately assert that for 12 years you, incomparably the greatest musician of the age – a man whose genius is a proverb wherever the English tongue is spoken – a man who can deal *en prince* with operatic managers, singers, music publishers and musical societies – when you, who hold this unparalleled position, deliberately state that you have submitted silently and uncomplainingly for 12 years to be extinguished, ignored, set aside, rebuffed, and generally effaced by your librettist, you grievously reflect, not upon him, but upon yourself and the noble Art of which you are so eminent a professor.

Yours faithfully

The pair continued to bicker by letter for a few weeks while Sullivan was gambling at Monte Carlo and seeing Venice. Their minds were eased by this paper warfare; and after it had lasted long enough for each of them to feel a bit hazy about its origin, the climbing-down process commenced. By the end of April it was arranged that the first production at Carte's new theatre should be a grand opera by Sullivan, who found the prospect so entrancing that he agreed to do another comic opera with Gilbert at once. In May they met, had a candid talk, and did their best to forget their recent correspondence. The calm was all the more enjoyable because of the preceding storm. They were like a pair of lovers whose happiest hours are those which follow a furious quarrel. Their two most popular works, and on the whole their best, were produced after angry disputes. *The Mikado* had emerged from the heated atmosphere generated by a lozenge; and now *The Gondoliers* issued from a contest between the authors, each of whom suffered spasms of rage because he was dependent on the other.

Again Gilbert showed himself to be in harmony with the main interests of his epoch, a child of his time. Ever since John Ruskin had, so to speak, put Venice on the map, it had become the ambition of every aspiring man and woman of the English middle classes to visit the place, and in the eighties they were being transported thither in hundreds by Thomas Cook and Son, under the guidance of Baedeker. It was an ideal setting for an opera, as it had been for a play in Shakespeare's time, and it enabled the merchants of London to sport vicariously in gondolas. Nothing could so happily have caught the holiday-spirit of the race, and the genial satire on equality and snobbery pleased a people who believed in democracy and behaved with self-interest.

Their quarrel having cleared the air, the collaborators worked in complete concord, Gilbert consulting Sullivan's wishes during the progress of the work, omitting 'dangerous dialogues' and re-writing songs. The opening performance of *The Gondoliers*, December 7th, 1889, was the most radiant and enthusiastic of all their first-nights, and they were so much moved by their ovation that they could scarcely speak to one another. But next morning Gilbert expressed his feelings on paper: 'I must thank you again for the magnificent work you have put into the piece. It gives one the chance of shining right through the twentieth century with a reflected light.' Sullivan's response was in similar vein:

> Don't talk of reflected light. In such a perfect book as *The Gondoliers* you shine with an individual brilliancy which no other writer can hope to attain. If any thanks are due anywhere, they should be from me to you for the patience, willingness, and unfailing good nature with which you have received my suggestions, and your readiness to help me by according to them.

It is fortunate that they exchanged these frank and friendly opinions at such a moment, for within a few months of that wonderful first-night they were exchanging equally frank opinions of a less friendly kind.

CHAPTER 13

On the Carpet

◦━◦━◦

From the time of Caesar Augustus triumvirates have never worked successfully. It almost invariably happens that two of the trio take sides against the third, or that one of them becomes negligible and acts as a buffer between his more energetic partners. In the case of Gilbert, Sullivan and Carte, each was at the head of his profession and a power in his own world; but as Sullivan hated business and disliked combat it was inevitable that he should side with the man who could save him from financial anxiety and give him sympathy. Gilbert was a stickler for rectitude, Sullivan a lover of peace, Carte a wary gambler. Temperamentally, as we have seen, the librettist and composer had nothing in common, their dissimilar natures, the one masculine, the other feminine, making an ideal fusion in art but creating antipathy in life. Their impresario had some of the qualities of each, but what he had in common with Gilbert was the competitive spirit that provoked antagonism, while Sullivan aroused his protective instinct. The famous quarrel, caused by the conflict of wills in Gilbert and Carte, was maintained by the inflexible conscientiousness of Gilbert and the easy submission of Sullivan to the man who shielded him from personal acrimony and relieved him from business responsibilities. The dispute began with a carpet and became serious with an affidavit. But anything would have been sufficient to start it because the subject of expenditure at the theatre had caused controversy from the time when the Savoy opened with *Patience*.

In the summer of 1882 Gilbert discovered that the nightly expenses of running the theatre were £130. He thought the amount outrageous and told Carte that it must be reduced. He pointed out that the gas bill at the Savoy was £10 a week more than it had been at the Opera Comique, in spite of the fact that the Savoy was lit with electricity, and that if their nightly receipts fell to £120 they would lose £3000 a year, whereas similar returns at the Comique would have brought them in £9000 a year. Three years later, during the run of *The Mikado*, Gilbert again complained that the expenses were not under sufficient control and said that he and Sullivan should take part in the business management. Carte refused to accept this view of their contract and a caustic correspondence ensued. Gilbert told Sullivan that if Carte were left to himself he might ruin the business. Carte retorted that he alone ran the risk of pecuniary loss. Sullivan did not participate in the discussion, but obviously sided with Carte because he had no wish to be bored with costs, accounts, and all the rest of it. Another three years passed and once more Gilbert had a row with Carte, calling him 'dictatorial'. This was followed by more indignant letters, and a report of the occurrence by Carte to Sullivan in which one phrase – 'You must stick to me' – suggests that two members of the triumvirate had already formed an alliance.

Such was the condition of affairs when, after a trip to India, Gilbert arrived home in the spring of 1890 and wrote a letter to Sullivan which appears here in full for the first time:

39 Harrington Gardens
S. Kensington
22nd April, 1890

My dear S

I've had a difficulty with Carte.

I was appalled to learn from him that the preliminary expenses of *The Gondoliers* amounted to the stupendous sum of £4500!!! This seemed so utterly unaccountable that I asked to see the details, and last night I received a résumé of them.

This includes such trifles as £75 for Miss Moore's second dress, £50 for her first dress – £100 for Miss Brandram's 2nd dress (this costly garment has now, for some occult reason, been sent on tour) – £450 for the wages of the carpenters during the time they were engaged on the scenery – Lubhart's charge of £460 for the gondola, the sailing boat, the 2 columns and the two chairs and fountain for Act 2 – £112 for timber – £120 for ironmonger – £95 for canvas – and so forth. But the most surprising item was £500 *for new carpets for the front of the house.* I pointed out to Carte that we (you and I) were, by our agreement, liable only for 'repairs incidental to the performances' – that new carpets could not possibly be 'repairs' – and that carpets in the lobbies and on the staircases in front could not, by any reasonable latitude of construction, be considered as 'incidental to the performances' – except in a sense that would include everything of every kind belonging to every part of the theatre. He angrily maintained that we were jointly liable for all upholstery in front (a contention that would justify him in entirely re-decorating and upholstering the theatre a month before we left the theatre for ever and charging us with two-thirds of the cost although the goods would at once become his property) – and emphatically declared that nothing would induce him to adopt any other view. I then asked him why, if you and I had to bear two-thirds of the expense, we were not consulted as to the advisability or necessity of spending so enormous a sum on goods which would at once become his property. He declined to go into this question. I then told him that if he adhered to his contention I should not commence upon a new piece unless a fresh agreement were drawn up. He replied that the only alteration he would agree to would be to put the rent of the theatre at £5000 instead of £4000 and that if I was dissatisfied with the existing state of things I had only to say so. I replied that I *was* dissatisfied, and he said 'Very well, then; you write no more for the Savoy – that's understood' – or words to that effect. I left him with the remark that it was a mistake to kick down the ladder by which he had risen – a sentiment which I hope will meet with your approval on general principles and also as singularly apposite to the case in point.

The clause in the agreement which deals with the question runs as follows: 'The said R.D'O.C. agrees to pay to each of them, the said W.S.G. and A.S., one third of the net profits earned by the representations after deducting all expenses and charges of producing the said operas and all the performances of the same, including in such expense a rental of £4000 per annum for the Savoy Theatre, and all rates, taxes, expenses of lighting, *repairs incidental to the performances*, and rendered necessary from time to time by ordinary wear and tear.' Not a word is said about *replacing* – we simply are liable for certain *repairs* and these are expressly described as 'repairs incidental to the performances' – a description that would be wholly superfluous if it were intended to include everything belonging to the theatre, whether in the lobbies, staircases, auditorium or stage.

I am sorry to bother you with this long letter, but I am sure you will agree with me that it is absolutely necessary that a distinct understanding should be arrived at, if we are to work together for Carte again.

Always truly yours
W. S. Gilbert

As already noticed, some of the most revealing passages in

Gilbert's letters were deleted from the final versions sent to the addressees. One sentence was omitted from the above probably because he did not wish to drag Mrs Carte's name into the discussion and get her into trouble with her husband: 'I was informed by Mrs Carte that it was Carte's practice, whenever a new piece was produced, to purchase whatever might be wanted for the front of the house, and add the amount to the preliminaries.' Another sentence might have evoked in Sullivan an opposite feeling to that intended, so it came out. After reporting Carte's phrase 'you write no more for the Savoy – that's understood', Gilbert had continued 'thus actually dismissing me from the theatre in which you and I have, by our exertions, raised him from penury to affluence'.

It seems that Carte also wrote to Gilbert repeating what he had said during their interview: that owing to the constant friction, their contract had better be terminated and another librettist engaged for the theatre. This letter has not survived, but Gilbert showed it to Jack Robertson, who appeared in several of his operas. Carte's defence at a later meeting was that Gilbert had over-estimated the cost of the carpet, which anyhow was rightly charged as a necessary wear-and-tear expenditure of the partnership, and that the excessive production costs of *The Gondoliers* were due to Gilbert. What actually occurred during their first verbal dispute will never be known. Carte's wife, who was present, asserted that Gilbert had been the first to say he would no longer write for the Savoy, and that he had started the quarrel by insulting Carte. But naturally she sympathized with her husband, and it is safe to conclude that all sorts of things were said in the heat of the moment that no one present could be expected to remember with any exactitude when silence was restored. As we have seen, both men had been simmering with vexation for a long period, and at last they boiled over with indignation.

What made matters far worse was Gilbert's discovery that Sullivan, a fellow-artist, took the part of the business-man whom he believed to be their natural enemy and exploiter. This inexplicable attitude, as he thought it, kept his blood at fever-heat and resulted in a violent scene between the three partners. At first Sullivan agreed that to avoid future misunderstandings a new contract should be drawn up; but when Gilbert pressed him to sign it at once, he said that it had better be held over until they wrote a new piece for the Savoy. On May 5th Gilbert reached a swift decision:

> The time for putting an end to our collaboration has at last arrived . . . I am writing a letter to Carte (of which I enclose a copy) giving him notice that he is not to produce or perform any of my libretti after Christmas 1890. In point of fact, after the withdrawal of *The Gondoliers*, our united work will be heard in public no more.

Apart from the lack of sympathy between Gilbert and Carte, and between Gilbert and Sullivan, certain contributory causes were at work to bring about the disruption. Sullivan was labouring on his grand opera, and the realization of his life's ambition was therefore dependent on friendship with Carte. But he was also afflicted with much pain at that time, and to add mental stress to bodily infirmity was more than he could face. He told a correspondent that he had a combined attack one day, 'my old physical trouble and Gilbert', and he knew that if he supported his collaborator he would have to study accounts and all the other tedious aspects of commerce. Gilbert too was not in a good state of health, his rage being exacerbated by gout, a temper-provoking malady. The third member of the triumvirate, Carte, was suffering from overwork and possibly an ailment known as swollen head, to which successful men in control of others are frequently prone.

As usual, Gilbert put the matter into the hands of his solicitors, and then asked Sullivan to back up his demand that the theatre accounts for the past years should be inspected:

16 July

My dear Gilbert

I don't quite see what I can do about the Savoy banking account or Carte's banking account at the present time. I have no grievance – no dispute, and I have raised no question which would justify me at this juncture stepping in with the demand that the Savoy accounts should be kept in a different manner. I have my own very strong opinion upon various points which I should under a new agreement strongly urge – nay, insist upon being altered. But the happy condition of affairs which would render a new agreement practicable and desirable seems to me further off than ever – indeed the deplorable step of calling in lawyer and accountant has rendered a satisfactory settlement almost impossible. My object now is to do nothing that will add fuel to the fire, and consequently I hold entirely aloof from taking part in this unhappy dispute . . .

Yours very truly
Arthur Sullivan

The Savoy profits were paid to the partners every quarter; but as the trouble over the April account had caused suspension of payment, Carte's solicitors advised him not to discharge the July account until the previous one was settled. Gilbert at once issued a writ for his share of the July profits; whereupon he received a cheque for £2000. But having studied the nightly returns he claimed at least £1000 more; and as his solicitors had discovered a serious discrepancy in the recent accounts, he decided that Carte was not to be trusted and applied for the appointment of a receiver at the Savoy Theatre. After several postponements, due to Gilbert's absence at Carlsbad for the treatment of gout, the case was heard at the beginning of September. In the course of evidence it was divulged that Gilbert's share of the profits on eight operas in eleven years had been £90,000. Carte's excuse for not letting Gilbert have what was due to him made an unfavourable impression, and he was ordered to hand over the £1000 claimed by Gilbert immediately, any balance still due on the July quarter to be remitted within three weeks. Having gained his main point, Gilbert, whose anger showed a hasty spark and straight was cold again, lost no time in writing to Mrs Carte proposing a reconciliation and suggesting that a legal arbitrator should decide the remaining points at issue between them. She agreed to meet him and talk things over. But unfortunately his handsome admission that he had spoken to her husband in wrath and made several unwarrantable charges was nullified by his request that all the accounts, from the very beginning of the partnership, should be examined by an expert. The olive branch that he offered to Sullivan at the same time was not without a legal thorn or two:

8 Sep. 1890

My dear Gilbert
You will I am sure readily understand the difficulty I feel in answering your letter. My old personal regard for you as a friend pleads very strongly to let the past five months be blotted out of our years of friendship as if they had never been lived through – as if the pain and suffering I (and I honestly believe you also) have

endured had been only a nightmare. But I am only human and I confess frankly that I am still smarting under a sense of the unjust and ungenerous treatment I have received at your hands.

If there is to be a reconciliation let it be a thorough one with confidence restored all round, not merely a patched up truce. But confidence cannot be restored whilst you still contend that no other course was open to you but to take the action which was an injury and humiliation to me. And you are doing yourself and your nature a gross injustice in pleading this. I would much rather believe, as I solemnly vow I do believe, that you plunged without forethought into these disastrous proceedings in a fit of uncontrolled anger greatly influenced by the bad health you were suffering from. I will never believe that except for this you would have turned round upon your colleagues, charging one with dishonesty, the other of practically abetting him, bad faith and supineness – putting the whole force of the law into motion in order to settle a wretched dispute over a small sum of money; as if you cared one rap for a few hundred pounds; it's not your nature. But what you unfortunately did care for was to shew your resentment in the most forcible manner and in such a form as to have given me the greatest pain and worry.

With the scandal of last Wednesday's proceedings still vividly before me, I could not sit down and discuss the original dispute calmly, and it would be folly to put myself into the position of hindering that which I earnestly assure you I am most anxious for – viz: a thorough and loyal reconciliation.

Don't think me exaggerating when I tell you that I am physically and mentally ill over this wretched business – I have not yet got over the shock of seeing our names coupled, not in brilliant collaboration over a work destined for worldwide celebrity, but in hostile antagonism over a few miserable pounds.

I am tempted to make a suggestion, which, whether you act upon it or not, you will I am sure receive in good part; and that is that you should withdraw your action at law against Carte and let the disputed matter be settled by a friendly arbitration (not a legal one of course) and not by ourselves. If that were done and the question finally decided, it would be a great relief to all of us.

Yours very truly
Arthur Sullivan

The self-pity in this letter, which is written with some of the sanctimoniousness of an archbishop, and above all the implication that Gilbert's gout had been chiefly responsible for the legal proceedings, provoked a tart rejoinder:

Breakspears
Uxbridge
9 Sept. '90

Dear Sullivan

The tone of your letter causes me to regret that I should have allowed a sentimental recollection of our long alliance to outweigh all consideration of the bewildering treatment I have received at your hands. But I cannot help reminding you that if, *after the discovery of an error of £1400 in four months' accounts*, Carte had consented to my examining the books of the past years (into which it is reasonable to suppose that other errors of equal importance may have crept) *no legal proceedings would have been taken*. And I must add that if he had not deliberately and arbitrarily withheld from me (on a plea so preposterous that the Court would not listen to it) money which you knew to be absolutely my own, I should never have taken the steps which caused you to array yourself publicly against me. It may perhaps interest you to know that as soon as I learnt that you intended to oppose my motion (you will remember that you did not give me the *remotest hint of this intention* when I told you what I proposed to do – you did not break it to me until I was anchored helplessly at Carlsbad) I telegraphed to my solicitor to confine himself to an application for the money due to me: he replied that owing to the form of the action, this was impracticable – that I must apply for a receivership or forego everything.

Finally I must, in common honesty, disclaim all right to shelter myself under the excuse that you have discovered for my course of action. I acted as I did simply because (as you had declined to interfere) I had no alternative except to bow to Carte's refusal to let me examine books which are as much mine as are the scenery, dresses and properties purchased out of the receipts, and to allow him to retain money long since due and constantly accruing which you know that he had no more right to than my watch and chain.

I deeply regret that I should have exposed myself to the magisterial reproof contained in your letter. I wrote in the afterglow of many memories and I am old enough to know that a man should distrust himself when he is under such influences.

Yours sincerely
W. S. Gilbert

At the end of September 1890 Gilbert bought a large house in what was then the country, quitting Breakspears and selling his London home, which had been chiefly notable for the many children's parties given by himself and his wife, when he usually seemed to be the liveliest child present, acting in charades, playing hide-and-seek, conjuring all sorts of marvellous things out of hats and pockets, and organizing everything with as much energy and absorption as he put into his theatrical productions. His new home, the name of which he soon changed from Graeme's Dyke to Grim's Dyke, had been built for Frederick Goodall, R.A., from designs by Norman Shaw. With the house went 110 acres of farmland, and in this green and leafy paradise he spent the remainder of his life, apart from holiday excursions by sea and a few months in London nearly every winter.

While he was busy moving, his solicitors were busy procuring evidence in support of his case against Carte, and they soon discovered, from particulars extracted from Carte's solicitor Stanley, that the oath sworn by Sullivan and Carte to protect their interests and prevent the appointment of a receiver was not valid:

> Graeme's Dyke,
> Harrow Weald.
> 14 Oct. '90.

Dear Sullivan

In my affidavit I swore that I had authorized no legal expenses which had not yet been brought into account, and that I believed there were no such expenses outstanding except, perhaps, for matters of insignificant amount.

You, on the other hand, swore not only that there were such legal expenses but that there were in particular legal expenses still outstanding in connection with an action that I had expressly authorized and that I had been present and had taken part in the various discussions relating thereto. According to Carte's and Stanley's affidavits, the avowed object of these statements (which were described by you on oath as being within your knowledge) was to afford a reason why I should be deprived of all my earnings then due and hereafter to accrue in connection with the Savoy Theatre until all questions between Carte and myself were settled.

It now appears that the action particularly referred to by you as one which I had personally authorized and the expenses of which were still outstanding, was the action commenced against us by Miss Lilian Russell, nearly eight years ago. It further appears, from a letter just received from Mr Stanley's firm, that all expenses in that action were paid and charged against the joint accounts no less than five years ago. It further appears, from the same letter, that the only legal expenses now alleged by Messrs Stanley & Woodhouse to have been still outstanding at the time of making your affidavit was an insignificant sum of £46 for matters which I did not authorize – upon which I was not consulted – and for which I am neither legally nor morally liable.

I am willing to believe that your affidavit (which, in effect, charges me with perjury) was made under an entire misconception, owing, no doubt, to deceptive representations which were made to you by persons interested in procuring your evidence. In view of the great importance naturally attached by the Court to the statements on oath of a man in your distinguished position, I must ask you whether you are prepared to give me in writing a distinct retractation of the clause of your affidavit to which this letter refers, with permission to make such use thereof as may appear to me to be desirable.

Yours truly
W. S. Gilbert

Sullivan cannot be blamed for refusing to go into the matter just then. He was immersed in his grand opera *Ivanhoe*, and his affidavit had been made on statements by Carte, with whom circumstances had compelled him to join. He wished to close the controversy, to have a free mind for his work, and no doubt Carte advised him that an altercation with Gilbert would merely distract him and harm their new venture. Carte's attitude, if not justifiable, was human enough to escape censure. Before all things he was a business-man; he resented Gilbert's attacks on his honesty; he believed that Sullivan's music was more certain to attract audiences than Gilbert's libretti; and a partnership with Sullivan alone meant that each of them would take half of the profits instead of one-third as hitherto. Moreover Sullivan could easily be managed by the oily one, who would be able to charge what he liked for theatrical expenses without risking hostile comment, the musician being too busy composing or gambling to bother about upholstery.

In January 1891 Gilbert published his *Songs of a Savoyard*, dedicating it to Sullivan, who wrote on the 28th of that month:

1 Queen's Mansions
Victoria St:, S.W.

Dear Gilbert

Although I had heard vaguely about the dedication of the *Songs of a Savoyard* it was only last week that I saw a copy of the book, sent to me by Mr Routledge. I should have written then to thank you for such a graceful and flattering compliment but I have not had a moment night or day to put pen to paper except in the case

of direct necessity. I do so now, with the double object of expressing my appreciation of the great compliment you pay me, and also
to say how sincerely I hope you will come to the new Theatre next
Saturday and hear *Ivanhoe*. I should take it much to heart if you
were not present, so pray come.

> Yours sincerely,
> Arthur Sullivan

If Sullivan believed that the dedication to which he referred
carried with it an oblivion of recent discord, he was quickly
disillusioned:

> Graeme's Dyke
> 30 Jan. '91.

Dear Sullivan

On the 4th July last a sum of £4000 was due to me from the
Savoy Theatre – my share of the quarter's profits of that undertaking. Of this sum, one-half was readily paid to me, but when I
applied for the balance (£2000) I was informed by Mr Stanley, the
solicitor of the Savoy Theatre, that it was thought better that this
balance should be withheld so long as there were any legal questions pending between Carte and myself. In order to recover the
money that my work had earned, and to prevent its application
in the future to the necessities of the new theatre, I commenced
legal proceedings against Carte in what, according to the advice I
received, was the only effective form open to me. You enlisted
yourself on his side (having previously assured me that you would,
in any case, remain neutral) and you joined with him in resisting
payment of the sum I claimed – not on the ground that it was not
due to me, but on the ground that certain legal expenses in an
action I had authorized were still outstanding, and that consequently it was impossible to ascertain what the quarter's net
profits would amount to. On the faith of this statement, made on
oath by a man in your commanding position, and endorsed as it
was by evidence to the same effect, sworn by Carte and Stanley
(to whom the costs in the action referred to were payable), my
application for the appointment of a Receiver was, as a matter of
course, refused, and a further term of delay was granted to Carte.
It subsequently appeared (as Mr Carte, by Mr Stanley, freely
admitted) that all the costs in the action referred to – that of
Russell v. Carte, commenced 8 years ago and settled a few months
after its commencement – had been finally paid and discharged
no less than five years since, and *that no fewer than 30 quarterly
divisions of profit had been made since those proceedings were instituted*. In a friendly letter to you I drew your attention to this

admitted fact, and, anxious as I was to believe that you had sworn your affidavit under the influence of mis-information, I gave you an opportunity of withdrawing, on this or some similar plea, the statement to which I have referred. In the course of an evasive reply, you curtly forbad me to make any further reference to those legal proceedings under peril of forfeiting your personal friendship. In reply to your expressed wish that I should be present on the occasion of the first performance of your new opera I have only to say that I shall be happy to accept your invitation if, before tomorrow evening, I receive from you an admission that the statements of which I complain were made under mis-information.

Yours truly,

W. S. Gilbert

Sullivan answered on the 31st:

My dear Gilbert

I thought that byegones were to be byegones, and that no further reference was to be made to any of the matters lately in dispute. But it is evidently not your intention to bury them, without exacting from me an admission which might be construed either as an apology or retractation. Forgive me for saying that I can neither apologize nor retract. I remained neutral (although reproached by you for my supineness) in the dispute between you and Carte, until my own interests were endangered – then I made an affidavit that the appointment of a receiver would be injurious to me. Then you made me a defendant in your suit, and launched forth an affidavit which certainly struck me as being extraordinary and which I was bound to answer. I have never alluded to your affidavits – never questioned the good faith upon which they were made – why should you question mine? You speak of my evasive reply to your letter. I thought my reply was pretty straightforward inasmuch as I gave you details of the matters upon which my affidavit was founded, and refused, as I do now, to admit that I was wrong. Surely, my dear Gilbert, you can afford to let things rest as they are now, and let us forget the past. Let your presence at the theatre tonight be an intimation that you are as ready and willing as I am to think no more of what has happened, and to allow nothing to disturb our old friendship.

Yours sincerely

Arthur Sullivan

P.S. I have been in such a drive today I could not write before. The enclosed stalls are not what I should have liked to send you, but the Royalties have taken two boxes out of six.

This called for three letters in quick succession, the first written at Graeme's Dyke on January 31st, the second from 18 Chesham Place, S.W., on the same date, the third on February 1st from the latter address:

Dear Sullivan

I am sorry that you have not accepted my offer. I have asked neither for an apology nor a retractation. I ask simply for an admission that the statement in your affidavit – that the profits of the quarter could not be ascertained because there were legal expenses still outstanding connected with an action I had authorized – would not have been made if you had known that these costs had been discharged in full five years ago (as in point of fact they were). If you will give me this, I will use the stalls with the utmost pleasure.

Yours truly

Dear Sullivan

I have no faith in Stanley and I want nothing from him. You deliberately swore that the costs in Russell v. Carte were still unsettled and by so swearing you defeated me and put me to an expense of £400 in costs. I have it in Stanley's own hand that all the costs in that action were settled 5 years ago, and so have you. I decline your stalls.

Yours truly

Dear Sullivan

My last letter to you was written in extreme haste and may not have conveyed what I intended to convey. I meant to say that a letter from Stanley, admitting that he had deceived you in the matter of the costs in Russell v. Carte, would expose him to an action for damages and might end in his being struck off the rolls. It is therefore hopeless to expect such a document from him.

I am, as I have said, most anxious to believe that you made the statement as to costs under a misapprehension, and I ask for no more than your simple word to that effect. I only ask you to say that, if you had known what you now know, you would not have sworn as you then swore. If – and the supposition is incredible – you are in doubt whether those costs had been paid you have only to look at your very carefully kept accounts of 5 years ago, and you will find that our third of the costs of Russell v. Carte were then charged against you. Carte will tell you that they had been paid – Stanley will tell you that they had been paid – yet you refuse to admit that, in saying they were still unpaid, you were acting under a misapprehension.

I am sorry to be the only discordant note in the chorus of praise with which your work was received last night. I would gladly have been present to render my tribute to a great work if you had rendered it possible for me to do so. As it is I will meet you when and where you please, if you think that such a meeting would promote a better understanding.

Yours sincerely

There are perhaps few experiences more enervating than arguing from a feeling of innocence against a man who is technically in the right. Sullivan was as weary of the subject as Gilbert appeared to draw refreshment from it:

4 Feb. 1891

Dear Gilbert

Little did I think that in asking you to come and encourage me with your presence on Saturday, I was reopening an unhappy controversy, which I firmly believed was settled and forgotten. We look at things from such different points of view that I fear neither will ever be able to convince the other. You assume I am in possession of facts of which in reality I am absolutely ignorant, and as you decline to receive the verification which I was desirous of obtaining from the person most competent to give it me, I am afraid the matter must rest where it stands.

Yours very truly

It is clear from this letter that Sullivan's affidavit had been sworn, not on his own knowledge, but on the evidence of interested parties, as indeed Gilbert had suspected:

5 Feb. '91

Dear Sullivan

If I did not reply to the letter in which you forbade me to make any further reference to matters connected with the action, it was because I was unwilling to prolong an unpleasant correspondence while you were engaged in the arduous task of producing your new opera – not because I was content to accept, humbly and submissively, the ignominious position in which you sought to place me.

It seems to be necessary to remind you that a man who solemnly swears to a statement, made in what he conceives to be his own interests, is bound to know that it is true. If it were sufficient that he had been told that it is true, anyone to whom Stanley chose to make that statement would be justified in swearing as you have sworn, and evidence would be multiplied indefinitely. In any case a man who has gained a personal advantage by swearing to a false statement under a misapprehension is bound in common justice and in common honesty to rectify his error when it is most clearly and unmistakeably brought before him.

(Gilbert here quoted from a letter by Mrs Carte to prove his point conclusively.)

I am heartily sorry that the attitude you have assumed appears to preclude all possibility of a complete reconciliation.

Yours truly

Gilbert's last shot in the campaign of the carpet was unexpected and deadly:

28 May, 1891

Dear Sullivan

... As a direct result of the action I commenced against Carte a twelvemonth ago, he has admitted an unintentional overcharge of nearly £1000 in the electric lighting accounts alone. He also admits that there are other items charged in the disputed accounts which should not have been charged and he expresses his readiness to put these matters right as soon as *The Gondoliers* is withdrawn. As you will, I suppose, benefit considerably by this re-adjustment of accounts I thought it possible that you might wish to share with me the costs of the action by which it was brought about.

Yours truly

After that, Sullivan ceased firing.

CHAPTER 14

Utopian

०◍◍◍◍◑◐

Carte's grandiose attempt to establish English Grand Opera at what is now called the Palace Theatre in Shaftesbury Avenue was fated to fail. Everything depended upon a sensational start, and his experience at the Savoy had warped his judgment. He thought that Sullivan alone would do the trick. But what was good enough for *Iolanthe* was not good enough for *Ivanhoe*. Walter Scott's novel, though far from his best, provided a magnificent grand-operatic story, but it demanded a Beethoven to do it musical justice, and someone more appreciative of Scott's prose than Julian Sturgis to write a worthy libretto. Moreover Carte had not mastered the art of puffery. He overdid the advance publicity, which implied that the new opera was on a level with the masterpieces of Mozart, Wagner, Gounod, etc., if indeed it did not surpass theirs, and, as 'G.B.S.' said in *The World*, 'it really does not do to spread butter on both sides of the bread'. However, Sullivan thought the opera his most important work; the opening night was a tremendous social occasion; the house was sprinkled with princes and peers; and the enthusiasm was immense. Queen Victoria, who had asked Sullivan to write a grand opera, sent her congratulations on his 'great success', and nearly everyone present on that distinguished occasion felt that a new era for serious music had commenced. But two casts had been engaged to play alternate nights: the expenses were huge, the audiences dwindled, and the opera ran for five months. On being told that Sullivan had expressed disappointment over the failure, Gilbert said: 'He's the sort of man who will sit on a fire and then complain that his bottom is burning.' Disliking what he termed high-class music, Gilbert nevertheless witnessed a performance of *Ivanhoe* early in February and even admitted that he was not bored: 'This is the highest compliment I ever paid a grand opera.' But the general public were listless, and

Carte soon abandoned his Royal English Opera House together with his castles in the air.

Gilbert was more tenacious of his dreams. No longer embarrassed by his late partner's criticisms, he resuscitated his lozenge, liquefied it, and, not unmindful of the success of *Dorothy*, arranged with Alfred Cellier to do the music. Their collaboration was settled immediately after the break with Sullivan, for on May 9th, 1890, Gilbert wrote to Horace Sedger, under whose management the piece would be presented:

> 39 Harrington Gardens
> South Kensington

Dear Mr Sedger

To be businesslike. As you know I have always drawn a very large income from the Savoy – from £10,000 to £14,000 a year. I do not expect to command the same terms at either of your theatres but I think my speciality is worth paying for. The terms I suggest are 15% on the gross receipts – the entire stage-management in the most comprehensive interpretation of the term to be mine. I to control the cast – that is to say I am to be at liberty to object to any proposed artist – though *not* at liberty to dictate who shall – all questions of scenery and dresses to be under my control, and my libretto to be spoken without any gags or other interpolations of any kind without my express sanction. The piece not to be produced until the composer and author declare it to be ready for production.

I hope you will not think these terms unreasonable, but I have always been absolute in the matter of stage-management and I believe that a large portion of such success as the libretti have achieved is due to my superintending the interpretation of my own ideas.

> Yours very truly

Cellier was in poor health and hinted that Gilbert should accompany him to a warmer climate the following winter, as he would like to work with, not apart from, his librettist. But Gilbert had no desire to work with his composer, and when the cold weather came Cellier went off to Sicily, Naples, Egypt and Australia. Naturally his movements caused misunderstandings. Gilbert's letter proposing alterations in the plot was forwarded from Plymouth to Naples and answered from Port Said. Cellier did not want any changes in the plot, as those which Gilbert suggested would clash with an opera he had already written. But owing to the delay Gilbert had practically finished the job before he heard from Cellier and wrote to say that he was altogether unwilling to undo what he had done: 'There seems therefore nothing for it but to put a definite end to a collaboration upon which perhaps (having regard to our respective temperaments) we never should have embarked.' A letter from Cellier's wife mollified him. Alfred had been ill, she reported, and had no intention of treating Gilbert with the slightest discourtesy – 'in fact he has always thought it an honour to collaborate with so distinguished and successful a librettist as you are' – and he would set to work at once on the opera as completed by Gilbert.

It must be remembered that there was a pronounced lack of honesty and scrupulosity in the theatrical world of Gilbert's time, and that his quarrels, though intensified by his choleric nature, were mainly due to the general laxity in business and manners. An ancient army phrase, 'Everyone is out of step except you', might be used against him; but just as one man in a company sometimes keeps step with the drill-sergeant's command 'left-right' while the rest are stepping 'right-left', so it was with Gilbert, who angrily declined to be cheated by managers or discourteously treated by collaborators. It was largely due to his bristly nature that theatrical people as a whole were gradually influenced to adopt a different code in matters of finance and consideration for others. Horace Sedger and Alfred Cellier were both taught to mind their p's and q's under his instruction. Sedger wanted to advertise their new piece as the class of thing then becoming popular. 'I must protect both Cellier and myself from the calamitous effects of popular cheap gush', Gilbert told him. Sedger also wanted Gilbert to reduce his demand for royalties. 'When I name terms, I never depart from them', said the librettist. After the contract had been signed Sedger complained that he had been 'unfairly cornered in the matter'. He was fairly cornered in saying so:

Dear Sedger

Your letter won't do. You have charged me, practically, with having swindled you, and I will have a distinct retractation and unqualified apology before I consent to deal with you except through the medium of solicitors. It is as well you should learn that charges of this class are not to be made against gentlemen with impunity.

Cellier's misbehaviour was partly due to bad health; in fact he died while the opera was being produced; but he did not appreciate Gilbert's systematic procedure, and when he wrote to say that he had postponed a rehearsal because the songs were not ready for the principals but would let Gilbert know the time of the next music 'call', he was made aware of his shortcomings:

25 Sep. '91

Dear Cellier

When we embarked on these rehearsals I entertained a sincere hope that we should get through them on an amiable footing. This it appears is not to be the case. Certainly I will not submit to be trifled with as I have been during the last week. You told me distinctly, before I read the piece to the company four weeks ago, that the music was 'practically finished'. The piece has been in rehearsal for 3 weeks and only four choruses – *and nothing else* – has been supplied. Moreover you were obliged to postpone last Friday's rehearsal because no more music was ready – a week has elapsed without rehearsal – and you are obliged to postpone today's rehearsal for the same reason.

You say that you will let me know the next music call. I need not dwell upon the fact that I am accustomed to be consulted as to all calls at which my attendance is advisable, because I think it will be better, in order to avoid further friction, that I should abstain altogether from your music rehearsals. Conduct them as you please, without reference to me, *and when every note of music of both acts has been learnt by the company* I will try to pick up the measures from Caryll. When I have got them into my head, I will commence my stage rehearsals which will occupy at least 5 weeks.

We now understand one another and you can take your own course.

Yours truly

P.S. I am sending a copy of this letter to Sedger.

His unsatisfactory dealings with another collaborator turned Gilbert's thoughts again towards a reconciliation with Sullivan, and when the music publisher Chappell expressed a hope that it might be effected he seemed favourably inclined. These letters tell the story:

4 Oct. '91

My dear Gilbert

Tom Chappell tells me that you propose that you and I should submit the matters which have been the cause of our rupture to a third party, and, according to his decision, that one or the other of us should confess himself to have been in the wrong, and thereupon we could resume our former friendly relations.

The matters originally in dispute being really all settled and forgotten, I feel that it would be a great mistake to reopen them now; for a reference to a third party would only produce interminable arguments and counterarguments without either side being convinced. I have no desire to rake up old grievances or to enter into fresh discussions as to who was right and who wrong. So far as I am concerned the past is no more thought of, and I am quite ready to let byegones be byegones, and to meet you at all times in the most friendly spirit; provided that the disagreeable events of the past eighteen months are never alluded to, or at least never discussed. I say this in good faith and I hope you will meet me in the same spirit.

Yours sincerely
Arthur Sullivan

Grim's Dyke
5 Oct. '91

Dear Sullivan

My proposition had its origin in a question put to me by Chappell as to whether there was any prospect or possibility of our working together again. I replied to the effect that, as matters stood – each of us honestly conceiving that he had been unjustly treated by the other – it appeared to me that such a cordial understanding as should exist between men working together as we had worked for so many years, could not possibly exist. He seemed disappointed at my reply and, at a subsequent interview two or three days later, I suggested that such an understanding might perhaps be arrived at if what I have always held to be the main question between us (that is to say, your affidavit of 3rd Sept.) were referred privately and in a friendly spirit to some intimate friend of both. Nothing is further from my wish than to enter into any discussion which might involve recriminations and perhaps intensify any feeling of unfair treatment which may exist in the minds of either or both, but I know you will agree with me that successful and cordial co-operation will be very difficult, if not impossible, if, when we meet, either of us has a living grievance up his sleeve. It is perhaps unnecessary to assure you that all feeling of bitterness has long since passed from my mind – but there remains a dull leaden feeling that I have been treated with inexplicable unfairness by an old and valued friend with whom I had been *en rapport* for many years and with whose distinguished name

I had had the good fortune to find my own indissolubly associated on a series of works which are known and valued wherever the English tongue is spoken. This is the present state of my mind as regards our relations towards one another, and if you can suggest any reasonable means whereby this cloud can be removed, it will give me infinite pleasure to adopt it.

Yours very truly
W. S. Gilbert

1 Queen's Mansions
Victoria Street
6 Oct. '91

Dear Gilbert

Let us meet and shake hands, and if you still wish to discuss the question of the affidavits (which was also the point upon which I felt most aggrieved) we can do so later. We can dispel the cloud hanging over us by setting up a counter-irritant in the form of a cloud of smoke. I am just off to the Waggs at Brighton to stay till Friday. Write me a line there

2 Adelaide Crescent

to say when you are likely to be in town.

Yours sincerely

7 Oct. '91

Dear Sullivan

I shall be very pleased to call on you – next Monday at 12 if that will suit you. I hope we may come to such an understanding upon the points of difference between us as will render it unnecessary to do as much as allude to them again.

Yours very truly

But on the day before they met Gilbert wrote to repeat the one grievance he had against Sullivan, giving chapter and verse concerning the affidavits, and saying that their renewed co-operation

could scarcely be carried on successfully unless we undertook it with our minds purged of all existing sense of grievance . . . If on the face of the facts I have here set forth you see your way to saying anything that can place us upon a thoroughly cordial footing, I am sure you will say it – if not, we must do as well as we can without it . . . If there is anything in my conduct from first to last as to which you think yourself entitled to an explanation, I shall be only too pleased to give it.

They met on October 12th and according to Sullivan were

reconciled and shook hands. Though each of them may have explained his attitude, neither was convinced that the other was right, as will duly appear; but they agreed to write another opera together.

Jockey Club Rooms
Newmarket
Wed. 14 Oct. '91

Dear Gilbert

I will try to settle for Tuesday when I get back to London, and will let you know. As regards the new piece which we hope to write together, I hope our understanding was clear: viz. that in view of two new pieces of yours coming out shortly, and of my being, not pledged, but in the middle of negotiations for a book, the time for writing and producing our new joint work was to be a matter for consideration and discussion. I say this because I am sincerely anxious (as I am sure you are) that nothing should ever arise which would lead to another misunderstanding between us.

Yours sincerely

15 Oct. '91

Dear Sullivan

Your letter arrived just as I was sitting down to begin upon a plot. It seems to me that if you find that the libretto for which you are in treaty is satisfactory, you will not be in a position to begin upon any work with me for a long time to come. As a matter of course you will want a rest after composing an opera and then will come the Leeds week (as I understood you to say) – so that I may take it that at least 12 and probably 18 months must elapse before you are ready to begin upon a piece with me. Now I need not say that I can't afford to remain idle during this long period – I *must* write and produce at least one libretto during this time. That I would infinitely rather do this in collaboration with you, goes without saying – *but write I must*. I am ready to begin *now* upon a plot – for you, I hope – but at all events for someone.

Perhaps when we meet you will be able to give me some idea when you will decide as to the libretto for which you are in treaty.

Yours truly

2nd Nov. '91

Dear Gilbert

I am today in a position to give you a definite answer as to my plans for the immediate future, as I have just settled the matter. As I told you, my negotiations had gone so far that provided the book offered me were satisfactory, I was bound to accept it. I have this morning accordingly agreed to set to work at once upon it. I look upon our renewed joint collaboration as merely postponed for a little time, and hope that we shall soon have another success together.

Yours sincerely

One of Gilbert's many attempts to see people as they are not, due to his dissatisfaction with people as they are, was made in *The Mountebanks*, first performed at the Lyric Theatre on January 4th, 1892. The dissolution of the lozenge into liquid did not help the plot, the grotesqueness of which is emphasized by his usual trick of mixing up the just possible with the highly improbable. But the piece was so well acted and produced that it ran for eight months, some four weeks longer than Sullivan's *Haddon Hall*, with words by Sydney Grundy, staged by Carte at the Savoy in September of that year. In spite of his autocratic conduct, Gilbert was much more popular with the companies they controlled than Sullivan. The performers, especially those who played small parts and the members of the chorus, trusted him implicitly, knew he would guard their interests, appreciated his generosity, found him genial away from work, tirelessly patient during work, ready to champion them in any dispute, and always polite in manners. When Horace Sedger, anxious to economize, arbitrarily dismissed about eighteen members of the chorus who were engaged for the run of the piece, Gilbert supported their appeal to the law and even got Carte to offer evidence that they were being victimized. Hardly another author, then or later, would have openly acted against the interests of the manager presenting his work, and therefore his own interests. But in this connection words speak louder than actions, and a few days after the production of the opera Gilbert received a letter from the female chorus superscribed 'From your Mountebank girls':

Dear Mr Gilbert

We feel we must express our deep gratitude to you for your great generosity and kindness in sending us all a week's salary last Saturday the 2nd.

We shall remember with pleasure the kindness and consideration you bestowed on us during the rehearsals, and could wish no better than always to be in your productions, to be ever under your kind surveillance.

Wishing you a long and most successful run with *The Mountebanks* and hoping you will have a most enjoyable holiday after all your hard work and anxiety.

(Signatures of the chorus ladies.)

He cannot have had much of a holiday because no sooner was one thing off his mind than another occupied it. Desirous to do George Grossmith a good turn, he changed a French farce, *Le Chapeau de Paille d'Italie*, into an operetta, called it *Haste to the Wedding*, and produced it, with music by Grossmith's son, at the Criterion Theatre on July 28th, 1892. It is an amusing trifle, which makes the reader wish that Gilbert had tapped more French farces for his plots. No longer having to supply Sullivan with sentimental songs, he abandoned himself to the mood of 'Bab', and there is an engaging air of imbecility about the whole piece.

Recovering from what he doubtless felt to be a lapse, he put his full power as a satirist into his next opera, which also benefited, as in the past, from a recent quarrel with Sullivan. *Utopia Limited* is the cleverest of his libretti, but it was nearly killed in the period of gestation. Ever since their time the general assumption has been that the renewed collaboration of the famous pair was carried through in a 'cordial and friendly' manner, but a study of Gilbert's papers reveals the measure of their cordiality and friendliness. Just after they had agreed to write another piece together Gilbert had decided that 'in order to avoid all chances of future calamity' he would rather take a percentage of the receipts for his portion of the work than share the profits, because on a profit-sharing arrangement he would require control, with his partners, over the expenditure. Sullivan had then made an agreement with Carte for the production of two pieces on a co-partnership basis, profits being equally shared between the two of them. The first piece was *Haddon Hall*, and in August 1892 he wrote to Gilbert suggesting that theirs should be the second piece. But Gilbert was under the impression that Sullivan had agreed to the same arrangement as himself, and in discussing the question with Carte he now suggested that, if they reverted to the old partnership, the rent of the theatre should be reckoned as £4500 per annum instead of £4000 as heretofore. This, he wrote to Sullivan,

would remove the only rock upon which we split during the 15 years of our association and there is good reason to suppose that, if that is done away with, no further difficulties of importance would be likely to arise.

In reply Sullivan reminded Gilbert of the percentage arrangement which the latter had himself suggested almost a year before, stated that a return to the old tripartite agreement would mean the annulment of his own contract with Carte, and begged that the matter might be held over for a few weeks, when he would be free to discuss it. Gilbert answered that he had understood both of them would be paid a percentage on receipts, and he was perfectly agreeable to this or any other method 'so that we are on the same footing'. But something in the tone of Sullivan's letter made him add:

> I am sure you have no such idea in your mind but I seem somehow to be in the equivocal position of urging you to embark upon an undertaking which you contemplate with something like apathy. I need hardly suggest that this is a position which neither you nor I would desire that the other should assume.

Two months went by and Sullivan remained silent. On October 20th, 1892 Gilbert wrote to complain of the wasted time, 'for it is impossible for me to concentrate myself upon a plot unless I know who is going to set it to music'. Sullivan informed him from Brighton that he would be back on the 29th for a day or two: 'Will you let me know if and when you are coming up to town and want a chat?' Gilbert thought this pretty cool: 'If I want a chat with you! Certainly, if *you* want one with *me*. That is to say if we both want one with each other.' He suggested a day and time, and from the Jockey Club Rooms at Newmarket a note came from Sullivan fixing their meeting but saying that he would not be able to start work till February. One of the curious things about these two is that their personal meetings were always so fraternal that they misunderstood one another. The obvious explanation is that neither felt at home in the other's company, and their mutual nervousness, added to an overcharged desire to be agreeable, produced an effusiveness which fogged the issue between them. In doing his utmost to make everything easy for his collaborator, each of them yielded more ground than he intended. This soon became apparent in the correspondence that followed their meeting:

Livermere Park
Bury St. Edmunds.
3 Nov. 1892

My dear G

I was in hopes that our conversation on Monday last had settled everything comfortably for the future, but your letter to Carte, a copy of which he sends me this morning, has I fear put fresh difficulties in the way. The enclosed memorandum in the form of a letter to you I wrote on Monday night – or rather early Tuesday morning, and it was not posted through an accident. I send it now so that you may see that our ideas of the understanding we arrived at differ materially. I had not, nor have I now, any intention of reverting to the old state of affairs, viz: of having a triple authority and triple control in the theatre. What has happened may happen again and I am too old now to be worried with ructions and disputes. The best thing to do is to avoid all chance of such things by taking the proper steps beforehand. The organization of the Savoy Theatre is changed since you were there, and the personnel is different; so as Carte and I are responsible for this, so Carte and I must have the entire control. The agreement between him and me cannot subsist and at the same time the *status ante quo* exist also. I am ready and willing to modify my arrangement with Carte so far as regards its financial conditions so as to let you in on equal financial terms. But for expenditure, accounts &c you must trust to my judgment, accuracy and honour. You misunderstood one remark of mine. I said it was understood that Carte would not spend any *large* sums upon furniture, decorations &c without consulting me, and I added that for any abnormal expenditure I should probably consult you, but I did not say I would not sanction it without your consent.

Take my advice and let matters be as I proposed. It will save all further trouble and remove a grave cause of possible dissension. I have done all I could to meet your views, with the desire of writing again with you, and I am sure you will never feel that your position in the theatre is different from what is was, or that your wishes will not be carried out as speedily and readily as formerly. I shall be back in town on Monday, ready to meet you whenever you like.

Yours sincerely
Arthur Sullivan

Grim's Dyke
4 Nov. '92

Dear Sullivan

Having regard to the tone and purport of your last letter I must assume that it was written with the definite object of putting an end to the possibility of a collaboration.

Yours sincerely,
W. S. Gilbert

1 Queen's Mansions
Victoria Street.
8 Nov. '92

My dear Gilbert

I am unfortunate in my letters to you, and it distresses me greatly that you should have misconstrued the 'tone and purport' of my last one. I am very sorry that you cannot see your way to agreeing to the arrangement which I thought would meet all difficulties and set us sailing again in smooth water; but you are the best judge of the course you should take, and it is of little use discussing by correspondence a matter upon which we seem so hopelessly at variance; and I don't want to quarrel with a man for whom I entertain a sincere regard.

Yours sincerely,
Arthur Sullivan

Grim's Dyke
9 Nov. '92

Dear Sullivan

When we met on Monday you proposed to me the following terms – that your agreement with Carte should subsist but that my interests should be in no respect prejudiced thereby, and that the profits of the piece should be divided by three and that we should each take a third part. To these I agreed. When the question of redecoration was raised you told me that by your agreement with Carte he could not spend more than a certain moderate sum on such matters without your express consent, and you added 'which of course I should not think of giving without consulting you'. No such word as 'probably' was used. 'Probably' means nothing and I certainly should never have accepted it as a satisfactory expression. A few general words then passed between us as to my stagemanaging the piece and as to my voice in the cast, and, as far as stipulations were concerned, the conversation ended, and I left you with the firm conviction that two men never arrived at a more distinct understanding. On my return home I sent a résumé of our conversation to Carte – setting it out in greater detail as that letter and its reply were to constitute the agreement. To that letter I received replies from you and from him entirely repudiating my view of the understanding, repudiating my statement as to the redecoration question, claiming for yourselves entire control of all matters of expenditure and stipulating that I should trust implicitly in all matters of account to your judgment, accuracy and honour.

Now any lawyer – even Carte's – will tell you that a man who is entitled to a share in profits is entitled to examine the steps by which such profits are calculated. I did not stipulate expressly for this as it is an inevitable incident of all sharing terms. I should as soon have thought of stipulating that there should be a balance in the bank to meet the cheque. But *you* did not stipulate, at our meeting, that this essential condition of sharing terms, this condition which is part and parcel, as a matter of course, of all agreements by which profits are shared, should be for once dispensed with. You omitted to disclose to me, at our meeting, that I was to be a financial leper – debarred from all right to examine into the propriety of your expenditure and the accuracy of your calculations, and waiting patiently at the stage-door for such a sum or dole as you and Carte may fling to me as my share of profits. But this is the position which on reconsideration you offer me after two months delay insisted upon by you as a preliminary to annulling your agreement with Carte and considering the question of my readmittance on my old footing!

Your rather baldly expressed reason for this is your objection to be disturbed by 'ructions and disputes'. This of course alludes to the dissensions that arose between us two years and a half ago. It was agreed that these dissensions were to be altogether discharged from our minds. But as you have inferentially alluded to them, let me remind you, in a few words, how these dissensions arose. I discovered, in April 1890, that Carte had considered himself justified, under our agreement, in applying £1400 of the first quarter's profits of *The Gondoliers* to redecorating and refurnishing the auditorium, and this without in any way consulting you or me as to the necessity or propriety of such an expenditure. It may be that the agreement justified this – he held that it did. I held, and still hold, that it did not. In the upshot I appealed to you. You replied that a new agreement must be drawn up in which such an act on Carte's part should be impossible and you even asked me to draft the heads of such an agreement. You then went to Newmarket for a week and on your return I proposed to submit that draft to you. You replied, rather angrily as I thought, that you were too busily engaged with your opera *Ivanhoe* to attend to any Savoy matters. Thereupon, indignant at this cavalier treatment at the hands of an old and highly valued collaborator, I dissolved our association. But although you declined to interfere in this matter, *it is a significant fact that you have not disdained to profit by my action to the extent of stipulating with Carte, in your new*

*agreement, that he shall spend no sum above a very moderate one on
redecorating and refurnishing without your express approval and
consent.* Nevertheless I, who discovered this all-important flaw in
our agreement with Carte, am as a consequence to have no voice
as to how the profits that my libretto may help to earn are calculated – no voice as to how much of those profits are to be taken
by Carte for his furniture and decorations.

(At this point Gilbert wrote a passage which he omitted from
the letter Sullivan received:

For this I am to confide blindly in your joint 'accuracy, discretion and honour'. Now however unimpeachable your honour
may be, I cannot forget that your accuracy and discretion plunged
you into the deplorable mistake of impounding £2000 of my
money – together with all accruing profits – upon a plea so inade-
quate that the Court of Chancery swept it away with a stroke of
the pen and ordered the moneys to be paid to me – half at once
and half in a month's time.[1] I have acted throughout, as you very
well know and as Carte very well knows, with absolute justice and
unimpeachable straightforwardness – my word as a man of honour
has never been assailed, and I find it difficult to express to you how
utterly painful it was to me to find that my old colleague and old
friend had arbitrarily insisted on my losing two months of my
time in order that, at the end of the two months, he might make
me the same proposition which I have all along declared that I
would not accept.)

As you know I have claimed throughout to be placed on the
same financial basis as yourself – this you have, in principle, freely
conceded – in fact your letter of 1st Nov. which you forgot to post
would, if it stood by itself, give me all I ask. But you have supple-
mented that letter with another in which, in terms that made my
blood boil to read, you imply that I am unfit to be trusted in
financial matters and insist that in all these affairs I am to confide
implicitly in your accuracy, honour and discretion. I assure you I
am not, as you would imply, in the habit of breaking my agree-

[1] Flatly contradicting Gilbert's affidavit, Sullivan had sworn : 'It is within
my knowledge that there are outstanding liabilities which have not yet been
brought into account . . . and I am aware in particular that certain liabilities
in respect of legal matters in connection with the performances at the Savoy
Theatre have been incurred and that such liabilities have not been brought
into account as I am informed because the Bill of Costs for such business
have not yet been rendered.' This statement was untrue, and Gilbert made
a note on it: 'See letter from Arthur Sullivan, Saturday (the day of the production of *Ivanhoe*), in which he admits that his information as to liabilities
not having been brought into account came principally from Stanley.'

ments or of distorting their obvious terms to meet my personal interests. I found fault with Carte for a certain act, and although you held aloof at the time you have fortified yourself against the possibility of its recurrence. I found fault with the expenditure on properties and carpentry, and Carte informs me that he now finds that in these matters an enormous overcharge was made. I found fault with the terms of a certain letter that I received from him, and you agreed with me that they were 'indefensible'. [1] And after all this endorsement, direct and indirect, of my grievances I am told that because I endeavoured to redress them by the only means that your *supineness* and *indifference* left open to me I am unfit for the financial society of men with whom I have been intimately and most successfully associated for fifteen years. For the piece I care little, but I cannot tell you how difficult I find it to sit patiently under the load of this intolerable insinuation, coming as it does from a man with whom I have been so long and so honourably connected.

Yours truly

1 Queen's Mansions
11 Nov. '92

My dear Gilbert

Your recollection of many past incidents differs so entirely from mine that a discussion upon them is useless, and I will therefore confine myself to stating what my feeling is about the present condition of affairs.

Two years and a half ago you threw me (and the Savoy Theatre) over, and voluntarily put an end to our collaboration. I went on for a long time without taking any steps to work with another author, whilst you at once sought out and obtained the services of another composer. Whilst I was very hard at work later, you made overtures for a return of our collaboration, and I agreed when my hard work was over to discuss the matter with you.

We met, and I suggested that instead of taking, under my agreement with Carte, half the profits of the Savoy Theatre, I would take one-third, so as to have the pleasure and advantage of working again with you. But I urged (and you agreed) that in other respects my agreement with Carte, which gives me amongst other things the right to examine the accounts and in some measure control the expenditure, was to stand; and now you are indignant because you cannot have the same right – a right which when you possessed it led to disputes and litigation and might do so again. You cannot for a moment imagine that I will ever again

---

[1] This is almost certainly the letter which Gilbert showed to Jack Robertson, who played the leading tenor part in *The Mountebanks*.

put myself into a position of being liable to suffer so much worry and anxiety as I did in the year following the production of *The Gondoliers*. I would rather give up writing for the stage altogether. At present we are in the midst of a great success at the theatre and dividing the profits by two. I offer (and Carte agrees) to divide them in the next piece (if you write it) by three – the management and control to continue as they are now. But you choose to indignantly refuse the offer, and to speak of yourself as a 'financial leper', evidently mistrusting my 'judgment, accuracy and honour'.

Yours sincerely
Arthur Sullivan

12 Nov. '92

Dear Sullivan

I was in hopes that our correspondence had come to an end, but there is one sentence in your last letter which I cannot pass in silence. You say that I made overtures for a return to our collaboration. Nothing can be further from the fact. At the urgent and repeated request of Chappell I agreed to meet you, on the distinct and definite assurance that you were willing to meet me. For ought I know or care the suggestion may have originated with you – it most certainly did not originate with me. If you have any doubt on this subject Chappell can solve it.

The rest of your letter carries its own reply with it.

Yours truly

But apparently it did not carry its own reply with it because Gilbert wrote again on the same day. The ostensible reason for his second letter was to obtain Sullivan's view on their South African royalties, but having dealt with that he continued:

Referring for one moment to the other matter, you will I suppose do me the justice to believe that mere gain of money is far from being the leading motive in my mind. But for the terrible insinuations against my honour and good faith which I conceive to be implied by the letters I have received from you since Monday week, I would have written with you on a percentage or without payment (as I did in *The Martyr of Antioch*) rather than not have written at all. Indeed I had already written to Chappell to that effect. You tell me that I practically doubt your honour in declining sharing terms that shut me out from all other financial interest. I do nothing of the kind. Do you suppose me to be so sordid and so unjust as to imagine that if you undertake that my share shall be the same as your own, I cannot feel sure that you will keep your word to the uttermost farthing? You know well that that is not my nature. Why, for 14 years of our association no financial diffi-culty even of the most insignificant kind ever arose between the three. And after this, to tell me that I am unfit to be financially associated because if I were endless difficulties and actions at law would arise, is indeed ungenerous. I think the least you can do is to withdraw the horrible imputation upon my honour and good faith contained in your two last letters.

14 Nov. '92

My dear Gilbert . . .

The charge you make against me of 'terrible insinuations against your honour and good faith' which you conceive to be implied by my letters, absolutely bewilders and shocks me. Without any dis-cussion or explanation I at once say God forbid that any such idea should be in my mind for a second, and I hope you will accept this as frankly as I mean it. Now – I am ill and nervous and I am going away at once – Wednesday morning – and I propose that we stop correspondence on this subject for a little while, for it really makes me ill going on in this somewhat acrimonious style with an old and valued friend. No good can come of it at present, and a little later we may both approach the subject in a less excited state of mind. In any case, as concerns work, I am no good for the next two or three months, and you in the meanwhile would be free to carry out any other work which may have suggested itself to you. When I have settled upon a halting place, I will let you know where it is.

Yours sincerely,
Arthur Sullivan

15 Nov. '92

Dear S

Your frank disclaimer of any intention to reflect upon my honour and good faith takes an immense load from my mind. I had got it, immoveably, into my head that your stipulations arose from doubts on these points, and by dwelling on the subject day and night I have magnified it to the proportions of a nightmare. Indeed it was impossible to consider any modus vivendi while this bogie remained unlaid.

If, when we met a fortnight since, you had proposed that I should take a percentage on gross receipts, as the simplest way of meeting a difficulty, I should have agreed to that, as I did to the proposition I conceived you to have actually made. Indeed Tom Chappell had previously strongly urged me to do so, and I feel sure that his advice was disinterested – for I have great faith in his integrity and he and I have always been on the best of terms. Suppose we let it rest thus – Let us revert to your proposition of last August. Let me meet Carte to arrange the terms (percentage on gross) you empowering him, as you did before, to act for you. Then I can set to work on the construction of the piece and have the first act ready for you by February or March or whenever you feel able to tackle it.

I hope your journey will set you up again.

Yours very truly

29 Nov. '92

My dear S

I saw Carte and Mrs Carte yesterday in accordance with your letter. Before going to them I made a rough calculation of the percentage that would correspond as nearly as possible with 'a third of the profits' (judging from past experience) and I made it to be eleven per cent. Turning to a letter of Mrs Carte's, dated December last (re *Iolanthe*) I find that she also discovered 11 per cent to be the average proportion. So I proposed 11% to them, leaving with them my figures for verification. They seemed to think it reasonable and are going to write to me after having communicated with you.

At the end of 1892 Sullivan went to the Riviera, where he remained until the following spring, having rented a villa called *Diodato* at Cabbé-Roquebrune. In December he sent £5 towards a fund sponsored by Gilbert for an old musician, and described his doings:

I take good walks every day (and of these there are abundance and variety) and rarely going into Monte Carlo which is very dull just now. I feel better than I have felt for months – sleep well at night – and am rapidly losing that horrible nervous depression I suffered from. I am sending you some sweets for Christmastime. Don't make yourself ill.

Some days later he wrote about the casting of the piece and added 'I hope Mrs Gilbert will get her Christmas Box (of sweets) and that you will not eat them all yourself.' On Christmas Day Gilbert reported that all was going well, that a few minor points could be cleared up when Sullivan returned and that he proposed to visit Monte Carlo in a fortnight to let his collaborator hear what he had written and make any suggestions or objections. On January 7th, 1893 he promised not to press for a special clause in the agreement so long as it was understood between them that 'if any permanent change in cast should be necessary after production, my opinion shall be consulted, and all reasonable weight given to any bona fide objection I may raise – I, on my part, promising to raise no objection on merely captious or vexatious grounds'. Sullivan wired that he was content. On January 15th Gilbert wrote that Carte 'who is perfectly maddening has been fighting every inch of the way with a dogged persistency that suggests rather that he is anxious to find a reason for breaking off negotiations than an anxiety to bring them to a successful issue', but the only words in this passage that reached Sullivan were that Carte had been 'fighting every inch of the way with a dogged persistency'. Gilbert asked for a clause in their contract 'that Carte will take all reasonable steps to prevent "gags" or interpolations in my text', but eventually they all thought that such points should be accepted without their appearance in the Agreement.

On January 19th Sullivan sent three propositions for the future disposal of their joint works, appending an invitation:

Now I think there is nothing in this letter to prevent your packing your portmanteau and starting at once. I urge this because I can take you in from now till 3rd February. On that day some other friends are coming for three weeks who will take all my spare bedrooms, so that I couldn't give you a room. Leave as soon as you can – don't take the *Club train*. Take the 11 a.m. to Paris (or the 10 a.m. from Charing Cross) and come on by the Rapide (which leaves the Gare du Nord) arriving at Roquebrune, where *all* trains stop, the next afternoon. They won't give you a ticket for Roquebrune, so take one for Mentone, and be sure to have your luggage examined at Calais or Paris – otherwise there is always a bother and delay here. Bring warm things, for though the sun shines it is pretty cold. Bring also (concealed in greatcoat pockets &c) your own cigars, as it is impossible to get a decent one here. Send me a wire 'I arrive such a day'. Yours ever A. S.

Gilbert started almost at once, and while at Roquebrune wrote to his wife:

Dearest Kits

I sent off a letter in a hurry this morning, so as not to lose a post – I now send you further details.

The reading went off *most successfully* – both Sullivan and Grove enthusiastic – declaring it's the best plot I've done. We have arranged all business matters on a satisfactory footing. This is a pleasant house standing in an orange garden close to the sea –

everything very nice and comfortable and informal. A.S. extremely pleasant and hospitable and much disappointed that I leave so soon as Sunday. We went to the Casino yesterday – I won fifty francs – we played billiards afterwards, and in the evening cribbage – for franc holes. We played three rubbers and I lost one franc. So at present I have not suffered much. I've just been into Monte Carlo to secure a sleeping berth for tomorrow's (Sunday's) train – which I have succeeded in doing. Virtuously disposed, I walked back – about 3 miles. The weather is lovely – like warm June weather in England. Wild strawberries ripe and oranges to be had for the picking. The Sutherlands are at Monte Carlo but I haven't seen them. Stock has just sent his rent, and I have a cheque from French for £22 odd. I had a wire from the Mertons yesterday telling me they were to leave London on Sunday. I shall join them at the Hotel des Deux Mondes on Monday morning. I don't think I shall stay over Thursday. Probably be home Thursday evening. I'll wire to Gurrany to have a fly ready, so don't trouble to send.

> Good-bye old Lady – no end of love from
> your affectionate Old Boy

Meanwhile Gilbert, who shared with Sullivan the feeling that small sums like £50 were beneath the consideration of men of honour but that large sums like £5000 were worth the consideration of men of business, had examined the question of receipts and had come to the conclusion that his estimate of eleven per cent on the gross takings would place him at a serious disadvantage. On reaching home he wrote to Sullivan:

> I had intended to mention the matter to you at Monte Carlo – for you and I always get on so much better in conversation than in correspondence.[1] But on reconsideration I thought it not altogether in good taste to broach such a subject while I was your guest.

He gave figures to show that the first quarter's profits would bring £3042 each for Carte and Sullivan but that his percentage would only bring him £2602; while the second quarter's profits would come to £4032 for each of them and only £2402 for him. However, he admitted the mistake had been his, and

> I am so far in your joint hands that I will agree without demur to any proposal you may make for amending my position, and I hope I need not reiterate that, whether you hold me to my ill-

[1] Yes.

considered bargain or not, I shall join cheerfully and loyally with you both in all the hard work before us.

His figures were based on the assumption that their new piece would repeat the success of their last; but as it did not, his arithmetical calculations were wasted.

While Sullivan was attacking the opera that summer, Gilbert was attacked by the gout and went swearing to Homburg.

> I am worse rather than better [he wrote]. My right foot (which I call Labouchere) is very troublesome, and I take a vicious pleasure (not unalloyed with pain) in cramming him into a boot which is much too small for him. My left foot (known in Homburg as Clement Scott) is a milder nuisance, but still tiresome, and would hurt me a good deal if he could.

In sending a new song for the piece, he said: ' "Court Reputations he'll revise". This flashed on me in a moment. Herein is the difference between a lyrical genius and a mere literary mechanic'; which shows that in flashes he had a right appreciation of his poetic gift. His passion for caricaturing elderly women, a form of literary matricide, had been steadily getting on Sullivan's nerves for some years, and the repetition of a faded coquette in the latest libretto was rather more than he could stomach. He said so:

> Dorney House
> Weybridge
> 1 July '93

Dear G

Had we been alone yesterday when you asked me about the part of Lady Sophy, I should have said what I am now going to write. The question at issue is between you and me and I did not want others to be mixed up in the discussion.

Hitherto I have written and spoken about musical difficulties only and there can be no question of the truth and force of my objections. But there is another matter and this I will, as privately between you and me, put forward with complete frankness, knowing that you prefer there should be entire openness between us.

The part of Lady Sophy, as it is to be treated in the 2nd Act, is in my opinion a blot on an otherwise brilliant picture, and to me personally, unsympathetic and distasteful. If there is to be an old or middleaged woman at all in the piece, is it necessary that she should be very old, ugly, raddled, and perhaps grotesque, and still more is it necessary that she should be seething with love and passion (requited or unrequited) and other feelings not usually associated with old age. I thought that 'Katisha' was to be the last example of that type – (a type which however cleverly drawn can never be popular with the public, as experience has taught me) – because the same point was raised then, and you even modified a good many of the lines at my request. A dignified, stately, well made-up and well-dressed elderly lady is a charming feature in a piece, and can be of real service to the composer, because the music he writes for her is so well contrasted with the youthful bustle of the other elements. On the other hand, the elderly spinster, unattractive and grotesque, either bemoaning her faded charms, or calling attention to what is still left of them, and unable to conceal her passionate longing for love, is a character which appeals to me vainly, and I cannot do anything with it. Let me here *most emphatically* disclaim any idea of calling your judgment to account – that is not my intention – artistically and from your own point of view you may be right.

I am only giving you my own personal feeling in the matter – telling you what I like and what I don't like. I like every word you have given me hitherto of the new piece, and I don't like the prospect of Lady Sophy in the 2nd Act. Furthermore, I am sure you won't take offence at my plain and outspoken opinion, for I court an equally frank opinion from you on anything in my share of the work which you don't like or which doesn't fit in with your intentions.

Yours ever sincerely
A. S.

Grim's Dyke
3 July '93

Dear S

As you know, I am always most anxious to meet your views in every respect and I believe I have never laid myself open to the charge of raising captious objections and making unnecessary difficulties. But the fault you now find with Act 2 brings me absolutely to a standstill. When I read the very elaborate sketch plot to you at Roquebrune last January – or early in February – you expressed full and unqualified approbation of every incident in the piece. Not to take advantage of a hasty or ill-considered expression of approval on your part, I left with you a verbatim copy of my sketch plot that you might digest it at your leisure. Since then I have worked steadily at the piece (save during the ten weeks of my illness) and at least five-sixths of it are finished. A fortnight or so ago (nearly five months after I read the plot to you) I received for the first time an intimation that you disapproved of the Lady Sophy business in Act 2 and made a suggestion the exact purport of which I did not gather from your letter, and so, while falling in at once with all your other wishes, I left the Lady Sophy business to be discussed when we met. It now appears, as I gather from your letter of today, that you wish her to be in Act 2 a grave and dignified lady to be taken seriously and apart from any grotesque suggestion. But (to say nothing of the fact that by investing her with a pathetic interest I should be laying myself open to the charge of repeating Mr Grundy's treatment of the Brandram part in the last act of *Haddon Hall*) I have in Act I committed her irrevocably to a more or less humorous fate, and in this you have aided and abetted me. Surely to make a sudden *volte-face* and treat her in Act 2 as a serious or pathetic personage (there being no single serious note in the piece up to this point) would be to absolutely stultify myself in the face of the audience. Possibly I may even now have failed to grasp your intention in its completeness. Possibly you may have failed to grasp mine. Most assuredly it is not necessary that she should be 'very old, ugly, raddled or grotesque' – she may be and *should be* (as I explained to you on Friday) a dignified lady of 45 or thereabouts, and no more ugly than God Almighty has made the lady who is to play the part. Nor do I propose that she should be seething with love and passion. She is in love with the King (as a lady of 45 may very well be with a man of 50) – but her frenzy is not of the gross or animal type at all, as you seem to imagine. Her position is this. Being compelled, by her duties as governess to the young princesses, to impose upon herself a restraint and an appearance of prudishness which is foreign to her nature, she takes the opportunity of being alone to express her natural dislike of conventional shackles. This she does in a strong quasi-dramatic scene (or by some other form of musical expression) with enough of suggested humour in it to keep it in harmony with the humorous and satirical character of the piece – and in this she declares her impatience of the Quakerish restraint which her position as the governess of the Princesses imposes upon her and her regret that, having regard to the scandalous conduct which is attributed to the King in the *Palace Peeper*, she cannot accept attentions which, but for these considerations, she would gladly do. The King overhears this with infinite pleasure and explains that the pars were all written by him. Embarrassed at the turn affairs have taken she is nevertheless bound to admit, now that his character is cleared, that the King is not wholly indifferent to her. She and the King, having thus come to an understanding, indulge in a joyous duet leading to a dance, which is witnessed and joined in by the two princesses and their lovers.

Now I am no apologist for my own humour. It is very likely that all this may be poor fun indeed, but in a matter of good taste I claim to be as good a judge as any man alive, and I cannot for the life of me see that in what I propose to do with Lady Sophy the canons of propriety are in the smallest respect disregarded. One thing is quite clear to me – this difficulty can be best settled by a personal meeting. If you think so too I will run down to you on Thursday next – or, if that won't do, on Tuesday the 11th – and I have no doubt we shall come to a pleasant understanding on this very important point.

Yours very truly
W. S. Gilbert

They came to an understanding that was probably not wholly pleasant to Gilbert, for the character of Lady Sophy in no way resembles his earlier scarecrows. Another set-back for him was Sullivan's inability to give musical expression to the Finale of Act 2. For the only time in the history of their collaboration he advised Sullivan to compose the music first, after which he wrote the words, telling his partner 'It is mere doggerel – but words written to an existing tune are nearly sure to be that . . . You may chop this about just as you please.' Gilbert believed that in the past the critics had failed to understand his pieces because they had not been given sufficient time to meditate upon them before writing their notices; so they were invited to witness the final dress rehearsal of *Utopia Limited*; and certainly the experiment seemed to brighten their intelligences, for nearly all the notices were favourable: even 'G.B.S.' in *The World* said that it contained the best work Gilbert and Sullivan had done together. The first performance took place on October 7th, 1893, and when the curtain came down on the last act the whole house shouted for 'Author', 'Composer', 'Sullivan' and 'Gilbert'. They made their usual entrances, one from each side of the stage. No doubt Carte had spotted from the beginning that if the two of them entered from the same side the contrast between their different heights would impart an element of comedy to the occasion; so the width of the stage divided them as they acknowledged the hurricane of acclamation. But on this occasion the audience wanted more than a bow and a nod, and Sullivan played up to them. He walked towards Gilbert with extended hand; his partner marched across to clasp it; and everyone howled happily.

But the run of the piece was not much longer than that of *The Mountebanks* or *Haddon Hall*. Though Gilbert had again absorbed the sentiment of the hour, this time he was wholly out of sympathy with it and ridiculed the popular belief in democratic progress. Utopia was in the air of the nineties, but *Utopia Limited* remained at the Savoy for little more than eight months.

CHAPTER 15

Gout

❍●❍●❍

Had it been less painful, Gilbert might have taken some pride in his gout, which suggested a long line of port-drinking ancestors. It was a gentleman's complaint, and made the victim use the language of an eighteenth-century country squire. But, as with Sydney Smith, it was the only enemy he did not wish to have at his feet. Sometimes it attacked him violently in both feet, sometimes only in a hand, sometimes in feet and hands. 'I have not been able to do anything but swear for the last eighteen days', he reported in 1893. When not swearing his impotence incensed him and he had to work his irritation off in demonstrations of ill-will. Answering an appeal by Mrs Carte for a donation to a charity for orchestral performers, he got rid of his bad-temper before displaying his good-nature:

I hate the orchestra. They take up a lot of paying stalls – they are the most cantankerous and independent set in the theatre – and they play so loud that my words can't be heard. Moreover, like many other high-souled and independent specimens of Nature's nobility, they are the first to come begging cap in hand when they are in difficulties. Having thus blown off steam, I have much pleasure in sending five guineas for the fund.

That was typical of the man. As in nature, calm followed the storm, and in his case gout and antagonism intensified if they did not cause the storm. His father had been subject to the same infirmity with similar results; yet he lived to a mellow age, 85, dying in 1890 at Salisbury, where his residence for some years in the Cathedral Close entitled him to be buried in the cloisters. He left about £8000, a quarter of which went to his daughter, Mrs Alfred Weigall, Gilbert giving her another thousand out of his share for looking after their father in his declining years. Their mother seems to have sunk into the shadow of the grave unrecorded and unlamented.

Although he frequently referred to it in his letters, no one made allowances for the part played by gout in Gilbert's many quarrels, except Sullivan, who as we have seen overdid the allowance. But the regular recurrence of the complaint, especially in the nineties, made him super-sensitive and precipitate in his dealings with others. His old enemy Henry Labouchere described him as spontaneous in conversation, never requiring a butt to be amusing, as a very pleasant companion and a most kindly man, 'but he was exceedingly touchy and prone to take offence about trifles. This I have remarked is very frequently the case with wits. Whilst they never spare others, they particularly dislike being laughed at themselves.' Gilbert was often advised by his friends to take no notice of journalistic penpricks; but all advice is useless unless it coincides with the wish of the person advised, when it is needless; and nothing could prevent him from headlong retaliation. Having scored his point, he became gentle and remorseful, not only forgiving his recent foe but willing to help the very person he had just invoked the law to punish. No better illustration of his nature in these respects could be exhibited than his actions in the case of Anna, Comtesse de Brémont.

In October 1894, while busy rehearsing a comic opera *His Excellency*, threatening an action against a newspaper for an offensive paragraph, and sustaining severe attacks of gout, he received a letter from Anna asking if she might interview him for a paper called *St Paul's*. He tartly informed her that his fee for an interview was twenty guineas. To which she returned:

> The Comtesse de Brémont presents her compliments to Mr W. S. Gilbert and in reply to his answer to her request for an interview for *St Paul's* in which he states his terms as twenty guineas for that privilege, begs to say that she anticipates the pleasure of writing his obituary for nothing.

It was an amusing gibe, rather in his own style of warfare, but it did not amuse him. He promptly wrote to *The Times* and *The Daily Telegraph* on the subject of 'The Lady Interviewer' and in the course of his letter referred to 'a lady who styles herself the Comtesse de Brémont', said that he was unwilling to place himself 'at the mercy of the good taste and discretion of this lady (who is known to me by repute)', and quoted her message, which appeared to justify him 'in declining the honour which the Comtesse de Brémont proposed to confer upon me'. He also sent a copy of what he called 'this specimen of feminine spite' to the editor of *St Paul's*, advising him to keep an eye on 'any article written by that lady and having me or my work for their subject'.

The publication of his letters in the two papers impelled Anna to bring an action for damages against him, and he supplied his solicitors with details. First of all he wrote to someone in New York about her title, and discovered that she was the daughter of an American, Mrs Dunphy, and had married a doctor named de Brémon, who described himself Comte de Brémont, as well as a Vicomte and a Baron, when he married Anna. But the Baron de Brémont, then alive in Paris, repudiated her right to the title. Gilbert had read an article in a Cape Town paper which contained unfavourable comments on Anna, and he believed his solicitors might collect a few facts of an awkward nature in South Africa, 'but time is important', he told them on the 23rd December, 1894, 'for I have to leave for the West Indies in three weeks, to recruit after a year of incessant gout, and I should like to push this matter well forward before I go'. The report by a firm of solicitors in Cape Town was more than awkward for Anna, whose career in those parts had been unconventional. She had published erotic poems, was expelled from hotels, had drunk more than was good for her and provoked scandal by her relations with actors and jockeys. 'Any Johannesburg man now in London could tell you endless tales about her', ran the report, which was as highly coloured as the nature of the subject demanded.

Armed with such testimonials, the case was a walk-over for Gilbert, whose legal representatives had no difficulty in proving that discretion was not among Anna's virtues. His resentment at once evaporated, giving place to charity, and he sent her a note: 'As I have no desire to put you to any further expense, I have instructed my solicitor not to apply to you for any costs in this action.' She thanked him for his kindness and deplored the pain she had caused him. He unreservedly accepted her expressions of regret and was 'quite prepared to regard bye-gones as having gone by'. In a letter to Lord Shand he confessed that he

was really sorry to see the poor woman vivisected in the witness-box – so I wrote to tell her I should not ask for any costs – and I received a very proper letter in reply ... so now, she is my sister. But this claim on the part of American citizens to interview any Europeans they may select, and hang them in effigy if they decline to submit, is an extension of the Monroe doctrine in a direction never contemplated by its originator.

While one woman was causing him some anxiety another was giving him much pleasure. At a party in the house of George Henschel he had been much struck by the singing of a pretty girl named Nancy McIntosh. Needing a soprano for the leading female part in *Utopia Limited*, he asked her to let Sullivan hear her sing. The composer too liked her voice, and they engaged her to play Princess Zara. She was an American, her father being President of a commercial company in New York, and ambitious to be a concert singer she had recently arrived in England to finish her studies under Henschel. Having made a success in the part, Gilbert engaged her for the soprano lead in his next opera, *His Excellency*, and she soon went to live with the Gilberts, becoming their adopted daughter. There is no doubt that she had an excellent singing voice, and as Gilbert took immense pains to train her as an actress she quickly became equal to the demands made upon her in that respect; but owing to his enthusiasm for anyone in whose ability he believed, he aroused some antagonism in those who were asked to share his admiration. This happened occasionally in the case of Nancy McIntosh, and when it did he took offence, apprehending hostility in what was merely a different point of view.

More disagreement between the Savoy collaborators had arisen during the production of *Utopia Limited*, and in a scrap of Nancy McIntosh's diary that has been preserved we have fragments of the story:

13 March, 1894.   'S has written breaking off collaboration. Mr G has written.'

16 March.   'Mr G called afterwards to tell me a new proposition from Carte.'

24 March.   'Mr G saw H(enschel) and it is settled that they are to write an opera together.'

7 April.   'Mr G told me of H's lying letter about me and that Carte won't produce his opera and that it may fall through.'

It did fall through, and *His Excellency*, with music by Dr Osmond Carr, appeared at the Lyric Theatre on October 27th,

1894, under the management of George Edwardes. The libretto was as good as most of those Gilbert had written for Sullivan, and the cast included three old Savoy favourites, George Grossmith, Rutland Barrington and Jessie Bond, besides Nancy McIntosh and another beautiful girl discovered by the author, Ellaline Terriss, who became the wife of Seymour Hicks.

The relative failure of *Utopia Limited*, for which he had prophesied a success equalling that of *The Mikado*, added to another quarrel with Sullivan, combined with the gout, did not create in Gilbert a favourable frame of mind for the direction of rehearsals. It would have required a sledge-hammer to make much impression on Rutland Barrington, but the sufferings of George Grossmith were such that even a gentle spirit like his was moved to remonstrate when Gilbert wrote him a stern note five months after the production of the opera. For seventeen years, said Grossmith, he had received letters of complaint from Gilbert without a murmur, but the last had gone beyond the bounds of his endurance. 'I hold a position in my profession which is nearly equivalent to the one you hold in yours, and I expect to be treated with a certain amount of courtesy.' A juvenile stage-manager had 'reported' him for gagging, and he objected to such humiliation, 'as I am not your servant'. He admitted that he and Barrington had occasionally indulged in some mild badinage on the stage, but asserted that he had never altered the author's lines. He felt that Gilbert should have politely asked him whether he had done so instead of accusing him of the deed. 'My occasional mild *interpolations* have been spontaneous, intermittent, and seldom repeated'. He then stated that when the business dropped during the frosty weather he had volunteered to play for nothing, and all the principals had reduced their salaries by a third; but instead of being thanked for helping to save a sinking ship, he had received a disagreeable and dictatorial letter addressed, not to his private residence at 28 Dorset Square, but to the theatre, 'and I presume you think *that* was an incentive to a nervous actor to play your work properly'. Gilbert regretted his hasty conclusion, but still disapproved of a performer's interpolated badinage, however mild. 'With reference to "gags", I am supposed to be adamantine, but this is not really so', he once declared:

I only require that when an actor proposes to introduce any words which are not in the authorized dialogue, those words should be submitted to me; and if there appears to be no good reason to the contrary, the words are duly incorporated with the text. I consider that as I am held by the audience to be responsible for all that is spoken on the stage, it is only right that nothing should be spoken that I have not authorized. Many 'gags' suggested by Grossmith, Barrington, Passmore and others, have rendered valuable service to my pieces.

It is practically impossible for a strong individualist, with a strict sense of fair dealing and a quick temper, to survive the production of his work in the theatre without an altercation or an eruption or both. The conjunction of Gilbert with his latest impresario George Edwardes was ominous, and the laws of nature would have had to be suspended in order to establish a completely harmonious association between the two; for the musical comedies presented by Edwardes temporarily supplanted in popularity the operas of Gilbert and Sullivan. There was nothing very remarkable about Edwardes except his success. He was a commonplace man, possessing business ability, the vulgar tastes of his day, and the intelligence (if that is the right word) to perceive what the public wanted; while Gilbert had given the public what he had hoped they might come to want, and finding that they liked it he continued to give it them. Gilbert and Sullivan created a taste, for which with variations Edwardes catered. The latter, who had been Carte's business-manager for some years, noticed that the comedians at the Savoy aroused more laughter the further they receded from the strict injunctions of Gilbert, noticed too that audiences wallowed in sentimental songs and liked the lovers to be more passionate than Gilbert permitted. When, therefore, he took over the Gaiety Theatre, he gave the comedians a free hand to be as funny as they liked, engaged composers to manufacture honey-sweet songs, and favoured highly romantic love duets. He had a staff of dialogue, lyric and music writers, and his success was due to their team-work. The confection caught on and shows like *The Shop Girl* and *A Gaiety Girl* made fortunes. A year after his presentation of Gilbert's comic opera he bought the lease of Daly's Theatre, which he ran with the Gaiety for many years, doing a series of musical comedies some of which were so prosperous that their names are still remembered, e.g. *The Geisha*, *San Toy*, and *The Merry Widow*. In partnership with other managers he also produced *The Duchess of Dantzic*,

Veronique, and similar works. Briefly, for a generation Edwardes was the chief provider of light musical entertainment in Great Britain, just as Carte had been for a shorter period before him. But while Carte had relied on Gilbert and Sullivan, his successor employed a small factory of public entertainers.

At first the Gilbert-Edwardes combination seemed to promise well. Edwardes paid £5000 for the entire London, provincial, American and colonial acting rights of *His Excellency* for three years, and two months after its production he asked Gilbert to write another piece for him. But four months later, in April 1895, the temperature of their relationship having dropped with the receipts, they agreed to delay their contract for a new opera. Gilbert had consented to produce *His Excellency* in New York, but when he heard that Edwardes had violated their agreement by disposing of the translation along with the acting rights in one country he refused to attend the rehearsals of the company engaged for the American season; upon which Edwardes wrote to accuse him of breaking his promise. The omitted portion of Gilbert's reply (printed here in parenthesis) is more illuminating than the rest of the letter despatched on September 12th, 1895:

Dear Edwardes

I have told you, three or four times, that I will not move a step in the American matter until you have admitted, explicitly, that in our contract for *His Excellency* it was never contemplated between us that the right of translation should accompany the acting right. When you have given me this admission and when you have withdrawn the highly offensive letter you sent me this morning I am prepared to consider whether the piece shall be lengthened and whether I am to go to New York for the first performance.

(It is to be regretted that you were so ill-advised as to send me the highly offensive letter I received this morning. The tone of that letter may serve to frighten choristers, but I assure you that it could have no other effect upon me than to aggravate any existing difficulties and to widen any existing breach. If I rightly understood you, you take upon yourself to threaten me with serious consequences unless I agree to superintend your rehearsals gratuitously and you further charge me with availing myself of an excuse to evade an undertaking that I had entered into. While this monstrous letter remains alive it is obviously impossible that I can enter into any personal relations with you.)

If, on consideration, you accept my conditions, I will meet you any afternoon this week at 3.30 – or on Monday at 4.30. If you decline them I must ask you to look upon this correspondence as finally closed.

Yours truly

Edwardes wrote on the following day to suggest that his solicitors should meet Gilbert's and settle the dispute. Gilbert answered on the same day: 'I have nothing to add to my letter of yesterday's date.' Edwardes complained by return that he had been 'most disgracefully treated' and stated that at Gilbert's express desire he had engaged Nancy McIntosh for the London and New York productions in the belief that this would influence the author to fulfil his agreement. Gilbert's rejoinder on September 14th began: 'Sir, your letter of the 13th Inst. is a tissue of untruths.' He then proceeded to unweave the tissue. Recapitulating his grievance concerning the translation rights, the disposal of which had been admitted by Edwardes, he summarized their dealings with his usual vigour and accuracy, making out that the manager had been unbusinesslike, evasive and dishonest. Two passages in his letter are of interest, the first dealing with Nancy McIntosh, the second being left out of the copy sent to Edwardes:

It is simply untrue that you engaged Miss McIntosh for America at my express desire. You told me that you were most anxious to send out as many of the original company as you could induce to go. Acting on this declared intention you offered engagements to Miss McIntosh, Mr Barrington, Mr Playfair, Mr Le Hay, Miss Alice Barnett, Miss Jessie Bond, Miss Ellaline Terriss and Miss Aylward – excluding only Mr Grossmith on the ground that his performance of the Governor was in your opinion unsatisfactory. You told me that you were most anxious that Miss McIntosh (of whose ability you spoke in the highest terms) should play her original part in the United States, but that the terms she asked, though not higher than she deserved, were more than you could afford to give, having regard to the enormous expense involved in sending a complete London company to the United States. You proposed a lower figure and I simply interfered as *amicus curiae* to suggest a compromise – which was adopted.

You tell me that I am the only person who has hitherto benefited by the piece. This may well be. A piece of mine in which the comedians are permitted to 'gag' as freely as they please – a piece in which four or five choristers are pitchforked, at one time, into principal parts, because you will not go to the expense of having those parts properly understudied by competent artists – a piece, in short, which is practically left by you to take care of itself without any managerial supervision worthy of the name – is not likely to be profitable to anyone but the author who is foreseeing enough to make arrangements that will protect him from the consequences of managerial neglect.

After this Edwardes must have climbed down because the only other item preserved in their correspondence is the copy of a wire sent to him by Gilbert: 'I understand piece to be produced Broadway fourteenth October. Shall I be safe in taking return berth in steamer leaving sixteenth October?' Edwardes was the type of man who, when cornered, would take the entire blame for everything that had happened on his own shoulders, hoping by the frankness and generosity of his confession to wipe out the fault and avoid reproach. Gilbert was too crafty to be taken in by such a stratagem, but so long as he gained his point he was not above closing an eye.

His Excellency started well and Gilbert wrote to Mrs Carte that 'if it had had the advantage of your expensive friend Sullivan's music it would have been a second *Mikado*'. But this is doubtful, for the fashion in light entertainment was changing, and though the public still flocked to see revivals of the old Savoy successes they wished the new shows to include more dancing, more clowning, and above all more romance than Gilbert allowed them. Carte urged his collaborators to concentrate on pure fun, to write 'a frankly comic piece – say, a modern farcical comedy to music'; but he too was a little out of date, the public displaying no desire to see an operatic version of, say, *Charley's Aunt*. Besides, Gilbert had already laughed at the army, the navy, the law, the church, medicine, aesthetics, politics, big business, the throne, and even in *His Excellency* the national anthem. There was nothing left to laugh at, and he was no longer the Gilbert of 'Bab' who indulged in laughter for laughter's sake. Still, he was willing to make one more attempt, and on April 7th, 1894 he wrote to Sullivan:

Dear S

Glad to get your letter. I shall be at your disposal when you return.

I much doubt our being able to get the piece ready by June –

and July would I think be quite out of the question. By the time you return April will be half through. To the 1st July will be about ten weeks. Now it will take *at least* six weeks to rehearse the piece *which will leave only four weeks* in which to write the libretto and compose the music! However, we can discuss this when we meet.

Convenu about the other author. One librettist is as good as another, if not better. Moreover this is the last libretto I shall ever write and it matters nothing to me who is to succeed me.

Yours very truly

Sullivan took the hint and composed music for a comic opera by F. C. Burnand, but their joint labours proved conclusively that one librettist was not as good as another, and the following year Gilbert provided him with something better:

River House
Walton-on-Thames
11 Aug. 1895

My dear Gilbert

I have studied the sketch plot very carefully, and like it even more than I did when I heard it first on Thursday. It comes out as clear and bright as possible.

I shall be very pleased to set it, and am prepared to begin (as soon as you have anything ready for me) and have written to Carte to tell him so. There is one very important suggestion I should like to make, which, if you see your way to accept, will relieve me of a vast amount of unnecessary technical labour, and turn difficult situations into easy ones for me. Of course I speak entirely from a musical point of view. How would it do to make Lisa the *principal* soprano part, and make Elsa the contralto. She might be the leading tragedy lady of Ludwig's troupe, and con- tralto of the Operatic company – not necessarily old, but (if played by Brandram) staid and earnest, a suitable wife for the manager, and from whose mouth the theatrically highflown sentiments from romantic plays would come very forcibly, especially as they would be uttered in rich contralto register. Then see what an advantage this will be to me. In all the concerted music there would be a soprano and contralto, instead of two sopranos, and when Countess Krakenfeld is the only female in concerted pieces we shall have the immense advantage of having a soprano and not a contralto at the top, getting plenty of brightness. This would make every- thing run as easily as possible for me, for I assure you I am, or rather have been, at my wits' end sometimes to know how to deal with concerted pieces which have no *middle* parts – i.e. no tenor or contralto, or where the top part is cramped by the limited range of the contralto voice.

So, if you see your way to fall in with this suggestion, you will lighten my work very considerably. Perry would make an admirable young shrewish, no-nonsense-about-her Countess Krakenfeld. I return the MS registered. Don't let the monkeys get at it. They might forestall Justin McCarthy in the *Pall Mall* and tear it to pieces!

Yours sincerely
Arthur Sullivan

P.S. I have made out a rough music plot from your sketch, as I always do, and enclose a copy.

Gilbert had poked fun at actors from the beginning of his career, and his final laugh was at their expense, bidding farewell to them with a few lines on his own capability:

> *Both A and B rehearsal slight –*
> *They say they'll be 'all right at night'*
> *(They've both to go to school yet);*
> *C in each act must change her dress,*
> *D will attempt to 'square the press';*
> *E won't play Romeo unless*
> *His grandmother plays Juliet;*
> *F claims all hoydens as her rights*
> *(She's played them thirty seasons);*
> *And G must show herself in tights*
> *For two convincing reasons –*
> *Two very well-shaped reasons!*
> *Oh, the man who can drive a theatrical team,*
> *With wheelers and leaders in order supreme,*
> *Can govern and rule, with a wave of his fin,*
> *All Europe – with Ireland thrown in!*

But just as Shakespeare's fun was not rollicking enough for Gilbert, his last opera with Sullivan was not frolicsome enough for the public, and *The Grand Duke*, first seen at the Savoy Theatre on March 7th, 1896, was seen there no longer after twenty weeks. The amazing pair, whose collaboration was unique in the annals of art, did not speak to one another again. Though each thought highly of the other's work their natures were so much at variance that they could not meet on the easy terms of other men. 'Sullivan never says much to me, and what he *does* say, I usually knock a lot off of, for discount,' Gilbert confided in the wife of Beerbohm Tree; 'but what he said to you he, no doubt, meant and it is very gratifying to know that he thinks so well of what I have done.' Such were the conditions of their relationship, and it is not surprising to hear that when *The Sorcerer* was put on towards the close of 1898 the two men bowed to the audience but did not exchange a word with one another. *Patience* was revived on November 7th, 1900, and Gilbert expressed the hope that Sullivan and he should bury all unkindness and take a call together. Sullivan wanted to do so, but he was too ill, and Carte shared the plaudits with the librettist. While messing about in the lake he was making at Grim's Dyke, Gilbert caught rheumatic fever and was ordered abroad by his doctor. Hearing that Sullivan was extremely ill, he wrote:

My dear Sullivan

I would be glad to come up to town to see you before I go, but unfortunately in my present enfeebled condition a carriage journey to London involves my lying down a couple of hours before I am fit for anything, besides stopping all night in town. The railway journey is still more fatiguing. I have lost sixty pounds in weight, and my arms and legs are of the consistency of cotton-wool. I sincerely hope to find you all right again on my return, and the new opera running merrily.

Yours very truly,

W. S. Gilbert

P.S. The old opera woke up splendidly.

Sullivan died on November 22nd, 1900. Gilbert was in Egypt, and on hearing the news he wrote to Sullivan's nephew expressing his sorrow and sympathy:

It is a satisfaction to me to feel that I was impelled, shortly before his death, to write to him to propose to shake hands over our recent differences, and even a greater satisfaction to learn, through you, that my offer of reconciliation was cordially accepted.

But however warmly they had shaken hands their differences would have remained, rooted in their natures. Fortunately their divergences in personality were complementary in art, and it is certain that if they had resembled one another at all closely the perfect unity of their operas could not have been attained. Though inspired by Gilbert's words, Sullivan's music gave them wings, and there emerged an ideal combination of charm and vivacity, delicacy and vigour, sweetness and strength. Had he lived at an earlier period, Sullivan would have produced the folk-tunes of a nation. As it was he composed its swan-songs. And when we consider that they came from a man whose illness was both constant and agonizing, we have to admit that history contains no parallel instance of so much joy and beauty created by one who suffered so much pain.

Gilbert's singularity as a librettist was due to his versatility. Many others had been able to write excellent lyrics or clever patter-songs or admirable comic verse or witty dialogue, but Gilbert could do the lot and each of them at least as well as the best of anyone else. Furthermore he created a world of his own, unlike any other, imposing his own personality on all its in-habitants, a burlesque world into which no real figure was per-mitted to enter. He showed a masterly restraint in maintaining the atmosphere of this artificial dreamland, never carrying a humorous idea too far, never allowing sentiment to become emotional, and never forgetting that the puppets should be subservient to the plot. He knew to a syllable the practical limitations of his medium and studiously kept within them. Even his satire, his most individual quality, never obtrudes. It is sufficiently superficial to be pleasing; it amuses without hurting. By satirizing everything in general, he satirized nothing in particular, and people willingly laugh at themselves when they are able to laugh at others. The Gilbertian cosmos could only have been fashioned by one who enjoyed life and sympa-thized with the predicament of his fellow-creatures; though some of his contemporaries may have felt that he only enjoyed quarrelling with them.

CHAPTER 16

The Embodiment of Excellence

❂❂❂❂

His reputation as a cantankerous man increased with the
years, not because he was any more perverse than the
average short-tempered human being who likes to have
his own way, but because, having several times exhibited
wrath, the rumours of his fractiousness were commensurate
with his fame. Quickness of speech was his real enemy. With
most people the first thought that enters their heads is kept
there. With Gilbert it slipped off his tongue before he was fully
aware of its birth in his brain, and was as quickly forgotten as
conceived. Had he lived in the previous century he would have
been a duellist, quick to draw his sword, impetuous in attack,
and a little uncertain of his own contribution to the quarrel
before he had finished wiping his antagonist's blood from the
blade. For example he must have said something that cut
deeply into the mind of Clement Scott but left no impression
on his own. That influential dramatic critic took his revenge
when *Brantinghame Hall* was presented in 1888, reviewing it
in a manner which evoked from the author:

I have no doubt that it will gratify you to know that you have
driven me from a stage, for which (in our days of friendship) you
have often declared that I was pre-eminently fitted to write.

Gilbert could not understand the cause of Scott's malice:

In what way I have incurred your enmity I do not know . . . I
have before me, as I write, a letter from you, written a few days
after a deplorable afternoon at Guildhall – a letter in which you
acknowledge in rapturous terms the service I had rendered you in
endeavouring to avert the disgrace with which you were – most
undeservedly – threatened – and in which you assure me that your
gratitude will be undying. It is interesting and instructive to read
this letter by the light of after events.

As we know, Gilbert behaved with the utmost magnanimity to Scott's widow.

But by the nineties his lightest quips were construed into venomous judgments, and his legal cases were regarded as the symptoms of an essentially belligerent nature. 'Here I am at last!' exclaimed the actor J. L. Toole on arrival at Grim's Dyke: 'I was afraid, if I put it off any longer, you'd bring an action against me.' The fact that he did not admire the Shakespearean performances of the leading actors at that time was interpreted as personal animosity, and one of his comments was so frequently repeated that it has become a common quotation. In whatever form it was first spoken, everyone now knows that he described Beerbohm Tree's Hamlet as 'funny without being vulgar'. When the remark had gone the round of the clubs and appeared in print Gilbert naturally denied having made it and Tree pretended that he had invented it. But a wit is scarcely ever witty at his own expense, especially when the raillery hurts his self-esteem, and we may feel confident of the phrase's originator when we read in one of Gilbert's letters:

> Do you know how they are going to decide the Shakespeare-Bacon dispute? They are going to dig up Shakespeare and dig up Bacon; they are going to set their coffins side by side, and they are going to get Tree to recite Hamlet to them. And the one who turns in his coffin will be the author of the play.

As author-producer he had no use for the actor-producer, and his view of both Tree and Irving was coloured by his knowledge that the author was negligible, the actor all-important, in their theatres. When asked whether he had been to see Irving in W. G. Wills's version of *Faust* at the Lyceum Theatre, he answered: 'Madam, I go to the pantomime only at Christmas', an observation that no doubt reached the ears of Irving. Many years later another leading actor did his best to laugh at one of Gilbert's impromptus. Sir Squire Bancroft was a punctual attendant at the obsequies of the eminent and a never-failing contributor to their floral memorials. When Gilbert heard that the famous elephant at the Zoological Gardens had expired, he asked quickly: 'Has Bancroft sent a wreath?'

Some 'stars' of the period had acted in his dramas and friction had resulted. He had quarrelled with the Kendals and John Hare. But he had again become friendly with Hare, and in the autumn of 1888 started to build the Garrick Theatre for him. During the work on the foundations one of London's many underground rivulets was opened to view and for a while it looked as if the site would be flooded. But to Gilbert's relief the water subsided. 'For some time I was in grave doubt whether to continue building or let the fishing', he said. The cost of the erection was estimated at £30,000, but by the time the job was finished in April 1889 it had risen to £44,000 and Gilbert had to borrow about £15,000, which meant an increase in rent, and a friendly but pointed correspondence between himself and Hare. 'I think you must still be under the impression that I have feathered my nest very comfortably at your expense', he wrote. 'If you will study the subjoined figures you will find that you are entirely mistaken.' The figures showed that the rent he was asking came to no more than $6\frac{3}{4}$ per cent on his total investment.

Now although you are a first-class tenant, you must see that investing £44,000 in the Garrick Theatre is not quite the same thing as investing it in Consols. You may be bankrupt or die – in the course of 21 years – in either of these cases the theatre would be thrown on my hands, perhaps for one or more years, during which I should receive no rent, but would have to pay ground-rent, mortgage, interest, rates, taxes and insurance to the tune of about £2300 per annum. There are many other contingencies and drawbacks that must be taken into consideration, but I have said enough to show that, in my desire to save you from falling into the hands of City harpies who would have made you bleed to the tune of 10%, I have plunged all my available capital and a good deal more into a most risky and utterly inconvertible form of security.

Hare admitted that he had viewed the matter entirely from his own standpoint, that he knew Gilbert had only built the theatre out of friendship for himself, but that owing to the unlooked-for increase of expenditure on the work he believed both of them were sorry they had ever heard of the site in Charing Cross Road. However, a full house brought in £234, the property was valued at £54,000 in 1889, and an offer of £60,000 was made for it in 1894; so Gilbert had no cause to regret his failure to buy Consols.

'A soft answer turneth away wrath', we are told; but an ironic soft answer incites wrath, and Gilbert sometimes said devastating things in a gentle manner. Justice Kekewich having admitted that he liked all the Savoy operas except *Trial by Jury*, Gilbert mildly remarked: 'He seemed to think that in holding the proceedings up to ridicule I was trenching on his prerogative.' Another Justice inspired a different kind of treatment. In the autumn of 1897 May Fortescue, an actress who had appeared in several of Gilbert's plays and operas, tried a short tour of his last full-length prose drama in the provinces before bringing it to London. It was called *The Fortune Hunter* and was at first printed 'for private use only', in which condition it should have remained, though it shows that the author was still receptive to the mental atmosphere of his age, for it contains the first attempt by a modern English playwright to portray a character who tries to psycho-analyse himself. It opened at the Theatre Royal, Birmingham, on September 27th, 1897, and the notices were so unfavourable that Gilbert went to Edinburgh for the second week of the tour to pull the piece together, announcing his arrival to his wife:

4 Oct. '97

Dearest Kits,

As my wire will have informed you I arrived all right (but half an hour late) and intend to return on Tuesday night by the train arriving at Euston at five minutes past seven. I found my sleeping berth was with another man – and every berth to Edinburgh was taken, but I found I could get a berth to myself (in another part of the train) as far as Carlisle – so I preferred that, and at 6 o'clock got into an ordinary first-class carriage – which I had to myself. Miss Fortescue is here – also Maurice whom I saw at breakfast this morning. He tells me that the business was magnificent at Birmingham. Of course I haven't any news, having only arrived an hour and a half ago. This is an old-fashioned and rather dingy hotel. I have a fair sitting-room but a ghastly bedroom. However, it's only for one night.

Good-bye, old girl. God bless you.

From your devoted
Old Boy

The dinginess of the Windsor Hotel did not improve his temper, already exacerbated by the criticisms of his play, and he was in the frame of mind that could only be appeased by a general slaughter of his enemies. 'He was bubbling over with indignation, and was, to put it mildly, in a fearfully bad temper', recorded the Edinburgh *Evening Dispatch* some years afterwards. 'Naturally, finding his subject in this mood, the interviewer gave him the necessary rope, and . . . Mr Gilbert did some noble slashing all round.' The arrangement was made by a friend of Gilbert's, who called at the office of the *Evening Dispatch*, asked a member of the staff, Isaac Donald, to interview the dramatist and gave him a card of introduction. The result appeared in that paper on October 5th.[1]

Starting quietly, Gilbert said that he had put more of himself into his blank verse plays, or they had taken more out of him, than the rest, and so he considered them his best work. As a business man he objected to so-called problem plays (in which no problem whatever was involved) because an exhibition of the seamy side of life kept respectable people out of the theatre and gave them a pretext to attack the stage. He confessed that his favourite Savoy opera was *The Yeomen of the Guard*, and that his best dramas were *Gretchen* and *Broken Hearts*, for into them he had put most of himself. Then the slashing commenced:

'Does it not occur to you that at the present day the numerous adaptations suggest a scarcity of British dramatists?'

'No, it does not. The fact is managers cannot judge a play when they see it in manuscript. If Pinero writes a play and sends it to Sir Henry Irving, it is accepted, not because it is a good play but because it is Pinero. If a stranger who may be a clever dramatist sends Sir Henry or Mr Tree or anybody else a play, it is not accepted, however good it may be, because they can't judge. Your manager nowadays crosses to France, sees a play that goes well, and how it can be slightly watered down to suit our censorious society, and immediately transplants it.'

'Then you have no sympathy with translations?'

'No! None! We ought to leave the French stage alone. They have good actors and atrociously bad plays. Their plays are much more analytical than ours, written for the most part in a quasi-Thackerayan manner. Sardou's plays elaborate character to such an extent that they might be pages out of Thackeray turned into French. Their actors, of course, can so speak and deliver speeches as to chain the attention of the audience, while ours, why, we have no actor who can make a thirty-line speech interesting! Whoever heard in this country "All the world's a stage" declaimed by a Jaques who did not in every line make it plain he had learned it off by heart. There is always the same dull monotony of delivery. Every living actor – Sir Henry Irving, Beerbohm Tree, Alexander,

[1] Printed here by permission of the *Evening Dispatch*, Edinburgh.

excellent though they may be otherwise – have that dull monotony of delivery. They keep to one note through the sentence, and finish a semi-tone higher or a semi-tone lower as the case may be.'

(Oddly enough, three days before this interview was published, Johnston Forbes-Robertson produced *Hamlet* at the Lyceum Theatre, London, speaking the verse with a beauty and naturalness unequalled in his own or a later generation. But as Gilbert had not been on speaking terms with Robertson for twenty years, he probably did not witness the performance.)

'In what direction would you say dramatic taste lies today?'

'In the direction of musical comedy – bad musical comedy, in which half-a-dozen irresponsible comedians are turned loose upon the stage to do exactly as they please. These are our popular pieces.'

'Have these pieces cultivated the taste for music halls, or have music halls, would you say, cultivated the taste for musical comedy – of the bad type?'

'Musical comedies and the music halls act and react upon each other. If these comedians are not in a musical comedy they are at the halls, and if they are not in the halls they are in a musical comedy. The public see that clever comedian Dan Leno in a musical comedy, and are inoculated with a taste for the halls, and so the disposition grows.'

'Then do you think the legitimate theatre, so called, is falling off?'

'The theatre is as strong as ever it was. At this moment, certainly, there are perhaps fewer original plays before the public than one would desire to see, but that is an exceptional phase. The press is largely responsible for the fact that there are so many adaptations on the English stage.'

'How is that?'

'Because they seem to draw no distinction between the production of an original play and the translation of a French one . . .'

'And do you seriously mean that you blame the press for the large number of adaptations on the British stage?'

'I do. I do not blame the actors and actresses. I blame the press for considering them seriously as original work. Why, I hear Sydney Grundy put on the same level as Arthur Pinero, while the fact is that Mr Grundy is only a translator. He is a creditable translator, but to put him on the same level as Mr Pinero is a monstrous injustice. Remember, I do not wish, in saying this, to decry Mr Grundy in any sense.'

'Where do you think Mr Pinero is at his best?'

'In *The Magistrate* and *Dandy Dick*, to which style I believe he will return. In wholly farcical plays he is at his best, and I like the quality of his work immensely. I think him a giant, but he finds his name bracketed with hacks.'

'Have you any further work in progress?'

'No! I will write no more plays. I mean to retire now. I am disheartened by the erroneous point of view from which criticisms are written in London. They never seem to dissociate the play from the author of the play. I am not complaining of bad criticisms. I have had plenty and have learned much from them. But there is such a tendency to look upon the author of a bad or an unsuccessful play, not as a poor devil who has tried his best, but as a man who has committed an outrage against nature. The critics attack him as if he were a scoundrel of the worst type, and they go on at it week after week. I don't feel disposed to put myself forward as a cock-shy for these gentlemen. I think it better to refrain from writing as I am not obliged to write. I prefer to work in a different groove where anything I may do will stand upon its own merits.'

'What do you think of your last work now playing in Edinburgh?'

'I think it has its faults, of course. Every play has. But I think it is very well acted, and that Miss Fortescue has got together a good cast. I want to take Edinburgh's opinion on the play before taking it to London. I have not seen the play from the front myself and I don't intend to. Indeed, I have not seen a play of my own from the auditorium for twenty-one years. Save a performance at Carlsbad seven years ago.'

'What was that?'

'It was *The Mikado*, played in German, and some of my own characters I hardly recognized, save for five minutes at a time, when off they would go into the adapter's bypath, and I became profoundly interested in what would happen next. Pooh-Bah, in fact, quite interested me.'

'How many dramatic pieces have you written during the thirty years you have been engaged upon such work?'

'Seventy-five, and this is the only one which has been on my hands.'

The morning after this interview appeared nearly every paper in Great Britain quoted the more vigorous passages, and when Gilbert received a copy some days later, having cooled down in the interim, he guessed that the actors and the adapter he had mentioned might not read his comments in a spirit of complacence. So he wrote at once to Henry Irving's secretary, and to Tree and Alexander personally, explaining that he had been misreported: he had merely said that the fashion of speaking blank verse, which they followed, was the wrong one. He also wrote to tell Sydney Grundy that he had referred solely to that writer's adaptations, not to his original plays. The reactions of the maligned actors were characteristic of them. Irving was the guest at a supper given by the Sheffield and District Press Club, and in his speech he spoke of Gilbert as having laid aside his lyre and 'chosen to dare the heights of the serious drama – with what success was shown by his very childish statements and his very jaundiced behaviour'. Tree, though disliking the man personally, tried to allay the storm by saying that Gilbert's reputation as a poetic dramatist entitled him to speak with authority, and even offered to testify to that effect at the forthcoming legal action. George Alexander acknowledged Gilbert's letter and noted its contents. Grundy put Gilbert at his ease, and received the following letter of thanks:

21st Oct. '97

Dear Mr Grundy,

Your very generous letter has removed a weight of anxiety from my mind. It distressed me beyond measure that it should be supposed that I had spoken slightingly of an author who has done so much excellent work for the stage and has always borne his marked successes with such becoming modesty. I well remember the admiration with which I learnt that you had declined to accept a 'call' for *A Pair of Spectacles* on the ground that the piece was practically a translation – a fact which I mentioned to the interviewer, but which he doesn't seem to have thought worth while to reproduce. I believe the words I used in my 'interview' were – 'Of course I speak of Mr Grundy only as an adapter', meaning of course only in your capacity as an adapter – no doubt an injudicious form of expression inasmuch as it was perhaps open to the misapprehension under which the interviewer seems to have laboured. The fact that you have written many original plays is too well known to admit of my describing you as 'only an adapter' – the statement would have been as open to obvious refutation as if I had described Lord Salisbury as a rabid radical or Mr Labouchere as a hot Tory.

Of course I shall make no use of your letter without your express permission, but if it should prove to be advisable to put it in evidence in my case against *The Era* I shall be much obliged if you will allow me to do so.

I am
Very truly yours
W. S. Gilbert

The case to which he referred was an action for libel brought by him against *The Era*, a weekly paper devoted to stage subjects. Commenting on the Edinburgh interview, *The Era* had said that

Mr Gilbert's abnormal self-esteem has with advancing years developed into a malady. In his own estimation he is a kind of Grand Llama or Sacred Elephant of dramatic literature. The mildest criticism on his work, the most gentle disapproval of one of his plays, is a crime of lèse-majesté for which, if it were in his power, he would punish the culprit severely . . . It is a significant fact that one of the first things Mr Gilbert did when he retired, as it was trustfully believed, from business was to become a J.P. It is evident that did we live under a more despotic dispensation he would commit all the London critics for contempt of court . . . Mr Gilbert's career has been a succession of combats with the object, alas! unattained, of vindicating the Gilbert theory of the universe against sceptics and rebels . . . his real kindliness and good-nature have simply been obscured by the abnormal protuberance of his bump of self-esteem.

For this somewhat partial pen-portrait Gilbert demanded £1000 damages. The case was heard in the Queen's Bench Division before Mr Justice Day and a special jury at the end of March 1898. Irving, Tree and Alexander were present in court. Marshall Hall appeared as leading counsel for the plaintiff, Edward Carson for the defendant. When Gilbert entered the witness-box he was examined by Marshall Hall:

'You have read what was said in the article about your bump of self-esteem. Do you regard that as written in joke or seriously?'

'I can hardly take it seriously, because I cannot suppose that anyone thinks I wish to reconstruct the universe. I am perfectly satisfied with Cosmos as it is.' (*Laughter.*)

'Is it true to say that you have had successive combats with anybody to vindicate your theory of the universe?'

'Oh, no! I have no theory of the universe, and I am not a combative man.' (*Laughter.*)

'Then with regard to the inability of any English actor to make a thirty-line speech interesting, was that a statement made by you?'

'It was not. I was asked whether I intended to write any more blank verse plays, and I replied that I did not. I was then asked if I thought that the taste for modern blank verse had entirely died out, and I said no – that what I objected to was the present fashion of delivering blank verse, which allowed the metrical, the iambic structure to dominate the sense, caused the audience to lose the thread of the discourse, and obliged them to give up the speech for a bad job and wait for the next speech in the hope that they would find better luck with it. (*Laughter.*) That statement was only intended to apply to blank verse. It would be most untrue to apply it to the great proportion of actors in regard to ordinary prose. It was not at all personal and referred solely to the principle upon which blank verse is spoken.'

'You did not intend those remarks as an insult to Sir Henry Irving, Mr Tree or Mr Alexander?'

'No, certainly not. It was merely my comment upon the state of the blank verse stage.'

'As a matter of fact, did you mention their names at all?'

'They were suggested to me by the interviewer, who said "Do your remarks apply to Irving, Tree and Alexander?" and I said "Yes, all living actors who deal with blank verse." '

Gilbert's cross-examination was conducted by Edward Carson, who thus had the honour of publicly sparring with two of the three greatest wits of that age. Oscar Wilde had won the word-combat between them, but was defeated by the evidence, and now Gilbert was about to score off him with every hit. Fortunately for his reputation he never had to cross swords with Bernard Shaw, who would have made mincemeat of him. The verbal duel now to be reported was as amusing as any duologue in the Savoy libretti, but the continued laughter aroused by Gilbert's rejoinders probably disposed the judge in the defendant's favour.

'You don't like reading hostile criticism?' asked Carson.

'I have a horror of reading criticism at all, either good or bad.' He admitted to a preference for reading unfavourable criticism: 'I know how good I am, but I do *not* know how bad I am.' (*Laughter.*)

After quoting a number of unpleasant notices of *The Fortune Hunter*, Carson said: 'You would admit that that is a formidable list of hostile criticism?'

'Distinctly I am quite prepared to admit that the play is a very bad play.' (*Laughter*.) 'A play that fails is for all practical purposes a bad play.'

'Did you observe from the public press that a short time afterwards Sir Henry Irving, at a dinner of the Sheffield Press Club, spoke good-humouredly but warmly about the criticisms upon himself?'

'I do not admit that he spoke good-humouredly but warmly. I noticed that he spoke most angrily and most spitefully concerning me. He described me as a librettist who soared to write original comedy.'

'You were not angry with Sir Henry Irving?'

'I was most angry at that coming from a gentleman whom I have never given any occasion for such an utterance.'

'Do you think that Sir Henry Irving spoke angrily?'

'I am sure he did.'

'And spitefully?'

'Most spitefully. I cannot conceive why he did so. I have never had an angry word with him, and I cannot conceive why he should be so spiteful.'

'Did you read what he said?'

'I read a report of it. I do not know whether it is accurate or not.'

'You say, sir, that you consider that Sir Henry Irving was angry at what appeared to be your opinion expressed to the interviewer. Did you ever write to the paper to contradict it or withdraw any single sentence of the offensive statement put forward about English actors?'

'No. I wrote to Sir Henry's secretary, and as I see him in court he may have the letter about him.'

'Don't you think it would have been only fair to have written and publicly withdrawn them in the press?'

'The matter was in my solicitor's hands and this action had been begun.'

Gilbert said that he had written to Tree and Alexander telling them that he had been misreported and that his remarks had only applied to the delivery of blank verse. Asked by Carson to signify the direction of current dramatic taste, he said:

'In the direction of musical comedy; bad musical comedy, in which half-a-dozen irresponsible comedians are turned loose on the stage to do as they please.'

'Will you mention one of them?'

'Oh, there are plenty of them!'

'I wish you would mention one.'

'Well, take the pantomime at Drury Lane Theatre with the great Dan Leno.' (*Loud laughter.*)

'But that only goes on a short time in the year.'

'It goes on for a long time in the evening.' (*Laughter.*)

'Do you really describe a pantomime as a bad musical comedy?'

'No, but I would describe a bad musical comedy as a pantomime.' (*Great laughter.*)

'That is very clever', said Carson when silence was restored. 'But I would like to know what you mean by bad musical comedies. Give me the name of one.'

'There are fifty of them.'

'Give me one.'

'I would say such a piece as *The Circus Girl.*'

'Would you call it a bad musical comedy?'

'I would call it bad. I believe the manager calls it musical comedy.' (*Laughter.*)

'Have they half-a-dozen irresponsible low comedians turned loose in *The Circus Girl*?'

'I do not know how many there are.' (*Laughter.*) 'Then there are musical comedies that have been played at the Gaiety. I do not know their names, but there is *The Shop Girl* and there is *The Bar Girl* I think.' (*Loud laughter.*)

'You mean the actors in these are irresponsible low comedians?'

'Not all of them. Certain of them are, as in the plays produced by Mr Arthur Roberts at the Lyric, where he says and does what he pleases.'

'He is an irresponsible comedian?'

'Certainly. Most irresponsible.' (*Loud laughter.*) 'And most amusing.' (*Laughter.*)

Gilbert refused to admit that a character in his *Rosencrantz and Guildenstern* expressed his own views on critics: 'I do not hold myself responsible for all the sentiments expressed by all my characters.' He said that as the critics did not discriminate between original plays and translations, there were fewer original plays on the stage. When at school he had translated the Greek dramatists, but had never claimed to be the author of their plays:

'I have always given Sophocles the credit for his share of the work in them.' (*Laughter.*) 'I once translated a French play, sitting up all night to do it, and I got £3000 out of it.'

'That was better than the bar?' remarked Carson.

'It is better than my experience of it.' (*Laughter.*)

'There is a passage here', Carson flourished a copy of *The Era*,

'in which you are described as Gilbert the Great, to which you take
exception?'

'Yes, I do not feel that I deserve the compliment.' (*Laughter.*)

Having failed to corner the plaintiff on those lines, Carson
tried to get an admission that he was quarrelsome. Gilbert
denied it. Was he not extremely touchy and quick-tempered?
No. Well, to take an instance, had he not quarrelled with
Clement Scott?

'Yes, I wrote to Clement Scott nine years ago complaining of a
criticism.'

'You said "I am determined not to expose myself again to your
insulting gibes"?'

'Yes, no doubt I wrote that.'

'You were cool and calm?'

'Yes, calm and deliberate. I don't know my temperature at the
time.' (*Prolonged laughter.*)

A further question elicited from Gilbert that he had brought
a law-suit against Horace Sedger, who had presented *The
Mountebanks*, but he refused to admit that he had quarrelled
with him:

'You were friendly with him afterwards?'

'I was not friendly with him before.' (*Laughter.*)

'Did you fall out with Mr John Hare at the Garrick?'

'I am not on terms with John Hare just now because he chose to
quarrel with me over the manner in which I referred to his action
in transferring the lease of the Garrick Theatre, which belongs
to me, to a syndicate formed to exhibit a music-hall dwarf.'

'It was all his fault?'

'There was no fault on either side.' (*Laughter.*)

'What damages do you expect for being called a Grand Llama?'

'I am not seeking heavy damages. I am bringing the action on
the article as a whole.'

Carson took his revenge for all the laughter of which he had
been the unwilling instrument in his speech for the defence,
when he commented so unfavourably on the plaintiff's character that Gilbert, unable to hit back, stormed from the court.
The judge's summing-up contained a sentence ('the plaintiff,
while objecting to criticism, had not been sparing in his own
criticisms of others') which had nothing to do with the case.
Even so the jury took two and a half hours to conclude that

they could not agree, which meant that each side had to pay its own costs. Gilbert gave his opinion of the case to Maud Tree in a letter sent from Sorrento on April 12th, 1898:

I have not worried myself at all about the trial. I resolved not to look at a newspaper, and, in short, I determined to clear my mind of it altogether. After all, I have done what I wanted to do. I was charged with having made an unworthy and malicious attack upon a body of men, many of whom I hold in high regard, and it was (as it seemed to me) incumbent upon me to refute the charge. The only way of doing this was to bring an action. The case would have been mine but for the judge who was simply a monument of senile incapacity. To the very last he hadn't the faintest notion as to what the trial was about. My case was comparatively trivial, but it is fearful to think that grave issues in which a man's fortune or a woman's honour may be involved, are at the mercy of an utterly incompetent old doll. Lawson Walton conducted my case with admirable dignity and restraint – Carson conducted his in the spirit of a low-class police court attorney. But I believe he did me no harm. I was particularly impressed with your husband's kindness in trying to make peace. As one of the men whom I was represented as having pointed at, it showed no little magnanimity on his part and one does not forget such things . . . I am not at all surprised to find that the Press strongly disapproves of actions for libel against newspapers.

Clearly Gilbert was not in a mood to endorse the opinion of the Lord Chancellor in *Iolanthe*:

> *The Law is the true embodiment*
> *Of everything that's excellent.*

CHAPTER 17

Talk and Travel

❦❦❦

Most people talk much and say nothing. Gilbert usually said something when he talked. But he was not in the ordinary sense a talkative man. He never monopolized the conversation, scarcely ever held forth at length on any topic, and seldom spoke for more than a minute at a time. He is chiefly remembered for short, snappy comments, and his contributions to club or table discussions were usually in the form of apothegms. He rather enjoyed inventing surprise endings to his brief anecdotes or descriptions. Once he spoke gravely about the virtues of a certain man whom he called a devoted husband, a model father, a loyal friend, honest, generous, just. 'I never knew such a paragon!' he concluded. Everyone was deeply impressed and murmured appreciation. 'I never knew such a paragon', he repeated reflectively, adding as an afterthought, 'and no one else ever did.' Another fellow was portrayed by him in affecting terms as a pattern of social charm, hospitality, sympathy and nobility of nature: 'But there was a slight flaw in his character which even his most attached friends regretted – he poisoned his mother and strangled his wife.' Such trifles were retailed in solemn tones, strengthened by dramatic pauses, and finished emphatically with a humorous eye-twinkle that his listeners found irresistible.

There is evidence that he occasionally held forth at length. P. G. Wodehouse once explained why butlers as a class were gloomy, one reason being that 'so many of their employers were sparkling raconteurs'. They were compelled to hear again and again the same old story told in the same old way, with baleful effect on their constitutions. In his youth P.G. had been taken to lunch at Grim's Dyke. Half-way through the meal Gilbert started to tell the sort of yarn that begins dully and ends brightly. Unfortunately the youngster, who did not think the anecdote a bit funny but knew it must be because of the teller's reputation, mistook a pause in the narrative for the moment when the joke had been reached, and discharged a hearty resounding laugh. The other guests seemed a bit puzzled, 'as if they had expected something better from the author of *The Mikado*', but in duty bound made mirthful murmurs and then drifted into general conversation.

It was at this point that I caught my host's eye [said P.G.]. I shall always remember the glare of pure hatred which I saw in it. If you have seen photographs of Gilbert, you will be aware that even in repose his face was inclined to be formidable and his eye not the sort of eye you would willingly catch. And now his face was far from being in repose. His eyes, beneath their beetling brows, seared me like a flame. In order to get away from them, I averted my gaze and found myself encountering that of the butler. His eyes were shining with a dog-like devotion . . . I had made his day . . . I suppose he had heard that story rumble to its conclusion at least twenty times, probably more, and I had killed it.

Such occasions apart, Gilbert's comedic gift was expressed in sardonic sallies, in repartees, in acid observations on people and things, of which a few specimens must be given.

At a public dinner Edmund Yates, editor of *The World*, usually a garrulous man, was noticeably quiet. 'What's the matter with him? Why this religious silence?' asked someone. 'He's probably thinking of the next "World" ', said Gilbert. Known to lack sympathy with the clergy as a class, the dramatist was asked whether he felt out of place in a company that included a number of divines. 'Yes, I feel like a lion in a den of Daniels', he replied. His experience of doctors was also unfortunate, and on hearing that a friend's son was going into medicine he remarked: 'I don't mind his going into medicine so long as his medicine doesn't go into me.' He disliked being fussed over, and when a woman exclaimed 'Oh, do take care! there's a wasp on your sleeve – it'll sting you', he reassured her: 'I have no great opinion of the intellect of the insect, but it is not such a fool as to take me for a flower.' Though he enjoyed good food, he was no epicure: 'My cook gets eighty pounds a year and gives me a kipper; Sullivan's cook gets five hundred pounds a year for giving him the same thing in French.' Occasionally he would indulge in a pun, but only if he thought it good. Apologizing for not having visited a female friend on account of a threatened attack of pneumonia, he said: 'It is well to be off with the old love before you are on with the pneumonia – same applies to neuralgia and neuritis.'

Perhaps his keenest sarcasms were reserved for plays and players. He thought poorly of nearly all his playwright contemporaries, and hearing that the next play by one of them, Henry Arthur Jones, was to be entitled *The Princess's Nose* he grunted, 'Hope it'll run.' In a letter to Maud Tree he gave vent to his feelings on the subject of Jones's *The Tempter*, a blank verse play produced by her husband in 1893. 'Blanker verse I never heard', he wrote, calling the piece

> gross and damnable – its literature, the literature of the servants' hall. 'Thou dost not love me as thou used to do'!!! 'Thou used'! Oh merciful father that stayest thy hand though thy rebellious children deserve the blow, save and protect us from this plague of Jones (which we have nevertheless rightly incurred for our many backslidings) through the merits of thy beloved Son, Jesus Christ, Amen. This is a form of prayer to be used in all Churches and Chapels throughout the United Kingdom and in the town of Berwick upon Tweed. 'Thou dost not love me as thou used to do'! It is as true in fact as it is false in grammar. *'Thou used'*!!! Farewell, I can no more!

For the sake of Maud Tree he went to all her husband's productions, first at the Haymarket and then at Her Majesty's Theatres. But he never said a word about Beerbohm Tree's acting, only praising his appearance in *Trilby* ('Svengali's make-up is marvellous – we could *smell* him') and his production of *King John*: 'The play is not one that I passionately adore, but the pill is so handsomely gilded that everyone will swallow it. The stage-management is superb. I had to go before the last act, as "I had a train to catch, O!".'

Some of his concise summaries of popular pieces in the first decade of the twentieth century appeared in a diary which he commenced at the beginning of 1905. He thought Barrie's *Peter Pan* feeble and silly; Shaw's *John Bull's Other Island* bizarre, sometimes amusing, but on the whole boring; *The Scarlet Pimpernel* just stupid; *When Knights Were Bold* 'banale'; and *Raffles* 'rot'. On the other hand he considered Pinero's *His House in Order* excellent. One of his judgments is curious and self-revelatory. Alfred Sutro's *John Glayde's Honour*, produced at the St James's Theatre by George Alexander in March 1907, was in Gilbert's opinion very well written but immoral, particularly the end. Glayde is a business magnate who has neglected his wife for twelve years while making money. She falls in love with an artist. Having made all the money he wants, Glayde returns, expects his wife to renew their relationship as if nothing had happened to cool her affections in the meantime, and orders the artist never to see her again. To allay Glayde's suspicions at a crucial moment, his wife lies to him, tells him that their life together will begin afresh, kisses him, and then escapes to the artist. Glayde follows her, and on finding that her passion for the other transcends what he calls her honesty, her truth and her shame, he leaves them together, saying to the artist: 'Take her, and help her – to lie and betray no more.' The end can only be called immoral on the assumption that it is moral for a man to neglect his wife and yet demand her love and fidelity. The piece was considered daringly modern by audiences at the St James's, but the audiences of the Court Theatre, recently weaned on the plays of Shaw, would have thought it hopelessly antiquated. The moral fog of Victorianism had lessened to a mist in the time of Edward VII, and Sutro, a typical Edwardian, was in a haze of uncertainty over right and wrong. His play is neither moral nor immoral; it is merely foolish; and Gilbert's attitude shows that in matters of sex he remained a true Victorian to the end of his days.

His flirtations were as innocent as his moral standards were strict, and in the multitude of loved ones there was safety, but he liked to hint darkly at possibilities. 'I am in love with most of the lady passengers', he wrote during a sea-trip to the Mediterranean, and at the age of sixty-six he said that he felt 'so safe and (involuntarily) good' because there was not 'the remotest chance of being a snake on another man's hearth'. Declining an invitation to a concert for the benefit of the Soldiers' Daughters Home, he confessed that he would like to see one of the soldiers' daughters home after the concert. 'When you go into someone else's bedroom in a hotel', he advised a friend, 'be sure it's the bedroom you want. I always do.' And in a letter to Maud Tree he criticized one of her husband's pieces thus:

Why does Magdalena love the King? He hasn't a redeeming quality. He is a base tyrant of the meanest type. Is it because he shows himself to her in his pyjamas? If I showed myself to ladies

in *my* pyjamas could I hope for such a result? If I thought I could
– but no – that way madness lies.

The pleasure of travelling abroad was heightened by the
pretty women to be met on steamers and in hotels. The Gilberts
made many excursions when there was no more need to furnish
libretti for the Savoy. They went by sea to Naples and other
Mediterranean ports, and in 1898 they visited the Crimea
which he found extremely interesting, having made a close
study of the campaign for which he had once volunteered.

There is a seaside resort, Yalta, which is one of the loveliest
places I ever saw [he wrote]. We had magnificent weather all the
way both out and home. Wherever we went we found a wet day
had just preceded us – in fact, we were chivying a wet day all
round the Mediterranean and all round the Black Sea. We caught
it up at last at Algiers, where it *did* rain. The ship was full of fubsy
old ladies and gouty old gentlemen – I called them 'The Old Curiosity Shop', which annoyed the old guys, who wanted to know
what I called myself. However, I never spent a more blameless
six weeks.

Towards the close of 1900 he went to Egypt to try a cure for
rheumatoid arthritis, and while there wrote two letters to a
friend, Mary Talbot, whom he called 'Cousin Mary' because
her mother was American. Both letters were sent from the
Grand Hotel, Helonass, Cairo, and they present an aspect of
his nature which is pleasantly at variance with that to which
some of his stage contemporaries were accustomed:

Dec. 30, 1900

My dear Cousin Mary,
     In the first place, let me tell you that I am writing under three
serious disabilities. Morning service is proceeding in the room
beneath me, and I cannot collect my ideas when Gregorian chants
are going on (I suppose it is the inherent piety of my nature which
asserts itself in spite of myself). Then a gale of wind is blowing my
paper about (I am writing in the open air); and lastly I am tor-
mented by a plague of flies, which settle on my face and hands
and will not be denied. I am sorry to say I cannot give a good
account of myself. I am just as great a cripple as when I left England. We have had an unprecedented amount of rain, five wet days
last week, and I have serious thoughts of starting for Margate,
which is drier, cheaper, and more bracing than this place. People
here say that they have never known so much rain to fall in

Helouan – as much fell last Sunday as in the whole of last year. I really have no luck. I have not left the hotel except to be wheeled to the sulphur-baths, which are rotten-eggy and do not seem to do me the slightest good. I am afraid I must reconcile myself to the prospect of being a cripple for life. In fact, the doctor here told me that he very much doubted if I should ever recover the use of my limbs. However, I'm not going to howl about it. I know, from your example, how delightful one may be despite a drawback of that nature, and how much enjoyment may be drawn from one's life under such conditions. But I should like to be able to wash the back of my neck. It is not a lofty aspiration, but at present it is the goal of my ambitions.

I am always your affectionate
Cousin Bill

Feb. 18, 1901

My dear Cousin Mary,

We had a frightfully narrow escape from destruction last Thursday. We all went by train to Cairo (my first excursion from the hotel) and when within about six miles of our destination the engine ran off the rails and tumbled down a steep embankment, dragging a third-class carriage with it and leaving our carriage half on and half off the embankment. We were in a long saloon carriage, and we felt a terrific bump which sent us flying forward half the length of the carriage on our faces. This was succeeded by a dozen more bumps of greater force, and we were all tossed about the carriage like parched peas in a drum. The engine, we found, was on its side alongside our carriage, and vomiting steam in great volumes. I was quite helpless, being unable to get up owing to my knees, and we expected the carriage to roll on to the engine, when I should certainly have been boiled alive in the steam. However, the carriage remained on the slope, and Nancy, by a tremendous effort, managed to get me on to my legs (my wife and she having got out in safety), and I also managed to descend. My wife had a bad bruise on the knee, and I had a very bad graze on the shin, with a bruise ten inches long and six wide – so that I am more of a cripple than ever. Seven people were killed and about twenty wounded – nearly all the occupants of the third-class carriage near the engine. Nancy was most plucky. She got up into the carriage again, collected all our traps, and finding that my hat had been shot through the window near the engine (on the further side from where we were) she clambered down and rescued it – seeing a frightfully crushed man nearby, a sight my wife and I happily escaped. Nancy then set off in the boiling sun to walk two and a half miles to old Cairo to get a carriage. She succeeded in this (after

having been hustled by a crowd of low-class Arabs) and returned
to the scene of the accident. I shall never forget the shrieks of the
wounded and dying, and we saw some awful sights into the bargain. We are none of us materially the worse for our adventure.
Both ladies behaved with extraordinary pluck and self-possession.
My wife's knee is practically well. It's extraordinary that, chucked
about as I was, my knees were never touched.

Always your affectionate
Cousin Bill

Occasionally Gilbert went for a short cruise without his wife,
and in August 1903 he accepted an invitation with a number of
other well-known people to make a trial trip on a new boat.
Meanwhile his wife travelled by their latest motor-car to visit
friends on the south coast. She was staying at the Sackville
Hotel, Bexhill-on-Sea, when this arrived:

Off Cowes
Sunday aft.

Dearest Kitty

Here we are after a very pleasant afternoon yesterday and a
bright but blowy morning today. The weather was so bad yesterday that we anchored in Margate Roads – having heard from a
passing vessel that there was a bad gale in the Channel. The
weather having moderated during the night, we got under way at
4.30 this morning and have crept down to the Needles against a
strong head wind – then we went about and are now on our way to
Southampton Water where we bring up for the night, leaving tomorrow (Monday) morning for the Thames. The weather, which
was fine but cold this morning, is now raw and overcast, but so far
without rain. As a cruise it has been a failure, but there are a
number of very pleasant people on board as you will see from the
enclosed list. Fildes, Burnand, Pinero, Dicey, Bancroft, Duke of
Abercorn, Sir Owen Burns and many others – in all about 120.
Gilbert Parker was to have come, but he has not turned up. Everything is extremely lavish – excellent meals and good cabins. The
ship is magnificent – the finest I ever was on – and they are building three others like her: Langbourne is to have one of them.

I am very anxious to know that you reached Bexhill safely and
that you fell into no police traps. We passed Bexhill at 9.30 this
morning – I tried to make you out at breakfast, but as you were
three miles off I didn't succeed, though I made out the hotel. I
hope you had no sideslips and that the rain kept off. Today I
expect you are off to Winchelsea and Rye and I wish I was with
you – it is really too raw and chilly for enjoyment on board. Give

my love to Nancy. I am looking forward to meeting you both at Crawley – and also to receiving a letter tomorrow morning.

With best love
Always affectionately your
Old Boy

Gone were the days when they had roughed it in a yawl and were looked after by a cook who waited on them at table in shirt-sleeves and no collar and was under the impression that 'the more you water gravy, the more gravy you get'. Now they did things in style, travelled in luxury steamers and stayed in expensive hotels. But in September 1905, on a holiday in the Italian Lakes, they were prevented from putting up at the most palatial establishment by the odd conduct of the manager, called by Gilbert 'the Belle Vue beast', who regretted that there was no accommodation for them, though they had booked rooms in advance. Upon enquiry, they discovered that Henry Labouchere, part proprietor of the place, was staying there. Gilbert considered the matter carefully and reached a conclusion:

> I never could understand his hostility (except that he is the avowed enemy of the whole human race) until I remembered that thirty-seven years ago I introduced him to the woman who is now his wife. I admit that, quite unwittingly, I did him an irreparable injury, and am disposed to regard his hostility in some measure justified.

This final fling would have amused Labby, but his wife Henrietta might have felt that Gilbert was still persecuting her.

CHAPTER 18

The Zoo and the Bench

❧❧❧

A French politician, Cardinal Richelieu, seems to have known more about human nature than an English professor, Sir Arthur Quiller-Couch. In the Cardinal's anteroom were two groups of pictures: those on one side depicted scenes of blood and violence, death in battle, assassination, torture; those on the other exhibited tranquil incidents of hearth and home, lovers' meetings, old folks' reveries, green meadows, blossoming trees, cows meditating, cats basking. The man who applied for a job was shown into this room and the Cardinal watched him through an eye-hole. If the fellow showed keen interest in the brutal episodes, he was classified as a timid peaceful soul for whom ruthless action was romantically fascinating and earmarked for a clerkly job; but if he remained rapt before the domestic sentimental scenes, his nature was instantly diagnosed as adventurous, pugnacious and pitiless, and thenceforth he was destined for disastrous chances, distressful strokes, and 'hairbreadth scapes i' the imminent deadly breach'. Quiller-Couch on the other hand noticed the amusement Gilbert extracted from fanciful savagery in *The Bab Ballads*, *The Mikado* and elsewhere, and deduced therefrom that he was 'thoroughly caddish . . . essentially cruel and delighted in cruelty'. Such moral judgments flowed easily from many Victorians and suggest that they were condemning something within themselves. Gilbert's form of amusement really proved that he was a tender-hearted compassionate creature who would not have harmed a fly. Cruelty is inherent in human nature, taking all sorts of forms, from the torture of human beings to the slaughter of animals, from idealistic rancour to malicious gossip. Whatever the form, it signifies a desire for power, and in Gilbert's case it was released in fiction and in wit. The physically cruel man, being insensitive and unimaginative, never indulges in sanguinary daydreams: he expresses his nature in action and recreatively wallows in sentiment. Gilbert's fictional sentiment was the obverse of his fanciful ferocity; but in real life he was essentially humane, his ebullitions of harshness deriving from a hasty temper aggravated by gout, an inability to perceive the true bent of his genius, and two features of his nature that may be traced to the conditions of his youth: an over-acute sense of hostility in others and an awkwardness with the outside world.

Apart from these distracting elements, he was a keenly sympathetic man, quickly relenting and apologizing when in the heat of the moment he had spoken unfairly to people and upset them. Uncomfortable with so many human beings, his deeply affectionate nature manifested itself with children and animals. He seemed to understand children intuitively and enjoyed playing childish games with them more than serious games with adults. He adored animals and hated blood-sports. 'Deer-stalking would be a very fine sport if only the deer had guns', he said, and when told that a fox enjoyed being chased by hounds he demurred: 'I should like to hear the fox on that point. The time will no doubt come when the "sport" of the present day will be regarded very much as we regard the Spanish bull-fight or the bear-baiting of our ancestors.' In his play *Gretchen* he put these lines into the mouth of Faust, who is seeking sanctuary in a monastery –

> As a poor, worried, over-hunted fox,
> Cursing his persecutors, runs to earth
> To lick his bleeding flanks in sulky peace,
> And brood, in solitude, on men and dogs!

His personal attitude was summed up without hypocrisy:

I have a constitutional objection to taking life in any form. I don't think I ever wittingly killed a black-beetle. It is not humanity on my part. I am perfectly willing that other people should kill things for my comfort and advantage. But the mechanism of life is so wonderful that I shrink from stopping its action. To tread on a black-beetle would be to me like crushing a watch of complex and exquisite workmanship.

There is an old story that a near neighbour at Grim's Dyke, Thomas Blackwell, whose firm was famous for their jams and other preserves, once complained that Gilbert's workmen had damaged something in his grounds. Gilbert, who was probably responsible for the story, replied: 'I am exceedingly sorry that my men should have damaged anything in your preserves. Pardon the word "preserves".' More to the present point, Gilbert certainly wrote the following letter to Blackwell shortly after settling at Grim's Dyke:

19 April, 1891

My dear Sir

Yesterday evening your keeper accosted my butler (who was shooting rabbits with my permission) and in very angry and boisterous tones complained that my dogs continually trespassed on your land, and threatened to do them an injury if ever he found them there again.

It is no doubt true that on a few occasions two of my dogs have wandered out of bounds, partly owing to the place being new to them and partly to the ruinous condition in which Mr Heriot left the fences. These fences I am having repaired and renewed whereever necessary in order that you may not be annoyed by my dogs – but that is of course not to be done in a day.

With respect to your keeper's threat, I feel sure that it has not your sanction. It is sometimes as difficult to teach a dog to respect a boundary line as it is to teach a pheasant to do so, and I am convinced that you would be as little likely to approve of your keeper shooting any dog of mine who may happen to stray on your land as I should be to shoot any of your pheasants that may happen to come over mine. I may state that as I do not breed pheasants I allow nothing to be shot but rabbits with which this place is infested.

I am, faithfully yours,
W. S. Gilbert

He was soon on friendly terms with Blackwell, which was fortunate because his estate became a sort of zoological gardens and the jam manufacturer's men might have shot all sorts of strange birds and beasts in the belief that they were upsetting the pheasants. In his idyllic oasis of lawns, flowers, trees, bracken, rhododendrons, fruit-gardens, ferns and bee-hives, he had made a lake of one and a half acres, and the whole place was a sanctuary for birds and animals, many of which were quite at home in his house as well. Dogs and cats had their baskets and stools for day-time naps; they dined with the family, each having its table-cloth on the floor. The Pekinese had their toys, taking them upstairs to bed and bringing them down every morning in their mouths. The French poodle scorned such trifles. One of the Pekes was responsible for the capture of a burglar by barking continuously outside a room on the top floor. A maid went in and a man rushed out. Sprinting for the nearest exit he barged into the butler and was successfully engaging with a footman as well when the gardener appeared. A three-to-one scuffle took place within hearing of the drawing-room where a female visitor was singing 'Oh, for the wings of a dove!' The sportsman being secured, and the movements of his limbs restricted by rope, Gilbert enjoyed a talk with him about burgling in general and his case in particular, the man admitting that if it had not been for the little dog they would never have caught him. When the police arrived Gilbert sent the prisoner off in a motor-car, saying he must be very much exhausted after the struggle. Incidentally, Gilbert's wife kept a truncheon by her bedside at night to ward off such intruders.

The residents at Grim's Dyke included two blue Persian cats, who disclosed a taste for envelopes, which were rolled into balls for their amusement, the sight of a letter inducing them to sit up and beg for the envelope. The female cat liked singing and climbed a chair to get near the sound, rubbing her cheek against the singer when possible. She permitted no fighting between the other residents and one day rushed at a collie dog that was attacking a Scotch terrier, which surprised them so much that they both fled, though it took the collie some time to detach her from his tail.

Gilbert's library was a favourite meeting-place of the animals. They went in and out through a wide French window, always open. But one of them became a little troublesome. He had a pet fawn, a fallow deer, that used to accompany him through the grounds, putting her nose into his hand and walking by his side. She became friendly with a donkey named Adelina (Patti), so called on account of a high voice. They went for walks together about the lanes, until the fawn discovered that the donkey could not follow her over fences and hedges, when she began to perambulate the countryside alone, visiting neighbouring estates and treating the food she found thereon as her own. Gilbert had to pay a lot in fines, tips and telegrams, because of this habit. At length she found her way to his library, which she entered so frequently, four times one afternoon, that he decided to send her away. She was taken to

Bentley Priory nearby, where she soon made friends with the other deer in the park. A year afterwards Gilbert was walking through the park, and seeing a herd of deer in the distance he gave the peculiar whistle with which he used to call her. Although a long way off, she instantly detached herself from the herd, came bounding towards him, put her nose in his hand, and kept by his side until he left the place. Four years later, tiring of herd-life, she found her way back to his library.

For several years he kept a number of monkeys, building a large house for them. But his favourites were a pair of lemurs, one of which started with a dislike of cigar-smoke, snatching a cigar out of his mouth and throwing it to the ground, but gradually acquired a taste for it and sitting on his shoulder would try to catch the whiffs. When free they would sometimes enter the dining-room and eat the nectarines and bananas or invade the strawberry beds. They were often liberated and it usually took several hours to capture them. On September 26th, 1905, Gilbert reported

a most interesting occurrence in our household. A baby, quite unexpectedly, has been born – to whom do you think? – to our two lemurs! It is the rarest possible thing for ring-tailed lemurs to breed in captivity. The Sec. to the Zoological Gardens . . . tells me that such a thing has not happened since 1881.

He noted the birthdays of 'Paul' in his diary, wherein all the deaths of his pets were mentioned, 'Paul's' being recorded on August 23rd, 1908, aged two years, ten months and twenty-eight days. If any animal appeared to be ill, he sent for a vet at once.

Throughout his life Gilbert never killed an animal, a bird, a fish or an insect. The pheasants in the neighbourhood soon got to know that the grounds of Grim's Dyke were an Alsatia and swarmed all over a place unviolated by sportsmen. The air was full of the song of birds, or, to quote an invitation he once issued, 'the gooseberry bushes are thickly hung with stomach aches; and while the cuckoo delights by day, the nightingale and the screech owl do their best to make night lovely'. Although it was sometimes necessary to exterminate pests, he never allowed his gardeners to kill a squirrel, the animal being endeared to him because it gave the name to the ten-ton vessel in which his adopted ancestor Sir Humphrey Gilbert, stepbrother of Sir Walter Raleigh, was drowned off the Azores in

1583 while on a third voyage to Newfoundland with the object of discovering the North-West Passage. The crest of W. S. Gilbert was a squirrel.

Residence at Grim's Dyke was not restricted to animals. The fan-tail pigeons occasionally hopped into the library to see what they could pick up, being partial to cigar-ends, and when he smoked out of doors several of them would sit on his shoulder and peck at his cigar. Once half a dozen turkeys, bored with the farmyard, strolled through the French windows and took up their positions on chairs, tables and desk. Gilbert's arrival caused their tumultuous departure with some damage to the ornaments in the room. At one time he formed an intimacy with a robin, which came to him from any distance within call, fed from his hand, and perched twittering on his head as he moved about the garden. While staying in London he paid several visits to his country home in order to see that the robin's meals were not forgotten. Siberian cranes occasionally stalked into the library, though their presence was not encouraged. A piping bullfinch which he had given to his wife became very tame, but one morning she noticed that it was nervous and piped dissimilar notes. Later in the day it was tame again and back to its usual musical form. This went on for more than a week, timidity and a different song alternating with friendliness and the old one. She remained in a state of deep perplexity until she found three bullfinches in the library, each closely resembling the other and each in a cage of exactly the same pattern. It was one of her husband's little practical jokes, which he contrived with as much thought and care as he gave to the stage-management of the Savoy operas. The butler had been taken into his confidence, and one cage was substituted for another with a different bird at regular intervals. For ten days he kept up the mystery, to his amusement and her amazement.

He liked parrots, one of which whistled tunes correctly, spoke long sentences, simulated the asthmatical cough of a previous owner, whose Irish stew was its favourite dish, and died at the age of 63. Another parrot, seeing so many ladies dressed for dinner, conformed with the fashion by pulling its feathers out. It sang a drunken song, followed by ribald laughter, an accomplishment acquired in earlier life. The parrots were often at large and usually enticed back to their cages with difficulty.

Some insects received a warm welcome at Grim's Dyke. One autumn a bee appeared in the library and seemed disposed to stay there. Gilbert called it 'Buzfuz' and fed it on moistened sugar. Though the windows were never closed, it preferred the sugar to the flowers outside, and to save it the inconvenience of the early morning dusting and cleaning a bed was provided in the form of a box. Occasionally it disappeared among the curtains, but it always returned for sugar and remained happily quiescent through the night in the safety of its cubicle.

Gilbert was not content with the peace and order of his private domain. Finding that Harrow Weald Common nearby was infested with all sorts of undesirable characters, poachers, footpads, vagrants, who molested respectable people, strewed the place with refuse, and sometimes set fire to the gorse, he took counsel with his neighbours, Thomas Blackwell at The Cedars, F. Gordon at Bentley Priory, and others. They empowered him to approach the Board of Agriculture on the subject. Their application was successful and a Board of Conservators was appointed, Gilbert and his neighbours guaranteeing £75 a year towards expenses. It is perhaps needless to say that Gilbert maintained a lengthy correspondence with the Board, which became acrimonious when they appointed a keeper to the Common. He threatened them with a cancellation of the subscription unless the guarantors had some say in the choice of the keeper. Eventually they caved in, and the Common was saved from the mismanagement of a public body as it had previously been saved from the depredations of ruffians.

The qualities of perseverance and obstinacy were highly developed in Gilbert. Once he had made up his mind that something was wrong, he worked unsparingly to make it right. His experiences in the theatre testify to this, and a single case in the province of public charity may be adduced in evidence. He discovered that the Hon. Secretary to the National Blind Relief Society, a clergyman named Pullein Thompson, was applying the funds in a peculiar manner. Gilbert collected full details of their disposal and carried the matter through with the persistence of a man who has nothing else to do, consulting solicitors, writing letters, interviewing everybody concerned, and eventually seeing the Bishop of London, who had described his conduct in questioning Thompson's veracity as 'suspicion run mad'. Votes of confidence in the reverend gentleman's uprightness did not deter Gilbert, who spent months proving his point and at length issued a pamphlet, privately printed for the information of the Charity Organization Society and entitled: 'My Case against the Rev. J. Pullein Thompson, Vicar of Christ Church, Chelsea, and Hon. Secretary to the National Blind Relief Society.' This was a form of unacknowledged public-spiritedness that made no appeal to those who advertised themselves as displaying a similar virtue.

But his ability in a recognized sphere of public work was widely acknowledged. In 1893 he was appointed a Justice of the Peace for the division of Gore in the county of Middlesex, after the following preliminaries: 'You have, I believe, studied the law as a barrister and have a sound knowledge of it?' queried the High Sheriff. 'That is so, but I hope you will not consider it an impediment', returned Gilbert. For the rest of his life he attended the first or second court at Edgware, usually presiding over the second, twice a week when in England, and from the late part of 1910 he divided his time equally between the Wealdstone and Edgware courts.

As a magistrate he combined sternness with kindness. Cases of poverty often moved him to pay the fines of those who would otherwise have gone to prison; but cases of cruelty were punished to the utmost of his jurisdiction. 'You'll do that sentence, notwithstanding the Home Secretary', he said to one delinquent of the latter class. He placed as much faith in the word of a civilian as in that of a policeman, which gave him the undeserved reputation of being hostile to the force, and he did not always see eye-to-eye with his fellow-justices. On May 27th, 1909, he wrote to the chairman of the bench, Irwin E. B. Cox: 'As I told you in court on Tuesday, I wholly disagree with the sentence that you passed on the man who was charged with assault, with threats, of a solicitor who had engaged against him in a previous case.' After giving reasons for his disagreement, he finished up:

I am sorry that I did not dissociate myself from your judgment at the time – but, in future, when I happen to be sitting with you, I must ask you to give full value to any arguments I may use that may be in opposition to your judgment, as I shall certainly take the course of publicly disclaiming concurrence with your decision.

He paid the fine and costs of the case privately to save the man from a month's imprisonment; and when another magistrate got to hear of this and complained, he asserted his sense of justice in a long letter.

The question of perjury constantly bothered him and he wrote to the Home Secretary about the oath taken by witnesses in petty sessional courts. He said that in the form of oath supplied to magistrates by the Justice Clerks' Association the adjuration 'So help me God' was omitted, and he wished to see it included as prosecutions for perjury might otherwise break down. The subject brought him into conflict with another magistrate who did not share his sense of public responsibility. A betting case was brought against the licensee of a public house, and as the verdict of the bench was sure to be followed by an action for perjury against the defendant one of the justices disagreed with the rest solely because he could not be bothered to go on with the case. Gilbert wrote a stern note to this easy-going fellow, concluding: 'It would be better for both parties that we should not sit together in the second court when that association can be avoided.' The case went to the Public Prosecutor, Sir Charles Mathews, who informed Gilbert privately that the magistrate concerned had been seen talking to the defendant during the lunch interval. Gilbert's annoyance with his associate did not affect his honesty and he denied the accusation, saying that the magistrate had lunched with his fellow-justiciaries. He then reported what had happened at his interview with Mathews to the accused magistrate. Mathews discovered what he had done and gravely reprimanded him. Admitting his error, which he said was due to his desire that the magistrate should not think he was acting inimically, Gilbert demanded the withdrawal of the reflection on his honour and good faith implied by the Public Prosecutor's statement that he had acted deliberately and intentionally. Sir Charles at once withdrew the reflection.

Sympathy in another's misfortune is too often a negative virtue. Gilbert implemented his sympathy with action. A man was arrested by a constable for being drunk in charge of a car, and the case came before Gilbert, who investigated it thoroughly and discovered that following a motor accident the man had been taken in a semi-conscious condition to a public house by some passing soldiers, who had revived him with spirits. Unfortunately he was a teetotaller, a drink or two had gone to his head, and when taken back to the car was found in that condition by the policeman. Gilbert wrote to the Chief Commissioner of Police at Scotland Yard, giving the facts and requesting that the charge be withdrawn. It was. Frequently he spent much time finding out the personal history and circumstances of those brought before him, and though compelled to punish certain offences he usually managed to compensate the offenders when they seemed to him more sinned against than sinning. One unhappy fellow who had tried to commit suicide was bound over with a warning: 'If you attempt suicide again, you will be brought before us and punished for both offences, but if you succeed you will be beyond our jurisdiction.' It was by the way an agreeable day for his companions on the bench when they were able to fine Gilbert for an offence under the Dog Muzzling Order. He would have liked to muzzle them instead of his dog.

He was a strict judge of motoring transgressors, though a careful discriminator between technical infractions of the speed limit, then twenty miles an hour, and careless or inconsiderate driving. He inspected the police 'traps' in his district to make sure that they were placed in positions where excessive speed was dangerous; and when the fellows then driving at fifty miles an hour on roads that were not suitable for half that rate were caught in a 'trap' and brought before him, the fines imposed were heavy enough to make them choose another district for fast travelling. One wealthy young man, who gave evidence in a manner that suggested he belonged to a superior breed, was fined five pounds for reckless driving and punished for his vanity: 'Had you been a gentleman, I should have fined you ten.' One June day in 1907 Gilbert had to take fifteen motor cases in his court. On the bench he was severe; but when a correspondent in *The Times* suggested that country dwellers should be allowed to protect themselves against the mechanical pests with a rifle, he made a joke of it and said that the country roads should be dotted at dangerous spots with advertisements: 'Motor shooting for a single gun.'

It was a time when most roads were narrow twisting tracks, when burst tyres were frequent, when pedestrians had not learnt to be conscious of the new form of locomotion, when horses were liable to jump into hedges and ditches at the appearance or noise of the magically moving vehicles, and when the drivers of horse-drawn carriages and wagons left their seats as a car came within sight or sound and covered the heads of their animals until the queer objects had passed out of view and hearing.

Gilbert himself was a keen motorist from the early days. In 1902 he bought an American Locomobile steam-car, and in October had his first accident:

> I made my début by spoiling a parson who came round from under a dead wall on a bicycle. He was pretty badly hurt. The car was turned over at a ditch. I was pitched over the dashboard on to my head (I saw many stars of beautiful colours and was quite sorry when they vanished), and my wife was pitched very comfortably into a hedge, where she looked like a large and quite unaccountable bird's-nest.

On December 21st of the same year he reported two more accidents:

> Yesterday we went to Chesham, lunched there and returned, all in three hours. We seem fated, however, to cause disaster. On Thursday, although we were only creeping on at two miles an hour, we caused a horse, which was driven in a trap by two ladies, to shy up a bank. The trap was all but capsized. One lady was thrown out and run over; the groom was also thrown out, and the trap went over his hand; and the horse then bolted with the other lady, but was eventually stopped without damage. Happily the lady who was run over was not much hurt. She good-humouredly explained it was 'only her legs'. She seemed, from her way of speaking, to have but a poor opinion of those limbs, and Nancy (who saw them) said they were not up to much. The ladies both said it was the horse's fault, as we were going as slowly as a wheelbarrow and showing no steam. Yesterday a tipsy man rushed out from behind a cart and was knocked down by the car. He apologized with drunken profusion of etiquette. This is the third accident we have had, and in each case have been held blameless by the damaged people.

He had been appointed Deputy-Lieutenant of the county of Middlesex, and this office, in addition to his magistracy, made him extremely careful to keep on the right side of the law. Taking no risks, he engaged a 'gentleman-driver' instead of the ordinary chauffeur, instructing him never to exceed the maximum limit of twenty miles an hour on the road. No doubt he also felt that as he would reach the grave soon enough there was no need to hurry while he was here. Thus the chronicle of his accidents is a record of other people's negligence. His Locomobile was followed by a 12 h.p. Napier, which gave place to a 16 h.p. car of the same make. In 1903 he was involved in a collision with a local omnibus, a very full account of which, and of the damage done to his car, was sent to the insurance company. The repairs took a longer time than he thought necessary, and when the car was returned it was not properly cleaned. His complaint was dealt with by S. F. Edge, a famous motor pioneer then connected with the Napier firm, who did not attempt to excuse his staff but frankly admitted that Gilbert knew as much about the business as they did, that he hoped they would profit by his knowledge, that there was no excuse for them, and that the management of the department concerned would be changed. He asked for the return of the car which would be thoroughly cleaned inside and out free of charge. If a sensible businesslike man like Edge had been in charge of the theatres wherein Gilbert's works were performed, there would have been little trouble with the author. But the motor industry was not crowded with good managers, if Gilbert's note to one of them in 1907 is an indication: 'I must press the delivery of the car at Grim's Dyke. If you have your rules, I have also mine, and when I purchase goods I expect to have them delivered to me at my address.'

His next car was a 9 h.p. Cadillac, which he retained after acquiring a 25–35 h.p. Darracq. In April 1909 he decided to have a Rolls-Royce, insisting that the selling firm should allow him £500 for his Darracq. The Rolls-Royce car arrived at the beginning of July, but it failed to give him satisfaction, and in September he demanded the return of the sum he had paid for it: £1399. 11s. Their reply he considered 'childish' and he informed them that 'a contract, duly entered into, cannot be repudiated on the ground that you have "over-looked" its main conditions. I shall perform my share of the contract and hold you strictly to yours.' As a result of some correspondence he agreed that they should put the car in order, but if his driver then found it faulty they must take it back. 'Of course its condition must be permanently satisfactory', he added. Apparently it was, for their correspondence ceased. The only recorded accident in this car occurred on April 9th, 1910, when it knocked down a woman mid-way between Edgware and the Hyde, Hendon. He took her to the Central London Infirmary close at hand and afterwards called to find out how she was. The doctor said that she was doing well and that he did not think her condition serious. On May 6th Gilbert heard that she was still suffering from the effects of the accident, but he refused to admit that even the faintest share of responsibility rested on him or his driver, since 'the accident was caused entirely by her culpable negligence in running from behind a stationary tram-car'. If she made a claim for compensation, he declared that he would fight it, and he referred her representative to his solicitors. The claim was dropped.

Once, on his way to London, a tyre went flat and a Stepney wheel was used. On the return journey a tyre burst, but he refused to stop and they drove slowly home on the rim of the wheel. The journey to London in the Rolls-Royce usually took about 40 minutes. But he did not always go by car, sometimes travelling by the Metropolitan Railway from Marylebone or Baker Street and motoring home from Harrow station. The platform chaos during the week-end rush hour at Baker Street provoked him to write a letter to the press: 'Saturday afternoon, although occurring at regular and well-foreseen intervals, always takes this railway by surprise.'

CHAPTER 19

Revivals

❦❦❦

The impact of a remarkable man's life on the world of his time may be likened to that of a stone thrown into the water. He makes a splash, which is followed by a wave or two of success, then a few ripples of fame, which grow fainter and soon disappear, leaving no disturbance on the surface to show that he had ever existed. There are some exceptions, and one of these was Gilbert who made three big splashes in his lifetime: the first as a dramatist at the Haymarket in the seventies, the second as a librettist at the Savoy in the eighties, the third as a classic at the Savoy in the early nineteen-hundreds; and the waves from this last are still undulating, the ripples still curling.

For him the first decade of the twentieth century was a period of revivals: his health was restored, his fairies were reborn, his diary was renewed, his letter-copying book was reopened, and his operas were reproduced. In 1893 his gout was so bad that he had to rehearse *Utopia Limited* on crutches. For several years the attacks were sometimes violent, sometimes slight, but always near at hand or foot. In 1899 he helped to dig the foundations of his lake at Grim's Dyke and contracted a worse disease from the wet clay. 'I had gout all my life till 1900', he said, 'when rheumatoid arthritis came along. They eloped together – the only scandal I ever had in the family.' This was not a clinically correct statement, because he suffered from rheumatic twinges for the rest of his life, but the condition in which he sought the climate and sulphur-baths of Egypt was at length ameliorated by a diet of vegetables, fruit and fish, and at the end of 1902 he was able to say

I am slowly getting stronger, but I am still rather Richardy (I hate the slang expression 'Dickey') in the knees. If my left knee were as good as my right knee, all would be well. It would even be well if my right knee were as bad as my left knee, because they would at any rate be pairs. However, I can walk five miles at a pinch.

He described himself as 'a crumbling ruin – a magnificent ruin, no doubt, but still a ruin – and, like all ruins, I look best by moonlight'. He prophesied that excursion trains would soon be run for trippers to gaze at him, as upon Tintern Abbey, and that he would be a favourite resort for picnic parties and sentimental couples. In the spring of 1903 he complained that 'my bones ache with rheumatism till I can almost hear them'.

However, his health was now on the mend and set-backs were due to youthfulness of spirits:

> I caught a nasty chill at the Waterlows from sitting on a damp lawn with distinctly the loveliest copper-haired lady I have ever met – at least it was that or eating the greater part of a large melon on Sunday night. These two causes tend to the same effect, so I can't say positively which of them is responsible for the fact that I haven't left the house since Sunday and have been living entirely on milk and rusks ever since.

His fondness for sweet things occasioned discomfort, but when chocolates arrived on his birthday he said that he would rather be bilious from such kind attentions than perfectly well without them: 'They came to console me for growing older – and the worst of it is that the older I grow the more consolation I shall need – and I'm not at all sure that in this case the demand will create the supply.' Though he looked upon seventy as the prime of life, he did not care to be reminded that he was quickly reaching that age: 'Personally I'm sick of birthdays; I've had so many of them, and they begin to pall, but (such is the inconsistency of the animal man) I feel I could do with a few more.' In November 1905, he walked to London.

> Not bad for a crumbling old josser of 69. By the way, I think this will be my last year on earth – you see, I am popularly identified with Topsyturvydom. Now 69 is still 69 if you turn it upside down. See? The same remark applies to 96. So if I escape this year I may go on to the higher figure.

But a fantasy of his, produced by Arthur Bourchier at the Garrick Theatre in May 1904, had not been topsyturvy enough for the public. It was called *The Fairy's Dilemma*, and was written partly in verse. Max Beerbohm in *The Saturday Review* said that it should have been written entirely in verse, adding that 'verse is not the only thing that it ought to have been written in; it ought also to have been written in the seventies'. Gilbert disagreed: he believed it would have been appreciated in the sixties. A favourable reception gave no indication of the feeble receipts, and the subdued applause of thinning houses betrayed a feeling that Gilbert once expressed when asked what he thought of a certain plan: 'Sir, I view the proposal to hold an international exhibition at San Francisco with an equanimity bordering on indifference.' Arthur Bourchier and his wife Violet Vanbrugh were anxious to make Gilbert comfortable and to do everything he wished at the rehearsals, which passed off without the least friction, though the amateurishness inseparable from the running of most theatres was marked: 'They are all very civil and kind, but it is different from the Savoy, where everything went by clockwork. There's a sad want of method at the Garrick, and I've had to put my foot down!'

There was no lack of method about Gilbert, who after a long interval, filled with work and illness, began to keep a diary again and to copy his correspondence, entering daily happenings in the former with the dutiful regularity of one who has nothing to say. Perhaps no man of his talent ever kept a worse record. It is simply a bare chronicle of visits and visitors, the daily round of games and other doings. The meagre comments are swamped by references to promenades and social engagements with women. It is, in short, 'an infinite deal of nothing'. Gilbert could never have written about personalities because they did not strike him as interesting, and he could never have written about himself because his interests were outside himself. He had scarcely any nostalgia for the past because he had lived fully in it, and little care for the future because he was wholly alive in the present. Nevertheless, though it would be impossible to minimize the unimportance of the diary as a human document, his lack of self-revelation is revealing. By showing us what he thought worth recording he displayed his limitations and inhibitions. He made the entries in French, saying, 'I am thus able to leave my diary about, as I know the servants like reading it.' But there was nothing in his memoranda to excite the servants' hall, and even the housemaids might have guessed the meaning of 'Premier cuckoo', since they had probably heard it in the grounds, or 'Premières fraises', since they may have noticed them in the house.

Let us glance at the entries for the years 1905–10 and see what we can glean. He duly noted each time he bathed in the lake, which was 170 yards long and 50 yards wide, and in the warm weather he bathed several times a day. Every game of croquet and billiards was mentioned, every walk in the grounds, every garden-party, every evening-party. Fifty-five guests came to one garden-party and music was performed by a Blue Hungarian Band. Charades, dumb-crambo and songs enlivened several dinner-parties. We learn that Kitty and Nancy went to church regularly, though they occasionally varied the experience by attending a Roman Catholic service or a Christian Science meeting while staying in London; that he was troubled at intervals with rheumatism in the leg and sometimes had to lie down; that nearly every day while they were in their rented London house during the winter they gave lunch-parties and nearly every night dinner-parties; that Kitty's 'At Homes' were crowded; that he took innumerable photographs and developed them; that he often played cribbage and bridge or read aloud to the domestic circle, Dickens for preference; and that they saw each New Year in with milk punch. He recorded the yearly arrival of mushrooms, strawberries, melons, nectarines, and asparagus. The planting of trees, the presence of friends and acquaintances, the paying of visits, the annual filling and emptying of the lake, the conferences with his lady visitors 'sur le haystack', the motor drives, the jig-saw puzzles, the state of the weather, the condition of his health – all these were matters of note, but not the state of his mind nor the condition of his emotions. He was very fond of croquet, in which he said that 'both sexes can join with propriety', but he does not seem to have been a skilful player. An entry in June 1906 runs: 'Je commence un jeu de croquet avec Nancy, mais je joue si abominablement que j'ai cessé – at j'ai développé de photos, au lieu.' But a year later he was able to report: 'Croquet avec Nancy. J'ai gagné!!!' And two years after that he won frequently.

Very rarely a phrase denoting personal feeling appeared in the diary. He disliked the work of Rudyard Kipling, and on April 29th, 1905, he attended the annual dinner at the Royal Academy: 'Le sacré Kipling dans mon voisinage.' He thought

the speeches dull and commonplace. From January to March
each year he took a furnished house in London and participated
in the tedious social swirl which persuades people that they are
living a full life. In 1908 he went to the Derby, winning the
second prize in a sweep (£75), and soon afterwards he saw Maud
Allan dance at the Palace Theatre, confiding in his diary that
the exhibition was 'Dégoûtant'. The following year he witnessed *King Lear* at the Haymarket Theatre, calling it a 'triste
et ennuyante représentation d'une pièce monstreuse', which,
of course, written in English, would have demoralized the servants at Grim's Dyke. Another event of 1909 was a headline
in an evening paper: 'Death of W. S. Gilbert in Great Agony',
to which he appended the word 'Liar'. This sort of thing happened on other occasions, and once he wrote to the peccant
editor:

> Sir – There is a line in your issue of yesterday that must have
> sent a thrill of joy through many a worthy home. I refer to a line
> in which I am referred to as 'the late W. S. Gilbert'. I am always
> sorry to spoil sport, but common candour compels me to admit
> (reluctantly) that I am still alive. Trusting that this will not
> inconvenience you – Yours faithfully.

Having re-started his diary he began to use a copying-press
once more, and after a lapse of twenty-five years we are again
able to read such letters as he thought worth preserving. On
December 8th, 1908, he wrote a series of specimen letters to
test the process, one of which ran:

> Gentlemen and Ladies
> This is written with copying ink in a stylographic pen with a
> view to ascertaining the effect in a copying press.
>   Yours obediently
>   W. S. Gilbert
>
> To the World at Large.

The new letters commenced with a correspondence on cigars,
a firm of importers being told that if Harrods and the Army
and Navy Stores could afford to sell the cigars he wanted at
105s. 6d. a hundred and yet make a profit, he did not see why
he should pay 118s.: 'These firms are not philanthropists – they
sell for profit as you do.' With another letter he returned a set
of Kinglake's *History of the Crimean War* owing to the dis-

creditable condition of the volumes, each being from a different set. This should have been explained in the advertisement, he said, and 'I could not possibly place such a shabby set on my shelves.' He also complained of the discoloration of a tent supplied by a well-known company. In fact he continued to teach business men their business.

'I fancy posterity will know as little of me as I shall of posterity', Gilbert declared. But that point was settled for himself and posterity by the revivals of the Gilbert and Sullivan operas at the Savoy Theatre from 1906 to 1909, when *The Yeomen of the Guard, The Gondoliers, Patience, Iolanthe, The Mikado, H.M.S. Pinafore* and *The Pirates of Penzance* were rapturously received by a new generation. D'Oyly Carte had died soon after Sullivan and his widow Helen reigned in his stead. At the end of 1905 she agreed to pay Gilbert £5000 in yearly instalments for the five-years acting rights of his libretti, to date from May 30th, 1905. Gilbert had a very high opinion of Helen Carte, who was not only a first-rate business woman but an extremely tactful person. She had been Carte's secretary before their marriage, in which capacity she had received a letter from Gilbert in 1883:

> I don't believe there is another woman alive who could have stated so complicated a case in such a masterly manner. Of the hearty zeal and goodwill embodied in your letter, and evinced in the tremendous efforts you have made on our behalf, I can hardly trust myself to write lest I should seem to be using extravagant terms. Let me prove how implicitly I believe in your brain-faculty and acute judgment by saying that, whatever your scheme may be, I will adopt it if you recommend it.

This letter is a credit to both of them, and it is sad to think that anything should have happened to lessen its validity. But from his correspondence about her revivals of the operas it seems that other forces were at work to bring discord between them, and we may guess that her manager, Boulton, and her musical director, Cellier, were largely responsible for what took place, since both of them knew that, given a free hand, Gilbert would insist on casting the pieces to his satisfaction, not to theirs. By ignoring him in so important a matter, they were asking for trouble, and their principal Helen Carte got it.

She wished to open the season with *The Yeomen of the Guard,* and in October 1906 Gilbert wrote to propose Nancy McIntosh for a leading part. Helen replied that her existing arrangements prevented her from offering an engagement to Miss McIntosh, but that she promised to engage the best possible casts for all the revivals. This made it clear that Gilbert was not going to be consulted over the casting, and he said that he was entirely against the London revivals being played by her touring company, that he could guarantee nothing unless his advice was taken about the casting, but that he would 'attend rehearsals and if I find the people practicable I will carry them through to the best of my ability'. Later he admitted that as he had no legal claim in the matter she could cast the pieces as she pleased, but he was 'surprised and not a little hurt' that his opinion had not been sought, and he reserved the right of publicly disclaiming all responsibility if the result should prove unsatisfactory. Her attitude seemed to imply that an author had no right to have his plays performed as he wished them to be, and when, to soothe him, she wired to ask if he would see a certain artist for a part, he curtly rejoined: 'As I have been totally ignored in casting the piece I prefer to leave the entire responsibility with you.'

Brooding over her strange behaviour, he wrote on November 16th, 1906:

> I may say at once that in casting the West End production of *The Yeomen of the Guard* without having consulted me in any way, you have placed upon me the deepest – I may say the only – indignity ever offered to me during my 40 years connection with the stage. That this indignity should have been inflicted on me by a lady whom, for more than ¼ of a century, I have always held in the profoundest esteem – a lady with whom during that long period I have never had a word of difference – a lady, moreover, whose attitude towards me, before and after I came into intimate business relations with her, has invariably been courteous and considerate to the last degree, renders her recent course of action in entirely ignoring me while casting the piece for production at the Savoy absolutely and altogether unaccountable.

In reply she expressed regret that he should feel as he did, gave the names of several artists in the past who had been taken from the provincial company to play parts in London revivals of the operas, and mentioned his refusal to see the particular artist she proposed. He answered by return of post:

Dear Mrs Carte

When Mr Pounds, Mr Lytton, Mr Evett and Miss Jay were incorporated with the London Company, it was with the approval and consent of Sullivan and myself. Your opinion of the people you have engaged may or may not be warranted by the result, but the act of engaging and casting them according to your own individual taste and pleasure, without any reference whatever to me, can only be warranted by strict interpretation of the agreement. You no doubt take your stand upon that, and as a matter of law you are entitled to do so, for I should no more have thought of stipulating that I should be consulted as to the cast of London productions than I should have thought of stipulating for punctual payment of fees. In either case I should have looked upon such stipulations as gross personal insults to yourself. If Sullivan had been alive you would no more have thought of casting one of the operas without obtaining his approval of every minute detail of the cast than you would have thought of setting the Savoy Theatre on fire.

I declined to see the artist you proposed to me because you had informed me a fortnight before that you had already settled the cast and would send me a list of it. I was not to be satisfied with such an *ex post facto* 'sop to Cerberus'.

It is a matter of no moment whatever to you, who have nothing further to gain by continuing to conciliate me, but the discovery of the contempt in which you hold my opinion on a point upon which you used to affect to regard it as paramount, has struck a blow at our lengthy association from which it never can recover. There is not another manager in existence who, agreement or no agreement, would have presumed to take upon himself to cast a piece of mine for a London production without having consulted my wishes on every point of detail.

As usual, Gilbert was irritatingly in the right, and short of a complete reversal of policy all Helen Carte could do, which she did, was to disregard everything he had said and assure him that she would always preserve the greatest regard and the most friendly feelings for himself. On November 26th he superintended the first rehearsal of *The Yeomen of the Guard*, jotting in his diary 'Assez bonne troupe excepté Serg. Meryll qui est terrible', and on the date of production, December 8th, he noted 'Médiocre représentation. J'ai eu une magnifique réception à la fin de la pièce.' Jack Point was played by C. H. Workman, who had appeared ten years earlier in *The Grand Duke* and was to play all the Grossmith parts in these revivals.

Gilbert once described him as 'an actor who has done me good service in the past'. There was a pleasant exchange between them at rehearsals when Gilbert remarked that Jack Point was caressing Elsie and Phoebe too realistically. 'Ah, yes, I see; you would not kiss them more than once', said the actor. 'Oh, indeed I would! but I must ask *you* not to', said the author. Gilbert received a fee of £200 for rehearsing the opera, but Helen Carte would no doubt have paid five times that sum for his approval. Instead she had to endure such reproaches as these:

> All the magnificent successes which we provided for you and which have poured thousands upon thousands of pounds into your pocket were all cast by Sullivan and myself without any extraneous aid worth mentioning.

> It is difficult to tell a lady, who is under overwhelming obligations to me and with whom during 25 years of business relations I have never had an angry word, that she has treated me with the profoundest indifference and contempt and inflicted a lasting injury on my work without employing expressions that are likely to be distasteful to her; but I must remind you that when an unoffending man has been so treated by a lady whose large fortune he has been so directly instrumental in helping to make, the offence lies with her in so treating him and not with him for protesting in plain terms against such treatment.

> With reference to your remark that the public do not appear to agree with me as to the general character of the performance (a point upon which I claim to be an infinitely better judge than they) I have only to say that if the cast were the very best that could possibly be procured, the indignity passed upon me in not consulting me with reference to it would be the same.

Helen Carte heard that he had referred to a member of the company (the diary tells us which) as 'the scouring of the provinces', but he hotly denied the report: 'For excellent reasons, I am extremely careful how I express myself within the walls of the Savoy Theatre.' But we are compelled to admit that, under stress, caution was not one of his attributes. Even the caution he did display was not of a kind to please Helen, who received this sample in reply to her request that he should undertake the stage-management of (i.e. produce) *The Gondoliers* in January 1907:

Dear Mrs Carte,

The cast of *The Gondoliers* is, with few exceptions, so very unsatisfactory to me that, in justice to myself, I am bound to disclaim all responsibility for it. As I have no desire to injure the prospects of the production by any public disclaimer, I propose to write to the critics of the principal papers to the effect that any credit that may attach to the selection of the cast of *The Gondoliers* will be due entirely to yourself and not in any single instance to me. While this is no more than the precise truth, it will leave the press at liberty to form an independent opinion as to whether your selection is judicious or otherwise. At the same time, I shall do my very best to present the company to the best advantage.

Yours faithfully

Helen interpreted this to mean that he intended to influence the judgment of the critics to the detriment of her season. She wrote to protest, and so did he:

90 Eaton Square
12 Jan. 1907

Dear Mrs Carte

I do not propose to write my contemplated letter with the view of assisting critics to form an independent opinion, as you admit in your letter of the 10th Inst. 'their independent opinion cannot be affected by the question as to who selected the artists'. My intention in writing it is perfectly obvious – it is to disclaim responsibility for a cast upon which I have not been consulted. As it is common knowledge among dramatic critics that, until the recent revival of *The Yeomen of the Guard*, I have always had an important voice as to how our operas should be cast, it is necessary for my own justification that I should place myself beyond praise or blame in the matter of the cast of *The Gondoliers*, in which I have had no voice whatever.

This is so obviously the interpretation – and the only interpretation – to be placed upon my proposed letter that I can only regard your assumption that it is deliberately intended to prejudice the minds of the critics to the damage of your artists, and possibly your business, as a gross and gratuitous insult. I have shown myself to be, in every respect, most zealous for the success of the revival – even going to the length of offering to pay the band for an extra night rehearsal rather than that the piece should be ineffectively produced. Having regard to the fact that before very long the copyright in the libretti will revert to me, my interests are intimately allied with their success, and I regard with dismay the fact that they are being produced in a manner which is calculated to do them an irreparable injury. In the interests of the pieces, and for no other reason, I have worked hard and incessantly to do the best I could with the material you have placed at my command, while for the artists upon whom you presume to assert that I am contemplating the infliction of a deliberate injury, I have nothing but gratitude for the unceasing efforts they have made to carry out my wishes to the best of their ability.

That the prospects of the revival might not be even remotely injured by a public disclaimer on my part, I proposed to communicate privately with the principal press critics to the effect that I am responsible only for the stage-management and not in any way for the cast, scenery or dresses as hitherto. Their independent opinion, as you frankly admit, could not be influenced by the question who selected the artists, and consequently no harm could possibly result to yourself or to them. Moreover, in order to dispel any suspicion on your part that in writing my proposed letter I was actuated by an underhand motive, I told you in advance of the course I proposed to take for the protection of my own interests – which I should certainly not have done if I had been actuated by the malignant intentions you have thought proper to ascribe to me. I must ask you to withdraw, explicitly and unreservedly, the grossly disgraceful and altogether unwarrantable charge you have made against me.

Helen wisely withdrew what she called her ambiguous statement which had been made in haste. Gilbert did his best with the cast of which he disapproved, and was given a 'Grande réception' at the final curtain on the opening night, having been at the Beefsteak Club while the piece was in progress. *The Mikado* was announced at the end of March, but to everyone's amazement the production was forbidden by the Lord Chamberlain because a Japanese prince was about to pay an official visit to England. In his evidence before the Committee on the Censorship in 1909, Gilbert said all that can interest us on the subject:

'I consider it was an unwarrantable and illegal act altogether. It was an act of depredation to take my play, which was worth £10,000 to me, and, without any communication with me, to prohibit its performance.'

The Chairman (Herbert Samuel): 'You would not have been a casus belli?'

'I should have made myself one had not the play been in the hands of Mrs D'Oyly Carte.'

'I mean a casus belli so far as the two Powers were concerned?'

'I do not know that the Powers were concerned. The *Mikado* music was, during the prohibition, being played on the Japanese ships in the Medway – a sort of musical comment on the absurdity of the prohibition.'

Asked by Lord Newton what really occurred, Gilbert replied:

'So far as I know, I was informed that the Lord Chamberlain had forbidden the production on the ground that it might give offence to our Japanese allies. The Lord Chamberlain did not do me the honour to communicate with me at all. He simply took my property and laid an embargo on it.'

'There was no correspondence and no interview?'

'Not before the stoppage of the piece. The Lord Chamberlain afterwards sent for me, and I had an interview at St James's Palace.'

'It was the autocratic action of the Lord Chamberlain?'

'So I understood from him, and that it was at the representation of the members of the Japanese embassy.'

Gilbert described the banning of *The Mikado* on account of the visit of Prince Fushimi as

a delicate and polite action on the part of a guest towards a host. The rights in the piece do not revert to me for three years; by that time we shall probably be at war with Japan about India, and they will offer me a high price to permit it to be played.

The action of the Lord Chamberlain provoked a humorous M.P. to ask the Prime Minister in the House of Commons whether, since Denmark was a friendly power, *Hamlet* ought to be performed, the Danish monarch therein being portrayed as a fratricide.

Patience was substituted for *The Mikado*, and Gilbert received, as for all the revivals, a fee of £200 for rehearsing it. He usually lunched at Simpsons, sometimes inviting a member of the cast who needed encouragement. On the first night, early in April, he dined at the Garrick Club, went to see the performing sea-lions at the Palace Theatre, and arrived at the Savoy in time for a 'Grande réception'. Early in June *Iolanthe* secured him a 'Magnifique réception'. The Lord Chamberlain having come to his senses, *The Mikado* was revived in 1908, Gilbert writing an *encore* verse for Workman. During the first performance on April 27th he dined at the Garrick Club, and after taking his 'call' at the Savoy he went to His Majesty's Theatre for supper with Beerbohm Tree, who had invited a hundred guests in his honour. *Pinafore* followed in July, and *The Pirates of Penzance* in December. Helen Carte's season lasted for more than two years, in the course of which the more popular operas were revived twice, and when *The Gondoliers* was done again with four or five new people in important rôles Gilbert insisted on taking a few rehearsals in order 'to get (in the interests of the piece) as good a revival as the material at my command will allow'. Rutland Barrington reappeared in his old parts, and the younger generation applauded every performance to the echo; but those who had seen the original productions were more critical. *Laudator temporis acti.* Every period, and much that happens in it, is wonderful to those who are young and vital enough to feel that mere existence is wonderful, and perhaps the chief solace of seniority is summed up by Justice Shallow: 'Jesus, the days that we have seen!' That, however, was not Gilbert's weakness. He complained to Helen Carte of 'the many exceedingly incompetent people, the terrible scenery and the atrocious dresses with which the reputation of the operas has been irretrievably injured'; and he said that 'nothing would induce me to accept a favour from her after the treatment I have experienced at her hands'; he told Richard Temple, an old Savoyard, that he hoped a wealthy syndicate would be formed for the proper production of the operas, starting with *Ruddigore*, as he was utterly dissatisfied with the recent revivals; and when Helen Carte tried to justify herself, he wrote on February 2nd, 1909:

Dear Mrs Carte

I prefer to believe what *I know to be the case.* You are not a free agent, or you would never have treated me with the gross insolence and black ingratitude which have characterized the Savoy methods during the past 2¼ years . . . the operas have been insulted, degraded and dragged through the mire and I have been exposed to humiliating ridicule in the face of the entire company. Blind and blatant ignorance accompanied by contemptible economy have characterized the productions of the past two years and people have been engaged whom the call-boy would have told you were ridiculously unsuitable . . . Probably you relied largely on Cellier for advice in acting the parts. Cellier knows whether a singer can sing in time and whether he has the requisite number of notes in his voice – but as a judge of the *quality* of a voice, or of the singer's capacity as an actor, he is useless. I have been pushed aside because Mr Boulton knew that I should not have been satisfied with the cheap and incompetent people whom he thought it advisable to cast in my libretti – and he has, I sincerely hope, suffered for his presumption. He has certainly made hundreds by his economies – but he has lost thousands.

Yours very truly

P.S. Probably you do not hear candid opinions about the character of your productions. *I do*.

It was of course the feeling that he had been treated as a negligible back-number that embittered him, for his opinion of the libretti was about as low as his opinion of the performing casts: 'I have been scribbling twaddle for thirty-five years to suit the public taste . . . Light flippery and amusing nonsense is what I have endeavoured to write.' 'But are you not proud of having acquired all this out of your own brain?' asked someone at Grim's Dyke. 'Not at all', he answered; 'it represents the folly of the British public.' Such was his estimate of the works that had inspired Sullivan's bewitching music, and which, because of that conjunction, may enjoy as long a stage-life as any of the classic English comedies. Apart from the famous libretti, four works by Gilbert are worthy of survival: the deliciously absurd *Bab Ballads*, the delightfully funny *Rosencrantz and Guildenstern*, both of which he would have dismissed along with the operas as twaddle, the charmingly sentimental period piece *Sweethearts*, and the farcical comedy *Engaged* which is the quintessence of that peculiar quality he brought to the language, known as Gilbertian.

CHAPTER 20

The Old Lion

◦⬤◦⬤◦

'Ｉf you want to gain your end', says Captain O'Hara in *The Ne'er-do-Weel*, 'never contradict flatly. Pull up short, and snap goes your hawser.' Gilbert's hawser continually snapped, and this bit of worldly wisdom put into the mouth of one of his characters is suggestive of the dipsomaniac who preaches with conviction in favour of temperance. He could not help contradicting flatly if convinced that he was right, and when he naïvely quoted a line from *Princess Ida* in a public speech – 'Everyone says I'm such a disagreeable man and I can't think why' – he was not flattered by the hearty laughter with which it was greeted. In later years he became less disputatious and more sensitive, his denial of the many caustic remarks attributed to him being due to a diminishing combativeness and an increasing consciousness that he had made an unnecessary number of enemies. But when he felt that he was being treated unfairly, the old retired lion could roar as lustily as the active animal of earlier years. At the height of his renown he had risked the loss of much money by the immediacy of his reaction to what he thought fraudulent dealing and it will soon appear that his temper was speedily aroused at the end of his life by what he believed to be dishonourable conduct. An instance of his too abrupt behaviour in a business matter may be found in his private papers.

A manager named Luscombe Searelle wrote from Johannesburg in April 1892 to ask if he might set music to one of Gilbert's libretti, explaining in a further letter that he had put on four of the Savoy pieces in South Africa, after having tried but failed to get into touch with Carte and Sullivan. Without pausing to wonder why an unscrupulous man should bother to make such an admission, Gilbert described this proceeding as 'akin in dishonesty to the act of a man who considers himself justified in stealing my watch because I decline to sell it to him', and went on to say 'I will not trouble you to explain upon what principle your "putting aside" a nightly fee – which you were careful not to remit to us – could possibly be accepted by us as satisfactory compensation for your insolent violation of our copyright.' But in November of that year Searelle came to England and sent Gilbert a blank cheque, asking him to fill it in for royalties on the performances of his operas given in South Africa, the actual sum being £188. 18s. Gilbert did not feel confident that this course was legal but agreed to discuss it with Searelle at his solicitor's office. Their meeting passed off amicably and Luscombe Searelle obtained the sole rights of producing the operas in South Africa. All of them had been previously pirated and mutilated by other managers, one of whom had already been informed by Gilbert that he had instructed his solicitors 'to take the necessary steps to prevent your carrying out your intention' of producing *The Mountebanks*: 'Their instructions are to spare neither time, trouble nor expense in order to effect this.' The arrangement by the Savoy triumvirate was that Carte should have the royalties on all performances in Cape Colony and Natal, and that Gilbert and Sullivan should benefit from those given in the Transvaal and the Orange River State.

Allied with his sudden bursts of annoyance and contradictoriness was a supernormal susceptibility to behaviour that could be construed as unfriendly. For example, there was usually some difficulty over the dogs he wished to take with him to the London house which he occupied for the winter months. For two or three seasons he rented No. 4 Grosvenor Crescent, S.W., but in the last five years of his life, 1907–11, he took No. 90 Eaton Square, S.W., paying £315 for the three months, January to March inclusive. The owner was Lord Normanby, who intimated that one dog was quite sufficient for human companionship. Gilbert wrote to the agents:

10 Sep. 1909

Dear Sirs

I hope Lord Normanby will reconsider his decision not to allow me to bring more than one dog to the house.

Last year I was allowed to bring two dogs on the understanding that if they stained any of the carpets, those carpets should be replaced at my expense, and nothing of the kind occurred. The two dogs that I wish to bring are the same as those I brought last

year and they are perfectly trained to the house. I may state that
the offending dog of the year before last is no longer in my
possession.

Yours faithfully

Precautionary permission was granted, but Gilbert scented a
slight:

16 Sep. 1909

Dear Sirs
    I regret the tone of Lady Normanby's letter. I am not in the
habit of evading my responsibilities. Whatever my dogs may spoil
will be replaced by me.
    I return the Agreement duly signed.

Although he did not bear malice he never forgot the affronts
of people who may have been innocent of offence. On July 4th,
1907, he attended Speech Day at Harrow School and replied
to the toast of the visitors, causing some consternation by
saying that it was 'the only place in the world where a line of
mine has ever been condemned as improper'. Only one person
present remembered that in 1872 Dr Butler, then headmaster,
had refused to let the boys see *The Palace of Truth*, performed
by the townspeople to raise funds for a hospital, unless the
hero's request to the heroine 'Meet me at 9 o'clock tonight
outside the garden gate' were re-worded 'Meet me at three
o'clock this afternoon.' Like all touchy men Gilbert was liable
to reach hasty conclusions on insufficient data. At the end of
1908 he resigned for no apparent reason from the Beefsteak
Club, and though he withdrew his resignation at the request
of the committee he seldom went there again, almost certainly
because he had overheard a disparaging criticism on his work
by another member. It is related that he once went into a room
at the Beefsteak, glanced round, and cried with amazement: 'A
dozen men, and I'm on terms with them all!' He was delighted
when he heard in February 1906 that he had been elected to the
Garrick Club 'on account of his public distinction'. Back in
1869 he had been blackballed by the committee in the belief
that he was someone else. Having discovered the error, they
asked him to put himself up for membership again, 'but it
occurred to me that as the mistake was theirs it was theirs to
rectify it', he said. 'Moreover, I am not one of those who turn
the second cheek to the smiter.' Even the dignified atmosphere

of the Garrick was not free from the currents of rumour, and he heard that a well-known American member named G. W. Smalley, who spent many years in England, had made a slighting remark about one of his poetic pieces. Again he drew too hasty a conclusion, and then withdrew it, but with a typical qualification:

27 March 1911.

Dear Mr Smalley

As a matter of course I accept unreservedly your disclaimer of any knowledge that the verse in question was mine, and that being the case I unhesitatingly withdraw my suggestion that your expressions of contempt were intended as a personal affront to myself. I may remind you that your 'soft answer' in its complete form only reached me this morning, and I hasten to admit that my accusations were unfounded and to express my regret that I should have made them.

At the same time I may be permitted to state, in palliation of my offence, that the lines you quoted are so widely known as having been written by me that I believe there are very few members of the Garrick Club who could not give you chapter and verse for them off-hand. It certainly never entered my mind to suppose that a gentleman so thoroughly up to date in all matters connected with literature and the drama as you are universally held to be could possibly be unacquainted with the fact that the lines in question are an excerpt from the very well known Savoy opera *Patience*, produced in 1880 and, since then, three times revived.

That the lines, taken by themselves, may possibly justify your contemptuous criticism I do not care to deny. If you read them with their context (with which you are of course unfamiliar) you may perhaps be disposed to modify your opinion.

I am
Sincerely yours

But Gilbert's nature, sensitive to fancied slights, was also sensitive to the feelings of others, making him anxious to help them and give them happiness. Hearing that an operation had been successfully performed on a friend, he wrote:

I've a hideous way of identifying myself with incidents of the kind when I know they are going to take place, and at 9 – 10 – 11 I couldn't help fancying – now the surgeons have arrived – now they are being shown into the room – now they are unpacking their devilish instruments, and so on . . . I wished I hadn't known when it was going to take place.

· 241 ·

His sympathy was comically expressed to another friend at supper: 'What will you have? Whatever you have I shall have; then I shall know exactly how you are feeling in the morning.' Sometimes his good wishes could make the recipient feel that they were worth a few sneezes: 'I hope it won't be a very bad cold; indeed I hope it will be a very good cold and go away at once.' A note in his diary for August 23rd, 1907, gives us a glimpse of his kindliness: 'Rencontre avec une petite fille près Victoria qui avez perdu sa tante. Je la trouve.' And a letter to a schoolgirl shows what a delightful host he must have been at the children's parties which he gave to the friends and families of his staff at Grim's Dyke:

My Dear Young Lady,
  (It seems absurd to address a young lady at school as 'Dear Madam') – It is my practice to decline to give my autograph to applicants, but on the other hand it appears to me that one ought never to deny anything to a young lady 'home for the holidays'. So you see that I am the victim of conflicting emotions. What shall I do? Toss for it! Heads I send you my autograph – Tails I write to tell you that nothing will induce me to do anything of the kind. Now for it! It's Tails! so I won't send it to you.
Yours very truly
W. S. Gilbert

His sympathy was not confined to the other sex. When a friend, C. E. Perugini, who had once been successful, asked for a loan of £100, Gilbert begged him to accept it as a gift, saying how easy it was for himself to send it, how difficult for the other to request it. He was able to put himself in his friend's place, to feel the discomfort of a proud man reduced to borrowing, and to recognize 'what is beyond all price – freedom from anxiety and complete peace of mind'.

Always good-hearted when his personal feelings were not hurt, he seemed to become mellower, not crustier, with time, and to take greater pleasure than ever in charitable deeds. He was honorary secretary of the Bushey Heath Cottage Hospital and helped many of those whose misfortune brought them there.[1] It annoyed him when Lloyd George's budget of 1909, with its super-tax, health insurance and 'dole', took the first

---

[1] Gilbert would be pleased that his home, Grim's Dyke, is now a Rehabilitation Centre for tubercular cases. The matron, Miss Elizabeth Siddall, was kind enough to show the author and his wife over the house and grounds, which remain much as W.S.G. knew them.

step to what is now called the Welfare State, and he drafted
a letter to *The Times* enumerating some of the public charities
to which he subscribed and the various improvements made
on his estate which had benefited many poor people.

> Henceforth [he announced], that is to say from the date at
> which the new Budget comes into operation, I shall discontinue
> my subscriptions to all charities which are intended to benefit the
> very poor and I shall confine my donations exclusively to a class
> which has not come within the purview of Mr Lloyd George's
> humanitarian scheme, such as underpaid curates, distressed
> gentlefolk and poor professional men.

His other improvements which gave employment to many
would also be discontinued.

> There is a certain luxury in helping poor meritorious persons,
> but if that luxury is to be taken from me and conferred upon a
> body of government officials I consider myself to be altogether
> absolved from that agreeable duty. In other words I do not feel
> called upon to give with both hands out of both pockets. I suggest
> this plan to all who do not stand in need of the radical vote, and
> who think it desirable to teach the poorest class of voters that
> there are other considerations to be taken into account beyond the
> weekly dole that will find its way into some of their pockets.

By that time he had received honours from his contemporaries and his sovereign. On December 30th, 1906, the
O.P. Club gave him a dinner. There were 450 guests, including
many survivors of the old Savoy company, and

> any amount of melted butter was (figuratively) poured down my
> back . . . It's well I don't believe all the good things that were
> said about me, or I should be suffering from a swelled head and be
> too big for my boots. As it is, both head and feet are normal.

But from his diary we learn that the dinner was too protracted
for one of his habits: 'Mon speech très bien reçu. Tout a pro-
gressé avec enthousiasme . . . Détestable temps en quittant.'

Six months after this event he was offered a knighthood by
the Prime Minister, Sir Henry Campbell-Bannerman, head of
the Liberal Party. He had already been sounded by the King's
private secretary and had expressed his willingness to accept it.
No doubt he felt that it was easy enough to pick up honours
if one cared to stoop low enough for them, but he had never
gone out of his way to please people of influence and his reply

to Sir Henry displays his lack of interest in such matters, for he does not seem to have been aware of the Prime Minister's christian name:

21st June 1907

Dear Sir Campbell-Bannerman

I am much obliged to you for your offer to submit my name to the King for the honour of Knighthood. It is an offer which I gratefully accept.

I fully understand that your letter is to be considered as absolutely private until His Majesty's pleasure is known.

I am

Very faithfully yours

W. S. Gilbert

On the 21st June he went to the Royal Garden Party at Windsor, and attended the investiture on July 15th at Buckingham Palace, where he was

duly tapped on both shoulders by Edward VII . . . I found myself politely described in the official list as Mr William Gilbert, *playwright*, suggesting that my work was analogical to that of a wheelwright, or a millwright, or a wainwright, or a shipwright, as regards the mechanical character of the process by which our respective results are achieved. There is an excellent word 'dramatist' which seems to fit the situation, but it is not applied until we are dead, and then we become dramatists as oxen, sheep and pigs are transfigured into beef, mutton and pork after their demise. You never hear of a novelwright or a picturewright or a poemwright; and why a playwright?

He called the title 'a tin-pot, twopenny-halfpenny sort of distinction, but as no dramatic author as such ever had it for dramatic authorship alone, I felt I ought not to refuse it'. He again spoke of it as 'a mere triviality', 'an unmeaning scrap of tinsel', and a reward for having brought up a family of plays 'without ever having had to apply to the relieving officer for parochial assistance'. He received four hundred letters of congratulation, and his wife about ninety-five, but he could not take the honour seriously. 'This indiscriminate flinging about of knighthoods is making me very nervous', he remarked; 'it's quite possible they may give one to my butler. He's a very good fellow, and I'm afraid it will upset him.' A female friend wanted to know whether she must now call him 'Sir William'? 'Call me "Bill",' he suggested. 'Very well, I'll call you "Sir Bill".' Gilbert would not have been 'Bab' if he had failed to reply: 'I'll do the billing if you do the cooing.'

All sorts of people now wanted to show him respect, and on February 2nd, 1908, a complimentary banquet was given him at the Savoy Hotel, with Lord Onslow in the chair and about 120 guests, including many leading figures in the legal and artistic worlds. The commencement of Gilbert's reply to the toast, which he noted as 'un succès fou', almost suggested that his last disillusionment had been destroyed by the universal demonstrations of good will, but he closed on a note that restored the disharmony associated with his name:

> With regard to the knighthood with which the King has been graciously pleased to reward my work, coming as it does at the close of a life of strenuous endeavour, I am disposed to regard it rather in the light of a commuted Old Age Pension; and if I may venture to make a suggestion to the Right Honourable gentleman at the head of the government, it is that a knighthood conferred upon all working men of 65 years of age and upward who are unable or unwilling to work would afford a cheap, effective and highly picturesque solution of what promises to be a problem of no little financial difficulty.

In the same month he headed a deputation of thirty dramatists or playwrights to the Home Secretary, Herbert Gladstone, on the subject of the censorship of plays. One of them, Granville Barker, described Gladstone as an ass and came to the conclusion that Gilbert and Pinero must be left to do the job as well as they could, because both of them, especially Gilbert, were 'so terrified at being mixed up with the disreputable drama that at the word "Shaw" so to speak they perform evolutions suggestive of flight'. As Pinero and Gilbert had nothing to say that could possibly shock a censor, they naturally favoured the safeguard of a stage-censorship; and when, in August 1909, they gave evidence before the Committee of both Houses of Parliament appointed to enquire into the subject, they voted for the retention of the office. Gilbert gave his reason:

> I think that the stage of a theatre is not a proper pulpit from which to disseminate doctrines possibly of Anarchism, Socialism and Agnosticism. It is not the proper platform upon which to discuss questions of adultery and free love before a mixed audience composed of persons of all ages, of both sexes, of all ways of thinking, of all conditions of life, and of various degrees of education.

This last point is still valid, because nowadays the majority of people have just enough education to assimilate misinformation without assessing it.

'Would you distinguish between the stage and a book?' he was asked?

'There is a very wide distinction. In a novel, when you read that Eliza slipped off her dressing-gown and stepped into her bath, there is no objection to it; but if that were represented on the stage it would be a very different thing.'

The question arose as to whether a play, once passed by the censor, should be subject to later interference by him, and Gilbert explained why it should:

If a strongly expressed love-scene takes place between a man and a woman seated at opposite sides of the stage, it may mean nothing; but if they are seated together on a sofa with their arms round each other's waists and the dialogue is punctuated by kisses, the effect may be very undesirable.

Asked whether he had read any of the censored plays, for example the *Oedipus Tyrannus* of Sophocles, he replied, 'It is many years since I read it, and then under compulsion.'

Restricted by his nature from the free treatment of certain subjects on the stage or in mixed society, his everyday club conversation was untrammelled. If he was Bowdler in the drawing-room, he was Rabelais in the smoking-room, enjoying and retailing stories with the gusto of one who had been a lifelong victim of propriety. 'Throughout the whole of his writings', said Lord Onslow at the dinner already recorded, 'there was not one single word that might not be enjoyed by the most innocent members of society. Sir William had never brought the flush of shame to the cheek of innocence.' Probably one of his objections to Shakespeare was that the Elizabethan enjoyed a stage-licence denied to the Victorian, and it is perhaps fortunate that he did not live to hear one of Shaw's characters say 'Not bloody likely!' in a stage drawing-room. Had he done so he would almost certainly have written a stern letter of protest to *The Times*, saying to himself as he finished it: 'So much for Mr bloody Shaw!' To the end of his life nothing could convince him that his blank verse plays, now unreadable and unrevivable, were not his best work. No doubt he thought that he had put most of himself into them because he had put the greatest labour into them, so making the common error of confusing diligence with merit. He was quite cross when Edith Browne, who was writing his Life for a series called 'Stars of the Stage', dismissed his serious plays as inferior work:

> 90 Eaton Square
> S.W.
> 10 March 1907

Dear Miss Browne

I return your proofs with some very candid and outspoken comments – particularly on the chapter in which you deal with my non-musical plays. You are good enough to chastise me, *ex cathedra*, as though you were an acknowledged and indisputable authority on the subject of dramatic composition and I an inexperienced neophyte. I have no desire that you should modify any views you may please to entertain concerning the success or non-success of those plays, but, to be quite frank, it seems to me that they might have been expressed with less 'cocksuredness'.

I say nothing about the lukewarm opinion you seem to entertain as to the literary quality of these plays (especially those in verse) except to express a wonder that the author of such a series of banalities should have been thought to deserve a biographer. I can hardly believe that I owe the compliment to the easy trivialities of the Savoy *libretti*.

> Yours faithfully

The biographer must have written an extremely diplomatic letter to get this in reply:

> 21 March 1907

Dear Miss Browne

Your very kind letter heaps coals of fire on my head. I hope I did not express myself too bluntly – at all events if I did, it is clear that I am forgiven.

Rightly or wrongly, in the pre-Savoy days I held the foremost position among dramatic authors (there were not many of them then) and it hurt me not a little to find that work which was so well esteemed when it was produced, appealed so feebly to so keen an intelligence as your own.

If I have done anything that appears to you to merit thanks, I am greatly pleased, but frankly it has afforded me great pleasure to work with you and I look back upon our interviews with cordial satisfaction.

> I am
> Very sincerely yours

The last line of his first letter to Edith Browne will explain why he was so angry with the editor of *Who's Who*. An application for a summary of his career was refused by him, with the result that he was described in that publication simply as Sir Arthur Sullivan's librettist, with the further result that he sent a very long account of his career for the next issue.

His enthusiasm for *Broken Hearts*, *Gretchen*, *Pygmalion and Galatea*, *The Palace of Truth* and *The Wicked World* was unquenchable, and he determined to make operas out of the last two. He began a libretto of *The Wicked World* on January 3rd, 1909, and finished it on February 26th, though he was occupied for several more days making improvements. The idea had been in his mind for some time and he had suggested it to Helen Carte in 1897; but her husband did not fancy a chorus 'composed entirely of ladies'. Nor did Arthur Sullivan, Edward Elgar, André Messager, Jules Massenet, Liza Lehmann and Alexander Mackenzie, to all of whom Gilbert proposed the subject. Then, on December 21st, 1908, he wrote to Edward German:

Dear Mr German

I have conceived the idea of a 3 act Fairy Opera, but the story involves a peculiarity which *may* stand in the way of its accomplishment. The peculiarity is that the chorus *must all be ladies*. You will be able to judge whether this would be a delightful novelty or an insuperable difficulty. As I see the piece in my mind's eye it might be productive of exquisitely beautiful effects – but your mind's *ear* may be altogether opposed to the notion. The story is eminently fanciful – in parts strongly dramatic, with a vein of playful humour running through it. There would be only three men's parts – a dramatic tenor – a vigorous baritone or bass – and a buffo who would be probably a light baritone.

If the idea commends itself to you and if your engagements would permit you to collaborate, I shall be very pleased to go into details.

Yours very truly

The idea commending itself to German, Act I was despatched to him immediately it was finished. The leading part, Selene, was written especially for Nancy McIntosh, and she practised her songs with German, who altogether approved of the choice.

When Sullivan died he left an opera *The Emerald Isle* uncompleted, and it was finished by German, who was the best composer of tuneful airs in England at the beginning of the century, his incidental music for Henry Irving's production of *Henry VIII* having won great popularity, which was consolidated by his scores for three comic operas: *Merrie England* (1902), *A Princess of Kensington* (1903) and *Tom Jones* (1907). He was not unlike Sullivan in character and attainments: in life, as in music, he loved harmony and shunned discord. His personality and his work appealed to such diverse characters and composers as Elgar, Sullivan, Mackenzie, Parry and Stanford.

But a backer was as necessary as a composer, and Gilbert had some difficulty in finding one. First he offered what he now called *Fallen Fairies* to Helen Carte 'in virtue of our long association'. But as the offer arrived within a week of the letter in which he had complained that under her management the revivals of the Savoy operas had been insulted, degraded and dragged through the mire, she found the prospect of renewed collaboration unattractive. Next he tried an enterprising American, Charles Frohman, who had produced *Peter Pan*; then the manager of the Haymarket Theatre, Frederick Harrison; then the lessee of the Prince of Wales's, Frank Curzon, who at first seemed keen, but Gilbert's terms cooled his enthusiasm. Seymour Hicks and Arthur Bourchier were also approached; but the business was settled by C. H. Workman, who had found some backers and wished to produce the Gilbert-German opera. It so happened that Workman's recent performances in the Savoy revivals had influenced Gilbert to write the chief comic part in *Fallen Fairies* for him.

A month before Workman had formed his syndicate Gilbert was in correspondence with Helen Carte about the Savoy operas not recently revived by her, which would be done by Workman after the new piece. He intended to make considerable changes in some libretti, small alterations in the others:

16 Apl. 1909

Dear Mrs Carte

The only suggestion I have to make arises out of your last letter in which you suggest that if you decide to produce, on tour, any of the operas that are not on your repertoire, after they have been produced in London, you shall be entitled to have the use of any alterations I may make or authorize.

It occurs to me that in such a case the amounts paid by Bertie

Sullivan[1] and myself (or by myself alone in the cases of *The Mountebanks* and *His Excellency*) should be returned to us – as (1) it would be the success of the piece in London that would prompt you to add it to your repertoire and (2) the alterations would probably be very material, especially in *Ruddigore*, *Utopia Limited* and *The Grand Duke*.

I do not make this a condition, as I rely upon your being appealed to by its reasonableness.

Yours truly

25 Apl. 1909

Dear Mrs Carte

I accept the terms contained in your letter of the 20th Inst.

It is understood that the understanding does not apply to slight verbal alterations – which you will be at liberty to use if you think proper to do so.

Yours very truly

Workman's syndicate wished to have some influence over the class of goods in which they were investing, but Gilbert refused to let them judge the merits of his work and insisted that Workman alone should make the decision. As a rule actors are not good men of business; the exceptions are not good actors. Workman, new to the job of management, had to steer a tricky course between the autocracy of Gilbert and the plutocracy of his backers. He halted between two viewpoints, eventually favoured the men who provided the money, and soon heard from the man who provided the brains:

3 June 1909

Dear Workman

Your letter has caused me inexpressible surprise and indignation. I told you, a fortnight since, what were the terms I should require for my libretto and referred you to German for the terms he intended to ask for his music. You took no exception to these terms and I regarded that point as settled subject to your approval of the libretto and music. I asked you, a fortnight since, if you were committed to any leading lady and you replied that you had arranged to engage Miss Spain, but only for one production, and that you had a perfectly free hand in that respect with regard to the second and following pieces. I then told you that Mr German and I had agreed that Miss McIntosh would exactly suit the leading part and that the libretto and music had been written with her in view. To all this you made no demur and again I considered

[1] Sir Arthur's nephew and legatee.

these matters as settled subject to your approval of the libretto and music. Having thus, as we supposed, cleared the ground, we took you into our confidence in full, and read you the libretto and played and sung the music to you. You expressed yourself as delighted with both and there appeared to be nothing left to be done but to draft and sign a formal contract. A week after the reading you wrote to offer us ridiculous and insulting terms and inform us that you were bound to Miss Spain for your first three productions (having previously assured me in terms that admit of no misunderstanding that you had engaged her for your first production only), some gentleman who is interested in her having contributed £1000 to your syndicate.

With regard to the terms, I never haggle. They are immutable and must be accepted or rejected *en bloc*. I have not a word to urge against Miss Spain for parts to which she is suited, but she is wholly unsuited to 'Selene'. Moreover I decline to have my libretto cast by a syndicate.

You have caused us to lose two months in idle negotiations and you have lured us into confiding to you the details of the music and libretto on distinctly false pretences. I decline to have dealings with a man who is capable of such conduct.

Yours truly

Workman decided that the wrath of Gilbert was more to be feared than the threats of Mammon, and duly grovelled. On June 7th Gilbert, opening with a severe reprimand, wrote:

The terms 15% on the gross receipts are extremely low and cannot be reduced in any way. My 10% is the fee that I have always received during the last 35 years, except when I was on sharing terms at the Savoy. It is what I received for *The Mountebanks*, *His Excellency*, *Utopia Limited* (with a guaranteed minimum of £6000 on certain conditions) *The Grand Duke*, etc. In the case of the two first pieces the per centage was turned into a payment of £5000, with contingencies. In those cases Cellier and Dr Osmond Carr received 5% on gross receipts. On all these pieces I have received 10%.

I do not press Miss McIntosh on you. I only say that German and I are completely satisfied with her – that I wrote the part for her and German the soprano music. If you can find a better at her salary (£25 a week) we will accept her – but Miss Spain, an excellent soubrette, would be quite out of place in a stately part calling for scenes of passion and denunciation. Miss McIntosh is an admirable singer and accomplished Shakesperian actress, with an individuality and appearance which are exactly what the part calls for.

Please let me know your decision at once as another manager is coming on Friday to hear the piece and music, unless I stop him. The cost of production might have been anything about £2500, but as a matter of fact it should not exceed £600.

Yours very truly

On July 14th Gilbert was able to advise German that everything had been satisfactorily settled with Workman, who had taken the Savoy Theatre and had 'contrived to get rid of Cellier' – François Cellier, whose behaviour as musical director during Helen Carte's season had riled the librettist. Having put everything in order, Gilbert left for Wiesbaden, where on October 2nd 'J'ascends dans le ballon.' Half-way through the month he returned home and discussed the cast with Workman and German. Auditions were held at the Savoy; the piece was read by the author to the company on November 8th; and Nancy McIntosh was rehearsed thoroughly at home. Workman did not turn up for the early rehearsals: he was, noted Gilbert, 'toujours malade'; but his particular malady was no doubt auctorphobia, for he did not dare tell Gilbert that one of his backers still wanted the girl he fancied to play the part for which Nancy had been cast. Workman must have suffered spasms of conscience every time he caught Gilbert's eye, knowing that he had practically promised his backer that Nancy would be relieved of the part at the first possible opportunity. Gilbert lacked the gift of ingratiation which German, like Sullivan, possessed in so eminent a degree, and he was quite incapable of putting people sufficiently at their ease to confide in him. Workman might have explained the awkwardness of his position to a man whose eyes did not see right through him and suspect treachery. As it was, his fear precipitated a catastrophe that might have been averted by careful management and skilful diplomacy.

In any case Gilbert was in no mood to be trifled with after his late experiences at the Savoy. Joseph Harker, who painted the scenery for the opera, described what occurred when the author called to examine it. The warmth of his greeting made Harker wonder whether age had turned the lion into a lamb. But when Gilbert saw the completed scenery, he wanted considerable changes. Harker replied that Gilbert had approved the original designs and that if he wanted them altered he must pay for the work and delay the production. The lion re-emerged and roared for ten minutes. 'I have seldom heard more violent abuse hurled by anyone than that with which Gilbert assailed me on this occasion', related Harker, who then told Gilbert that such behaviour was not to be endured and that he refused to be bullied in such fashion. Gilbert stamped and snorted his way out of the studio, and at the close of the final dress rehearsal before a picked audience publicly stated that everyone except the scene-painter had assisted him loyally.

On the first night of *Fallen Fairies*, December 15th, 1909, Gilbert dined at the Beefsteak Club, spent the rest of the evening in Nancy's dressing-room, and received a 'Belle réception' at the end. The criticisms were not enthusiastic, possibly because fairyland in Gilbert's verse was quite as carnal as anything in the real world of prose and much sillier. On December 22nd Workman wrote to say that a member of the syndicate did not like Nancy in her part and that she must leave the cast. Gilbert went to see Workman, who must have had such a trying interview that his attitude stiffened; and Gilbert broke the news to Nancy, who received it with fortitude. In order to buttress his shaky position, Workman reported that at one performance nine people had left the theatre in protest. Gilbert replied: 'If, as you told me on the telephone, nine people rose from the stalls during her final scene and left the theatre in disgust (which I do not for a moment believe) it was because you sent them there to do so.' He said there was overwhelming evidence that Nancy had been magnificent in her part and had aroused more enthusiasm than Workman himself or anyone else:

> In short, I am firmly convinced that, to serve some ulterior end of your own, you have wilfully and deliberately concocted this utterly unfounded charge – intended to oust her from a part to which, in the opinion of both author and composer, she is exceptionally well suited. It is on that assumption that I shall rest such proceedings as I may be advised to take.

He then resorted to that embodiment of excellence, the law, addressing Workman:

27 Dec. 1909

Sir,

This is to give you notice that I intend to apply today to a Judge in Chambers for an ex parte injunction restraining you from playing *Fallen Fairies* this evening except with Miss McIntosh or her accredited understudy Miss Venning in the part of Selene. I give you this notice that you may be in a position to face the contingency.

> I am, &c.

But his solicitor Birkett said that he could not obtain a writ that day (Monday) because it was a Bank Holiday.

On the 29th he took German in a taxi to see Birkett: 'German joue le fainéant, et ne désire pas se mêler avec un procès. Alors l'affaire est terminé.' But the fact that German played the 'fainéant' did not lessen Gilbert's energy. German had written that he was satisfied with Nancy in the part and that the action of the syndicate in dismissing her was 'intolerable and of course violates our contract with them'. Gilbert reminded him of this:

> I am sorry you disapprove of my resorting to law proceedings . . . I must tell you frankly that I have no alternative but to pin you down to the terms of the two letters I have quoted . . . You will no doubt remember that when we were on our way to Birkett's you said to me 'Miss McIntosh sang magnificently on this final night.' I replied 'You really think that?' and you answered 'Yes, she sang magnificently.'

Unable, without the support of his collaborator, to institute proceedings to stop the performance, Gilbert brought an action on Nancy's behalf for breach of contract, and on January 13th, 1910, he was able to act solely on his own behalf, sending a note to Workman:

> Sir
> I write to confirm my telegram of this afternoon – 'I forbid you to introduce into Fallen Fairies a song that has not been authorized by me. Gilbert.'
> I shall apply tomorrow for an injunction.

He took the well-known actor Cyril Maude and the famous dramatist Arthur Pinero to see his solicitor in support of his affidavit. Workman gave in, and at the end of the month asked the librettist and the composer if they would guarantee the theatre expenses for two weeks on the chance that the opera might be nursed into a success. They declined, and the show came off after a run of six and a half weeks, Gilbert instructing his solicitors to stop the proceedings against Workman and the syndicate on condition that they paid their own costs.

He never forgave Workman for his slippery conduct, and refused to let him revive any of the Savoy operas. Workman had intended to follow *Fallen Fairies* with *Ruddigore*, but at the end of 1909 Gilbert asked Malone, manager of the Adelphi Theatre, if he would like to do it. Writing for himself and Herbert Sullivan, the librettist of *Ruddigore* made a remark that would not have pleased the composer: 'We propose to cut out a good deal of the heavy music in Act 2.'

On May 30th, 1910, Helen Carte asked whether Gilbert wished to resume control of the Savoy operas, her acting rights having lapsed. He replied that 'the bottom has been knocked out of their value for production in London by the circumstances attending their recent revival. Many years must elapse before the operas recover their former *prestige*.' He therefore had no wish to resume the performing rights, which were again bought by Helen, who paid £5000 for another five years. Before she did so Workman got to hear that the rights were in the market, and begged Herbert Sullivan to obtain Gilbert's permission to let him make an offer for them. Herbert arrived at Grim's Dyke with the actor's proposition on June 22nd, 1910. Gilbert did not keep Workman in suspense, writing on the same day:

Sir

Mr Herbert Sullivan has shown me your letter *re* Savoy operas.

I do not intend to waste any epithets upon you – you can easily supply them yourself. It is enough to say that no consideration of any kind would induce me to have dealings with a man of your stamp.

I am, &c.

It was the last roar of the old lion, though he emitted an occasional growl almost to the end of the next chapter.

CHAPTER 21

The Hero of the Piece

❦━❦━❦

Adapting Henley's lines on Stevenson to our subject, we
may roughly characterize Gilbert's nature as containing

A deal of Johnson, just a streak of Steele;
A little Herrick; Landor most of all;
And someone who can only be called 'Bab'.

The outer man gave no hint of this odd combination of qualities,
though his female friends might have discerned the chivalry of
Richard Steele, his male friends sometimes heard him explod-
ing with the wrath of Walter Savage Landor, his readers could
occasionally perceive in his lyrics the quality of Robert Herrick,
many children were treated to the absurd fun of 'Bab', while
not a few of his acquaintances were made aware of the down-
rightness and uncommon sense of Dr Johnson, for instance the
barber who asked when they might expect anything further
from his fluent pen. 'What do you mean, sir, by fluent pen?'
demanded Gilbert. 'There is no such thing as a fluent pen. A
pen is an insensible object. And, at any rate, I don't presume
to enquire into your private affairs; you will please observe the
same reticence with regard to mine.'

But few would have guessed that the slightly pompous man,
with the martial carriage and genial ferocity of manner, who
showed them over the house and grounds of Grim's Dyke, was
the English Aristophanes, as someone called him, the most
successful dramatist of his age. His height and sturdy build
gave him dignity, his dictatorial speech could make him awe-
some, but his jovial fresh-coloured face, laughing eyes and
amusing comments neutralized the somewhat formidable effect
of his deportment and enunciation. His touchiness was soon
apparent, and visitors were careful to avoid uncongenial
themes, but his intercourse varied considerably: with those he
liked he was witty and free; with those who did not arouse his

interest he was polite but curt; with those he distrusted or disliked he could be ruthless. His domestic arrangements were in the hands of a very competent wife, who never contradicted him and who retained his affection and confidence partly by self-effacement but largely by sympathy and understanding. Knowing the effect of hostile criticism upon him, she let him see only such press-cuttings as dealt tenderly with his work. She was the sort of person whom visitors called 'a nice little thing', but she was the right wife for him and those who thought her colourless were perhaps colour-blind. A remarkable man often attracts the sort of woman who fancies his wife is not good enough for him; but it is usually the remarkable man who is not good enough for his wife. The Gilberts were as perfectly matched as is possible in connubial relationship, and both of them were sensible enough to know it. 'Anniversaire de mon mariage: causerie et promenade', is a grateful entry in the diary for August 6th, 1906.

He was liked by his staff at Grim's Dyke, of which there were twenty: eight in the house, twelve out of it. His butler was with him for 26 years, three of his gardeners for 14, 12 and 11 years, his chief motor driver for 8 years. An occurrence in his early life was repeated in 1910. A footman, Arthur Dowling, left suddenly, and when a new employer wanted a certificate to his character Gilbert was strictly fair, stating that Arthur had been with him for eighteen months, that he was honest and efficient, 'an excellent servant, clean in person and in his work'. He had however been discovered 'under the influence of liquor, though he was certainly not drunk', and on being reproved by his mistress had thrown up his situation and left without his wages. A former employer had given him an excellent character and Gilbert said that he would have kept him in consideration of his efficiency and good conduct if he had wished to stay. Such contretemps were not confined to the staff. Occasionally a friend deserted Gilbert without giving notice:

1 July 1909

My dear Lady Betty

Nancy tells me that you told her that I have written a letter to you that had offended you beyond all possibility of forgiveness. Of course you and I know very well that my letter contained nothing that was not germane to my argument, and that it was expressed temperately, though decisively, throughout. A dismissal on your part has long been looming in the background, and if you wish to use my inoffensive letter as the peg upon which to hang an excuse for that dismissal, it is, of course, entirely at your service for that purpose. I am sorry that you should have expressed yourself as you did to Nancy, as she credits me with a sense of chivalry which is inconsistent with my writing an offensive letter to any woman – least of all to one whom I have always regarded with such profound esteem.

It seems strange to be dismissed without even so much as a poor 'good-bye'.

Yours always
Gillie

Gilbert's interest in the theatre was kept alive by his work for the Academy of Dramatic Art and his membership of the Dramatists' Club. He was on the council of the A.D.A. and discussed such grave matters as the separation of the sexes at lunch, the election of a new administrator, the taking of more commodious premises in Bedford Square. He lunched regularly with the Dramatists' Club at the Criterion Restaurant, the Café Royal, the Burlington Hotel, and elsewhere; and it is interesting to remark the presence of Bernard Shaw at one of these meals on February 2nd, 1910, along with the usual crowd, Arthur Pinero, R. C. Carton, Anthony Hope, James Barrie, Cecil Raleigh, and a newcomer Somerset Maugham, not to mention '&c'. His keen interest in photography took him frequently to the cinema in Bear Street, Leicester Square, and he remained a fairly constant playgoer when in London. Other activities occupied his time besides swimming, entertaining, bird-watching, animal-fondling, and the magistracy. He submitted to the discipline of being painted by Herkomer, and he even consented to be President of the Grim's Dyke Golf Club. Motoring was a steady source of enjoyment and he recorded his least exciting trips, such as the July day in 1909 when they went to Chenies, saw the church, took photos of the sextoness, and lunched at the Bedford Arms, where he left his kodak and had to retrieve it later. Aeroplanes were novelties in those days and he was careful to mention that on April 27th, 1910, his wife and Nancy caught sight of two, but he did not. However, he made up for the loss by studying the stars, having built an observatory and purchased a telescope, spending much time in erecting the first and arranging the second.

Although, as the barber implied, his pen was not as fluent as heretofore, he could not wholly abandon it. With born writers the itch to write is endemic, the practice of composition a drug. Having determined to write no more libretti after *The Grand Duke* in 1896, a determination he forewent in 1909, he agreed to write the stories of two Savoy operas for elaborate illustration and publication. In January 1908 he knocked off the story of *Pinafore* in six days, receiving £750 advance on a 10% royalty; and in August of the same year he took a fortnight over *The Mikado*. The publisher did not want to bother him over the illustrations and was rather alarmed when Gilbert bothered him:

3 May 1910

Dear Mr Bell

I cannot at all understand how you came to suppose that I had no desire to be consulted as to the illustrations in Vol. 2, when I had expressed the strongest disapproval at not having been consulted as to the illustrations in Vol. 1.

I am quite at a loss to understand the reason of the conspicuous discourtesy with which I have been treated in this matter, and I must decline altogether to associate myself with the publication.

Yours faithfully

With most successful authors a letter like that would suggest literary vanity. With Gilbert it simply points to the personal discomfort attending him through life, deriving from causes already indicated and demanding the exercise of good manners and consideration from those with whom he came in contact. 'I don't think I am a vain man or I shouldn't have so poor an opinion of what I do', he wrote to Maud Tree. Modest about his works, he lacked self-pity, the offspring of vanity, and also the conviction of so many vain people that they could run the universe much better than those who make a business of religious and political conduct. He belonged to no party and no creed, though his sympathies lay with the conservatives and the established church. Perhaps he may be described as a radical conservative and a christian agnostic. He believed in doing good but not that it was necessary to accept a dogma in order to do it.

Whatever inconveniences he underwent in the outside world, he always found comfort at home, and the only serious uneasiness he experienced was the departure of Nancy for Los

Angeles to visit her relatives. On January 3rd, 1908, he sent her a few lines:

> Dearest Nancy
>   . . . I write this for fear you might think that I had forgotten a duty which was also a pleasure . . . I haven't any more news. My wife sends her best love and all wishes for a happy New Year *which we hope and trust you will spend with us*, but we seem to see difficulties ahead. I only hope you are not going to chuck us after so many years.
>   Kind regards and all good wishes to your father and brother.
>   Your affectionate
>   Judge

He had once given her a photo of himself, writing on the cover: 'For Nancy. With a heart full of love.' Both the Gilberts were devoted to her, and she to them. Her assistance was invaluable in the organization of parties and the entertainment of guests. 'We have a largish dance tomorrow', Gilbert had once written before she joined them, 'so the house and all in it are upside down. Poor Kitty looks quite odd and unusual, upside down.' Nancy helped greatly in keeping things right side up. She soon returned from California, and Gilbert bought her an annuity of £500. Later he did the same for his wife and himself, paying £8475 for theirs in 1910.

Nancy accompanied them on most of their journeys abroad. Twice they visited Wiesbaden, where Kitty and Nancy received treatment. Once they stayed at Territet on the Lake of Geneva. In September 1908 they went up the Adriatic to Fiume and Venice, taking Messina and Palermo on the way. Coming back they stayed, as before, at the Hôtel Regina in Paris, where 'J'ai acheté une tiara pour Kitty – £450.' Three months later they heard of the terrible earthquake at Messina. In May 1910 they made a sea-trip to the Azores, visiting Lisbon (with a glance at Cintra and Montserrat), Gibraltar, Santa Cruz, Las Palmas and Madeira. The return journey was rough and on June 6th he noted 'malade et au lit toute la journée', but he felt better next day and was able to go on shore at Vigo. Most of the daily entries in his diary consisted of three words 'Rien de remarquable.' In the autumn of that year, unaccompanied by his wife and Nancy, he went on a voyage to Constantinople, telling a friend before leaving: 'I have been strongly advised to ally myself at once with the Young Turkish Party, but unfortunately I was not furnished with her address, so I scarcely know what to do.' He left for Marseilles on October 12th, arrived at Constantinople on the 28th, returned via Ajaccio, where he had his hair cut and saw Napoleon's house, and reached home on November 6th. 'Rien à noter', is the refrain of his diary, but happily some letters written to his wife have survived, proving that the diary might have been expanded without detriment to truth:

> Near Messina. 7 a.m.
> Tuesday

Dearest Kitty,

My wire will have told you that we reached Palermo safely and I shall post this at Messina which we reach in about an hour. I have done a stupid thing. I left England without visiting cards and without a passport, and they won't let you land at Constantinople or Smyrna without one – and Hogg is in the same fix. So we are going to call on the Consul at Messina and get one from him and then get it visa'd by the Turkish consul. Dossé tells me that this will be quite simple. We have had lovely weather and calm seas so far, with a full moon (or nearly). At Palermo I went to see my friends the dried monks – then to the Royal Palace – and then to a curious old ruined church, built in 1150 – then to the Cathedral. I did not go to Monreal. I get on capitally with my table companions who are all very pleasant people. Here is a plan of the table –

The Sea		
W.S.G.		Hogg
Sir F. Mowatt		Doctor
Miss Mowatt		Miss Kerr
Capt Mowatt		The other Miss Kerr

The waiters and stewards are very attentive and the food &c is just as good as it was on the Mantua – in fact, just the same.

A man introduced himself to me as having been at our Harrington Gardens dances and dinners – Mr Tennant, son of the Tennants of Richmond Terrace and brother of Dorothy Stanley. He is quite a pleasant man and I have introduced him to Mowatt who knew his father and mother. Mr Roberts (the stout man on the Solsette whose arm was so badly bitten at Venice) and his wife

turned up at Marseilles a day late and without a scrap of luggage.
They went by rail from Dieppe to Rouen and then came on by
motor, but they neglected to reclaim their luggage (which was
booked to Paris). Roberts went back to Marseilles to try and get it
and was to join us at Villefranche, which he did, but without luggage. Yesterday he and his wife went shopping at Palermo and
bought enough to carry them on. I must wind this up now as we
shall be at Messina directly. I am anxious to get letters, but, owing
to the strike, I don't know when that will be. I hope you are both
well and enjoying yourselves. I need not say that I miss you
greatly and heartily wish you were here. I hope your mother is all
right.

Good-bye, old girl, best love to Nancy and yourself

Always your devoted

Old Boy

Approaching Katakolo, Greece.

Wednesday, 19th

Dearest Kitty

We left Messina yesterday evening and shall reach Katakolo, on
the west coast of Greece, this evening. I did not go to Taormina,
but remained at Messina all day. The city is a pitiable spectacle –
miles and miles of ruined houses, with many dead bodies buried in
the debris – the smell of the bodies quite perceptible. There were
extraordinary sights to be seen – in one case the corner of a house
was left standing, 50 feet high, all the rest of it having fallen away,
but on the top floor of that corner was a glass door, *with every pane
entire*. It is impossible to conceive the desolation of the place without seeing it. Several shops are open on the ground floor of houses
of which all but the ground floor has fallen away. The people seem
cheery – there is lots of work to be done, but they are too lazy to do
it. I was told by the British vice-consul that they are having the
time of their lives, as they live rent-free in huts supplied by the
American government, with an allowance from the subscribed
funds. He told me that the poorer classes would be glad of an
earthquake every 5 years. There are several streets of temporary
sheds – suggestive of an American mining town in the wilds.
We took a carriage in the morning and drove about the town for
2 hours and went on shore again after lunch and walked through
the streets. Altogether it was a most curious experience. Tomorrow
I shall go with Cook's party from Katakolo to Olympia – where the
Olympic games used to take place, but I don't look forward to the
expedition, which is an all-day affair, with any pleasure.

The time has passed very pleasantly so far, fine weather and
smooth seas. I have changed my cabin which was quite forward to

one more amidships. Our party at table are all very jolly and we get on capitally together. The Man With Eight Servants has made several advances to the Mowatts, myself, and others of our party – but he is regarded with scorn and abhorrence by all of us. He asked most affectionately after you and Nancy and desired to be most kindly remembered. I am very anxious to get letters and papers. I suppose that will not be until we reach Athens. Having come away (like an ass) without passports, I shall have to get them at Athens. Dossé has promised to work it for me.

Good-bye, old girl. Give my best love to Nancy.

Always your affectionate

Old Boy

P.S. I hear that an English contractor has undertaken to clear away all the ruins and re-build the city on plans supplied by the Italian government, in 5 years.

Approaching Smyrna.

Tuesday morning, 25th

Dearest Kitty,

We had a day and a half at Athens, with glorious weather – 80 degrees in the shade. We arrived on Sunday and devoted the day to the Acropolis, Temple of Jupiter, &c, and I took about three dozen photographs, all of which were quite successful. We had a capital, though expensive, guide – procured for us (Hogg and me) by Dossé – he was, in point of fact, a first-class courier. On Monday we set about getting passports from the British Consul at the Piraeus and then having them visa'd at the Turkish consulate – or we should not have been allowed to land at Smyrna and Constantinople. This took up the earlier half of our time and the rest of the day, until 3 o'clock, we devoted to the Museum – which, no doubt, you recollect. Then we had to go on board, and we started at 4.15.

There is a long excursion from Smyrna to Ephesus – rail and on donkeys – but this we shall not do. Tomorrow we go to Bronsson (near Constantinople) and on Friday we shall be at Constantinople, where I hope to get letters and papers, as I have not had a line from home since I left, 13 days ago. Of course I couldn't have had any before Athens – and there the mail was late, so we had to leave without it. It is very annoying to be so long without hearing from you, but it isn't your fault or mine. I hope Nancy is taking successful photographs. Give her my best love. I suppose you got my wire from Athens telling you that I was quite well. I bought a huge sponge there for 10 francs – it would have cost 30/- in England. I know you love a bargain.

The food on board is not so good as on the Mantua. The fish is poor, the eggs twangy, and the meat tough. The service is excellent. I have admirable stewards and the ship is very comfortable. There are no particularly interesting people on board except Mowatt. His daughter and the two young ladies who sit at my table are difficult to get on with. Hogg and I get on excellently. He is quite a good fellow and very considerate. There are several passengers one can talk to – but none of them much above the average.

Good-bye, old girl. Best love to you. I am passing the time pleasantly but I shall be very glad to be home again.

Always your devoted

Old Boy

P.S. We have had ideal weather throughout, and the sea quite calm. We shall be at Smyrna in an hour. As I post this at sea it will go for a penny.

The year of Gilbert's sea-voyages saw two notable public events: the death of Edward VII and the trial of Dr Crippen. On May 20th, 1910, Gilbert witnessed the funeral of the monarch who had knighted him from a house in Southwick Street but did not obtain a very good view of the procession. The arrest of Crippen was recorded in his diary on August 1st, and in September, obtaining a ticket from Sir Charles Mathews, he attended five hearings of the case at Bow Street. The prisoners were committed on the 21st, and during his voyage to Turkey he bought a copy of *The Daily Telegraph* at Smyrna in order to read a report of the first day's trial at the Old Bailey. For some reason, inscrutable to those who find crime more depressing than thrilling, the trial of Crippen aroused universal interest, and a man who chopped up his wife and ran away with his typist soon became a mythological figure. The drama of their arrest on the Atlantic Ocean, wireless being used for the first time to effect the consummation, may have had something to do with the mass excitement. Gilbert, always attuned to popular emotion, could not keep the subject out of his conversation and remained on tenter-hooks until Crippen was convicted.

The case haunted him and gave him an idea for a one-act play, the scene being a condemned cell in which a criminal undergoes the agony of suspense just before his execution and dies of heart-failure at the moment of his reprieve. Gilbert had a flair for histrionic talent and chose an actor who had made his fame in comical characters to play this gruesomely tragic part. On December 21st, 1910, James Welch, who had 'created' Lickcheese in Shaw's *Widowers' Houses* and the Waiter in *You Never Can Tell*, lunched with Gilbert at the Junior Carlton Club, and reacted favourably, if curiously, to the author's verbal account of his grim playlet *The Hooligan*. 'Il en est charmée', reported the diarist. Gilbert obtained permission from the head of the Criminal Investigation Department, Basil Thomson, to collect details of the last hours of a condemned man, for which purpose he visited Pentonville prison, where Crippen had been hanged. He spent eight days writing the sketch in the second half of January 1911 and then read it to Welch, whom he took to Pentonville. He had a slight disagreement with Welch at the first rehearsal and left the theatre, but the actor wrote to apologize, and all was well. *The Hooligan* was first seen at the Coliseum on February 27th, 1911. Kitty was present with some friends, but her husband remained at the Beefsteak Club, calling for them afterwards. Welch made a hit with the sketch, paying Gilbert £75 for the first fortnight, £50 for the second, and securing the acting rights for two years thereafter with a further sum of £200.

Apart from turning an early prose skit into a play for the students at the A.D.A. (*Trying a Dramatist*) Gilbert wrote no more. He had begun to prepare his reminiscences in the spring of 1910, had authorized the firm of Macmillan to publish the book, and had spent one day in March and one in April on the job. But his temperament rebelled against such work and he probably destroyed what he had written. One day a friend called at Grim's Dyke with a journalist who wished to prepare an obituary notice for the file of *The Times*. Gilbert laughingly supplied as many details as he could remember.[1] He showed no lack of vitality, no loss of memory, no lessening of interest in whatever took his fancy. And he was as prickly as ever. Early in April 1911, he went to see his one-time protegée, now a 'star', in a play called *The Popinjay*. This was Julia Neilson, whom he had discovered and trained as an actress. She had played leading parts in revivals of *Pygmalion and Galatea*, *Broken Hearts* and *The Wicked World*, and he had written the chief character in *Brantinghame Hall* for her, which had resulted in a long engagement with Beerbohm Tree and established her as an actress. She gave him a photo of herself, writing on it

[1] Information supplied by Mrs Constance Mathews.

'To my Dramatic Daddy.' He had even been partly instrumental in getting her a husband, for she met Fred Terry, whom she afterwards married, in Tree's revival of Gilbert's *Comedy and Tragedy*.

After seeing *The Popinjay* he wrote to congratulate Julia on her performance, but received no reply. It was his nature to put the worst construction on any word or deed or oversight that seemed to set him at naught, and this kind of thing had happened before. One actress who was wholly indebted to him for engagements had behaved like 'an ungrateful little cat, and looks upon all I have done for her as in the natural order of things.' Another, Marion Terry, had been greatly helped by him in the early stages of her career, but after she had made a reputation he did not hear from her for some time. His reply to a request she then made carried a reproof:

June 27, 1889

My dear Marion,

If you are the Miss Terry whom I knew very well some years ago, I shall of course be very pleased that you should play *Engaged* for your brother's benefit. But not having heard of or from that young lady for about 3½ years, I concluded that Abraham had taken her to his bosom.

Yours affectionately
(if it is the same girl)
W. S. Gilbert

But he viewed Julia Neilson's seeming negligence as a case of flagrant ingratitude, and his sensations may be compared with those of a husband who, catching sight of his wife mixing arsenic with his food, feels disappointed in her. On April 19th, 1911, Gilbert wrote again, but the 'My dear Julia' of the first letter was toned down in the second:

Madam,

As you have not thought it incumbent upon you to acknowledge, in any way, the very courteous letter I wrote to you a fortnight since, congratulating you on your performance in *The Popinjay*, I am forced to conclude that, for some reason quite unknown to me, you are disposed to regard me as a stranger.

In these circumstances it occurs to me that you may be unwilling to remain under a weight of unnecessary obligation to me and that, with a view of removing some of that weight, it may be agreeable to you to return the sum of one thousand pounds which

I handed over to you twenty-two years since. It is true that, at the time, I made no condition of repayment, as it was intended to relieve you and your mother from a stress of pecuniary obligation, but as you stated that you should always regard it as a loan to be repaid if ever you were in a position to do so, I have no hesitation in bringing the matter under your notice.

Yours faithfully

Julia Neilson assured the biographer that she had written to acknowledge Gilbert's first letter, so hers must have gone astray. It is scarcely necessary to add that Gilbert was not in need of repayment. After his death his estate was valued at £112,000, and it is clear that he was more concerned to be generous with irony than stingy with money, though quite capable of telling someone that he 'never wanted to receive a letter from anyone else, except of course those containing cheques'.

At the age of 74 he enjoyed both health and wealth. He ate what he liked, drank what he fancied, went where he wished, and did what he wanted. Acknowledging some oysters, he said, 'We are all prepared to die in excruciating agonies on the altar of friendship', but he could never resist such pleasures:

I always yield to temptations. Even Providence yields to them. If I do a rash thing, I'm told I'm tempting Providence; and if Providence can't resist *my* humble temptations, how can I be expected to resist His? So I don't; in I always go, head over heels.

Sometimes he felt down in the mouth for no particular reason, and then he resorted to the Book of Job, his favourite work in literature, or Dickens, his favourite author. 'Men of my age are like trees in late autumn', he wrote; 'their friends have died away as the leaves have fallen from the trees', and in March 1911 he described his condition: 'The old crumbling ruin has been propped up and under-pinned, and will, I think, stand for a few months yet.' From two references to a truss in his diary, it appears that he had ruptured himself, but this did not check his activity, and when advised not to walk from Harley Street to Eaton Square soon after lunch he was indignant: 'Walk! Of course I'll walk. I walk six or seven miles a day. I never wore a pair of glasses in my life and I still feel eighteen.' He remained brimful of fun as well as energy. Cyril Maude's daughter, Margery, wished to take a snapshot of him and he posed in the ridiculous attitude of a ballet-master. On seeing the photo he wrote underneath it: 'How ill white hairs become a fool and jester!' It was a period when The Women's Suffrage Movement was rampant, and reading that some suffragettes had padlocked themselves to the railings outside the Prime Minister's official residence shouting 'Votes for Women!' he said, 'I shall follow suit. I shall chain myself to the railings outside Queen Charlotte's Maternity Hospital and yell "Beds for Men!" ' In fact he managed to enjoy old age, calling it 'the happiest time in a man's life', but adding mournfully, 'The worst of it is, there's so little of it.'

Early in May 1911 he suffered from rheumatism, his wife treating it with turpentine and wool. But he was soon well enough to bathe in the lake, to attend the magistrates' court, and to round up two gazelles which had taken refuge in his library. On the 26th he attended a Thackeray centenary dinner in the Middle Temple, afterwards going to a reception where he met Pavlova, whose dancing he much admired, and Nordkin. He left the party at 12.52, reaching home at 1.20 a.m., doing the ten miles in 28 minutes, which slightly exceeded the speed-limit. On Sunday the 28th he bathed in the morning and again in the afternoon, played croquet with Nancy before and after lunch, went for a walk in the grounds, listened to Nancy singing after tea, and had his third dip in the lake before dinner. He mentioned these facts in his diary, concluding with:

'Nous avons lâché les lemurs.'
'Premier melon.'

Monday, May 29th, was a fine day. He motored to London to visit his friends Sir Charles and Lady Crutchley and to watch the Annual Parade and Inspection on Oak-apple Day at the Royal Hospital, Chelsea, of which Sir Charles was Lieut.-Governor. The Inspection was held by Lord Roberts. They asked him to stay for lunch, but he made the excuse that he wished to see the actress May Fortescue, who had been thrown from her horse in Hyde Park and was laid up. He then went to the Junior Carlton Club, and astonished W. H. Kendal, who was lunching alone, by asking if he might sit at the same table. They had not spoken to one another for many years, but Kendal replied that members of the Club could sit at any table they liked. Gilbert joined him and talked of their old days together as if nothing had occurred to damp their ancient friendship.

He asked after Madge Kendal, and eulogized their acting in his plays with such warmth that Kendal's surprise overcame his appetite. Having eaten a hearty meal, Gilbert rose, shook hands vigorously, went away, returned to shake hands, retired, came back for a last handshake, and disappeared. Then he called on May Fortescue, who was lying in a dark room; remained chatting with her for a short time, and spoke to her mother before leaving the house. 'I won't ask you what you think of her appearance, for you can scarcely see her', said the mother. 'Her appearance matters nothing; it is her disappearance we could not stand', said Gilbert.

He had arranged to bathe with two girls that afternoon: Winifred Emery, niece of Mrs Cyril Maude, and her pupil Ruby Preece. He took a train from Marylebone station, met them at Harrow, and drove to Grim's Dyke. The two girls, neither of whom could swim well, were soon in the water. Ruby suddenly found that she was out of her depth, got frightened, and cried to Winifred for help. At that moment Gilbert appeared, called out, 'It's not very deep; don't splash', plunged in, and swam towards her. 'Put your hands on my shoulders and don't struggle', he said as he reached her. She obeyed, and he sank almost at once. She went under for a moment, but found on coming up that she could just stand in the water. When she got to the bank there was no sign of Gilbert, who had died of heart-failure from the sudden exertion to rescue her.

As a young man he had gloried in the thought of a hero's death in action and had volunteered for the Crimean War. Over forty years later he experienced the same emotion and volunteered for the South African War, but his age disqualified him. When past seventy he said that he would like to die on a summer day in his own garden. Both aspirations were fulfilled, for he died in action on a day of sunshine, swimming to save a life in his garden lake.

Index

(N.B. All Gilbert's writings are listed alphabetically under his name.)

and developed, 87 ff.; they supplant Offenbach in England, 88; dispute re Westminster Aquarium, 91–2; his Diaries, 95–101, 226 ff.; attends Queen's Levee, 97; enters into partnership with Carte and Sullivan, 103 ff.; they produce in U.S.A. to frustrate 'pirates', 104 ff.; his jealousy of Sullivan, 108; his defence of Carte, 108; his methods of composition, 114 ff.; builds house in Kensington and rents another at Harefield, 114–16; first rift in partnership is bridged by *The Mikado*, 118 ff.; his production technique, 121 ff.; the Savoy triumvirate allots partner's functions, 123 ff.; his attitude to women, 124–5; he criticizes *Ruddigore* music, 126; quarrels with Sullivan and Carte, 127 ff., 132 ff.; reconciliation follows with *The Gondoliers*, 134–5; the 'carpet controversy' with Carte, and resultant separation from Sullivan, 136–40; he applies for a Receiver at the Savoy Theatre but is willing to refer dispute to arbitration, 141; he buys Grim's Dyke, 144; he associates Sullivan as co-defendant in his suit against Carte, 145; he refuses invitation to Sullivan's *Ivanhoe*, 148; a proposed collaboration with Cellier leads to disputes with his manager, Sedger, 152–4; further collaboration with Sullivan is mooted by publisher Chappell and, after prolonged bickering over terms, compromise is achieved with *Utopia Limited*, 154–74; his views on orchestras, 176; effects of gout on his conduct, 177 ff.; after more partnership quarrels, he collaborates with Osmond Carr, 179–80; his views on 'gagging', 180–1; short and stormy association with George Edwardes, 182–4; his last contact with Sullivan and his grief at Sullivan's death, 186–7; an analysis of their divergent personalities and qualities, 187–

188; his opinion of Tree's 'Hamlet' and of Irving's 'Faust', 190; he builds Garrick Theatre and rents it to Hare, 191; his last prose drama, 192; his views on 'problem-plays', actor-managers, translations from French plays, music-halls and musical comedies, 193–6; his views are challenged by Irving, 196; his libel action against *The Era*, 197–202; his conversational methods, 203 ff.; his views on contemporary dramatists, 205–6; his love of children and animals, 212–17; life at Grim's Dyke, 214–23, 227 ff.; public and charitable activities, 217–18; his views on perjury, 218 ff.; his actions as J.P. re motoring offences, 220 ff.; his own motoring accidents, 221–223; becomes Deputy Lieutenant for Middlesex, 221; his dislike of Kipling and Maud Allan, 227–8; extensive revivals of his works lead to disputes with Carte's widow, 230–7; he attacks the Lord Chamberlain's ban on *The Mikado*, 234–5; he speaks disparagingly of his libretti, 237; sharing arrangements for foreign royalties, 239; he quarrels with the Beefsteak Club, and is elected to the Garrick, 240; his generosity to friends, 241 ff.; his children's parties at Grim's Dyke, 242; his reaction to Lloyd George's Budget, 242–3; his knighthood, 244; complimentary banquet at Savoy Hotel, 245; he opposes abolition of the censorship, 245–6; considers his blank-verse plays his finest work, 246–7; has controversy with *Who's Who*, 248; collaborates with Edward German but quarrels with the managing Workman-syndicate, and breaks finally with Workman, 250–5; his character, interests and hobbies, 256 ff.; his work for the Academy of Dramatic Art, 258, 265; various journeys abroad, 260 ff.; attends King Edward's